SELLING STEVE JOBS' LIVER:

A Story of Startups, Innovation, and Connectivity in the Clouds

Merrill R. (Rick) Chapman

ISBN: 978-0-9672008-4-2

Distributed to the book trade worldwide by Softletter, Inc., 12227 Chapel Road, Clifton, Virginia 20124. Phone 860.860-7549. Email orders rickchapman@softletter.com, or visit https://softletter.com.

Produced in the United States of America

ACKNOWLEDGEMENTS

I first need to thank my daughter, Lilith R. O'Connell, Esquire, for her assistance in writing the judicial decision chapter and advising me on the legal issues raised in *Selling Steve Jobs' Liver*. I also want to express my appreciation to my friends Randy Hujar and Gary Skiba — Randy for his advice and information on the manufacturing and marketing of the uLivv, Gary Skiba for his insights into the psyche of the programming mind. I also want express my gratitude to Joe Dacy II, author of "**Esquelle and the Tesla Protocol**," for his *Liver* copyedits and critiques.

Finally, my deepest thanks are reserved for my wife Ruth, who during the editing of both my novels has read them back to me line by line and provided me with invaluable advice and assistance. I could not have finished them without her.

Cover and Logo Illustration

Steven Wells of **Thinkwells Works**
Connect online at: **ThinkWells-Works**

DEDICATION

To Ruth, Lili, Jim, Winston, Evie, Caleb, Hunter, Daphne, and Lulu, and at the Rainbow Bridge Charlie, Winston and Oliver.

PREVIEW

"You're late," I said. "You were supposed to be here at nine."

"The subway train from Brighton was slow."

"Forty-five minutes slow?"

Boris said nothing and refused to make eye contact with me or Ignacio. After a second, I said, "OK. We'll let it pass this time. Did you send me or Ignacio your resume? Your CV?"

"I didn't receive anything yet," Ignacio said. I hadn't either.

"Here is resume." He reached into the pocket of his jacket with his large, furry hand, pulled out two crumpled paper documents consisting of three pages stapled together, and handed one to each of us.

I scanned the resume and sighed internally. It was barely English and littered with misspellings. It also sported a yellowish stain I assumed was either tea or coffee. This would not be a long interview.

"Why didn't you email this?" Ignacio said.

"Uncle Illarion said I should be careful about sending out too much information about myself online. He has asked me to keep a low profile."

"Boris, I don't think he meant paper resumes," I said. "Let's go into the conference room and find out more about your skills and if you're a fit to the Reliqueree culture." We walked into the conference room and seated ourselves around its oblong table. In his chair, Boris began a slow, barely-perceptible rocking motion.

TABLE OF CONTENTS

PROLOGUE

The West Side traffic brought the limo to a standstill, leaving me, Ignacio, my partner and co-founder of Reliqueree, and Sheridan, the firm's PR head, stranded in a long line of idling cars. After a couple of minutes, I decided to put the wasted time to good use. I pulled out my iPhone and checked our social media dashboard. "uLivv," "Trans-Livvient" and "Reliqueree" were all trending on Twitter. The media coverage of the grand opening of our first store had generated almost a million more likes on our Facebook page. The CEO of HP had asked to connect with me on LinkedIn yesterday. Traffic on our Pinterest and Instagram sites was going to explode once video and pictures of the gala event hit the Cloud and the blogs.

Next I accessed our accounting system and compared December's sales against November. I smiled as the numbers displayed onscreen. We'd killed it. And even though the holidays were over, January sales were projected to exceed December's by 200 percent. Hmm. We'd calculated we had enough stock in reserve for years, but even I hadn't forecast this level of demand.

"Call Michael," I instructed the phone. Michael was my fiancé's brother and also responsible for our important processing operations. He'd left early for the store with Angie to enjoy a private tour of the interior. He answered.

"Hi," he said. "Where are you?"

"Stuck in traffic just a few blocks away." I knocked on the Plexiglas window behind the driver. It rolled down.

"Yes, Mr. Pennington?" he said.

"How long before we clear this? Should we just get out and walk? I'm from New York. I know where I am."

"GPS says we should work through this in about 20 minutes. That enough time?" the driver said.

"Yes." I'd given us an hour to reach the store and was ready to stop the limo and lead everyone on foot to 14th Street if need be. As I'd told the driver, I was native stock, nobility so far as the rest of the region was concerned. New Yorkers were arguing Thomas Paine when the hillbillies from New Jersey and Connecticut were still making their mark.

I resumed my conversation with Michael. "Have you seen the sales figures?" I said.

"I did. I had my doubts about this whole thing earlier, but it's amazing how it's taking off and..."

I interrupted him. "I'm worried about inventory. Are you sure we'll be able to meet demand?"

"Relax. We have enough material to stretch from the Earth to the Sun two times and back. And that's factoring in the estimated wastage. Years of sales."

"Yes, but 25 percent is 'dark matter.'"

"Still more than enough. And aren't you planning a 'Plus' Edition?"

"Yes. It should be a killer if it's positioned and marketed properly."

"Angie says 'Into the Blue' orders are flooding in," Michael said. "The platform is growing. I know I'm not a marketer, but I've learned a few things watching you in action. People are buying into the company's vision. I'm not sure you'll need the rest of the inventory."

He was right, but I worry a lot. It's because I care. Steve Jobs cared.

If you're an entrepreneur, your middle name is "Worry."

"What's the turnout like?"

"The place is packed," he said. "Every press invite was picked up half an hour ago. Stern, Roose, and Stevens are here."

"Terrific. How about Boris? Has anyone heard more about May?"

"Angie spoke to Illarion. He says it appears ICE screwed up. O'Connell is working on it. Should only be a couple more days. She spoke to Boris and he said he'd be there on time. She said he sounded fine."

"Excellent." With May gone, Boris' stress levels had gone stratospheric, but with everyone's help, he seemed to be coping. Once she was back, I was sure he'd calm down. "We should be there soon. Talk more then."

"Wait, Angie wants to speak to you. She wants to know..."

Another call came in. I looked at the number. Todd Birnbaum. Amazon's top biz dev guy. I hadn't thought this day could become any better, but apparently I was wrong.

"Tell her I'll see her in a few minutes. Amazon just called. I'll fill her in when I get there."

"OK," he said. I disconnected and took the call.

"Nate Pennington. How's it going, Todd."

"Hi, Nate. Look, Andy wants to discuss purchasing. And I want to clear up any misunderstanding from DEMO."

The last DEMO had been held in September in Phoenix. Bezos and Birnbaum walked out on our presentation a couple of minutes after it began.

"Tell him not to worry about it. I'm sorry we didn't communicate our vision to you more effectively. By the way, Forbes just moved Reliqueree into the number 15 spot in their top international brands list. I'll bet we crack the top 10 within six months."

"What's wholesale going to look like?" Todd said.

I'd been looking forward to this moment for months. "I'm sorry, Todd. We're not doing straight wholesale. We're going wholesale plus MAP. We'll be reasonable on the discounts. No problem with the non-disclosure agreement. But we control our pricing and brand equity."

In the MAP model, the manufacturer controls and set their pricing. In straight wholesale, the retailer. Amazon enjoys controlling pricing models and regards MAP as a Tool of Satan. Only companies with strong brands and sky-high demand can insist on MAP.

"Amazon doesn't buy under MAP. You know that, Nate. We buy straight wholesale."

All Apple products are sold to Amazon under strict MAP agreements. The reason is if you can't buy an iPhone from Amazon, the customer will go somewhere else. And then keep returning to that somewhere else to buy other stuff.

"Yes, Todd. You know, there's an industry rumor going around that your boss and Tim Cook crossed paths at a TED talk in Vancouver and Andy muttered the words 'straight wholesale' where Tim could hear it. The next day, Andy gets a phone call and after it's over, leaps on a plane to Cupertino, takes a taxi to One Infinite Loop, changes into a wetsuit, and is escorted up to Tim's office where he sits in a chair and balances a colored rubber ball on his nose while clapping his hands together going **'arf,' 'arf,' 'arf.'** But I'm sure it's just idle buzz."

There was a long pause on the line, then Birnbaum said, "Uh, yes. Let's connect tomorrow and resume our talk. We're going to be looking for 40 points. Good luck with the store opening."

"Thanks, Todd. Talk to you."

I disconnected and looked across the seat opposite me at Sheridan Bettar. A native New Yorker like myself, Sheridan was of Irish/Lebanese extraction and very attractive, with long silky black hair, blue eyes, and an excellent figure. She was a top-level PR operative, with a strong background in high-tech and excellent knowledge of where the industry was trending. When she contacted someone in the industry, they answered back.

"Have you heard anything from The Woz yet?" I said.

"Yes. I've heard back from Mr. Wozniak."

"And?"

"And I warned you to let it go. He's not a fan. We're fortunate he's been quiet during the launch. One of the first rules of effective PR is that when a rattlesnake bares its fangs at you and you hear a 'skritcha, skrticha, skritcha' sound, you don't ask its motivations. Be grateful it's allowed you to back away without being bitten."

"What did he say?"

She pulled out her phablet and read. "Please inform Mr. Pennington I'm not interested in participating in or commenting on his company and product. Inform him that I believe he represents what is evil about technology today. He is a ghoul and his product a travesty. And do not send me anymore uLivvs."

I leaned back, disappointed. Since the launch, I'd been trying to persuade The Woz to engage with us and give the uLivv a chance. It just seemed right to virtually reunite the Two Steves, but right now the second wasn't interested. I pushed the whole issue out of my head until tomorrow. I wasn't going to let it spoil today.

The limo remained stuck in traffic and I began to mentally review my "to do" list for the next several weeks. There were three major tradeshows Reliqueree would be at exhibiting at in January and February. I was scheduled to visit Shenzen in a couple of weeks to look at prototypes for the next generation uLivv. After my discussion with Todd Birnbaum, a trip to Seattle also needed to be added to my itinerary.

And in March, the wedding.

I looked to my right at Ignacio, who was typing on his laptop. After several seconds, he felt my eyes on him.

"What?"

"What are you working on?" I said.

"Running some tests of Boris' latest code and analyzing the emulator results. So far, no issues with ChatGPT.

"Good." I paused, then said, "Ignacio, I need to ask you. Am I doing the right thing by marrying Angie? Am I being fair to her and our child? Doesn't she deserve better?"

"I'm not sure what you mean."

"Reliqueree's growing fast. You've seen the sales figures. You know that for the next several years, I'm going to have to play the role of hard-charging, high-tech startup CEO. Long hours on the road, more hours spent on marketing, social media, pitching the IPO, leading the team. I don't want to be a phantom husband and a stranger to my child. After Lisa was born, Steve Jobs didn't have time to be a good father to her for years."

"Didn't he claim he was sterile and that she wasn't his kid?" Ignacio gave me a friendly punch on the shoulder. "Not going to work today. They didn't have DNA testing in the 70's."

"Aren't they going to induce next week if she doesn't go into labor?" Sheridan said. "'Fair' isn't relevant anymore. From Angie's perspective, 'long overdue' and 'I've been more than patient waiting for you to do the right thing' are more germane."

"Besides," Ignacio said, "this is the 21st century. No need for you to be a phantom anything. You can work anywhere productively, including home. We can set up video conferencing, server access, file synchronization, anything you need from any location."

"I prefer a more hands on management style."

"You don't have to compromise," Sheridan said. "You can video conference **and** pitch in with diaper changing. That's as 'hands on' as it gets. Besides, if you try to back out of the wedding, her uncle will be upset and this is a bad time to anger your primary supplier."

She made sense. On our last trip to Shenzen to inspect the first uLivv prototypes and discuss the manufacturing schedule, Tony Song had met us at Hong Kong Airport, taken a close look at his niece's swelling baby bump, flashed me a genial smile, and personally driven us to SongTech HQ. From a business standpoint, the trip was a huge success. At the factory, a uLivv planning and implementation team was waiting to work with us on quality control and fulfillment. From the first decisions on the early prototype through final production, we'd enjoyed nothing but fast turnarounds and flawless execution from our Middle Kingdom partners. Family matters in China.

Tony had made his point about Angie's impending motherhood before we'd boarded our flight back to the U.S. At the airport, he'd presented me with a lovely personal gift, a custom-bound, richly illustrated hardcover history of China. Bookmarks had been placed in the sections dealing with the importance of marriage and "face" in Chinese culture. Another was placed in the chapter describing the Chinese justice system and the execution of malefactors via the traditional "death by a thousand cuts." Formally known as "slow slicing" (*"lingchi"* in Chinese), the process involves tying a person to a wooden frame and cutting the flesh from their body a chunk at a time until they die. *Lingchi* was banned in China in 1905, though periodically a revival of the practice is recommended in the case of telemarketers, spammers, and Jehovah's Witnesses.

"You're both right," I said. "After all, 40 **is** rushing up on me. It's probably time I settled down and embraced new challenges and responsibilities."

I looked out the window to see a leggy young girl stride by on the sidewalk wearing jeans, boots, and a stylish jacket draped over a very attractive figure. She appeared to be in her early twenties, her profile sharp against the crisp winter air, honey-brown hair glinting as the weak afternoon sun caught the highlights. Internally, I sighed.

Finally, traffic began to move and five minutes later we were pulling up in front of the store, one of dozens planned over the next 36 months. Reporters, cameras, and news trucks were camped around the entrance. Wuhan had finally cleared the city and New Yorkers had returned to their old habit of packing themselves together like sardines. Buyers were lined up several blocks down both sides of 14th Street. Camera drones buzzed above capturing aerial views of the scene. New York may be the Big Apple, but when it comes to technology, it's small chips in comparison with the Left Coast and the Valley. Reliqueree was the biggest high-tech news to hit the City in decades.

Sheridan had worked hard to ensure the Mayor would attend the grand opening and as I watched, His Honor's limo drove up to the front of the store and he stepped out. The press and cameramen rushed over and cut him off momentarily from our view. It was a good opportunity for me and my retinue to slip quietly past the crowd and inside. The security guard scanned our passes and we were in.

The inside, as Michael had said, was packed, with the invitees wandering about gazing at the uLivvs on display, picking up various accessories, scanning the software kiosks, and inspecting the "Into the Blue Bistro." A microphone and podium were placed in front of the Bistro and a symbolic yellow ribbon stretched across the main cashier's station. I spotted Angie surrounded by several reporters, who seemed fascinated by what she was saying. Either that, or they were trapped in the gravitational field she exerted on nearby objects as she came to the end of her ninth-plus month. We briefly made eye contact, and I moved on.

I also picked Gruezén out from the crowd, scanning the interior with an expression of faint dissatisfaction. Designing and merchandising our first store had been a rush job and we'd had to cut more corners than he'd liked. He pulled out his phone and took voice notes as he threaded his way through the aisles.

A group had made their way to the rear of the store and was staring upwards. What drew their gaze was "Digital Remembrance," a majestic oil mural being projected onto the ceiling at Retina resolution. It was a tableau rendition of Steve Jobs surrounded by other famous figures in high tech and sure to be widely discussed and streamed.

The lawyers and I had tussled over the use of Jobs' likeness, even though I'd reminded them repeatedly New York does not recognize a right of publicity after a celebrity's death. When you care about something deeply, you fight for it. After all, Steve Jobs had cared so deeply about creating a great company called Apple that when he named it Apple, there was **already** a great company named Apple founded by The Beatles. And even though Apple (Steve's) promised Apple (The Beatles) it would stay out of the music business, that didn't stop Apple (Sculley's) from adding a music synthesizer to its computers in 1986. Apple (The Beatles) sued. In 1991 (Apple, The Beatles), sued Apple (still Sculley's) again over the issue of packaging music with the Macintosh. Then, in 2001, Apple (Steve's again) released the iPod. I'm pretty sure Apple (The Beatles) sued over that as well, but I've lost track. If you find this difficult to follow, imagine what the attorneys on both sides of the cases had to endure.

But the important lesson is the one Steve Jobs taught us all. *"Your time is limited,"* he wrote. *"Don't let the noise of other opinions drown out your own inner voice."* I was following Steve's sage advice and not allowing legal lemmings to prevent me from listening to **my** inner voice. And given the uLivv's sales and the outcome of our recent legal battle, I thought it a good bet Jobs' estate would eventually be open to a licensing deal.

I checked my phone. 12:55 pm. The whole event was scheduled to kick off in five minutes. I went over to Sheridan.

"Everything on track? Any problems? Have you seen Boris?"

"No, but Michael told me he's here," she said. "It's all going off like clockwork. At 1 pm the Mayor's going to speak for a few minutes, then hand the podium off to you. There's an iPad with a teleprompter app loaded with your remarks. You're scheduled for five minutes. Don't go overtime. Then the Mayor and you will cut the yellow ribbon, we'll let the general public into the store, and you'll be available for on camera and streaming interviews for the next 30 minutes. After that, we're done. By the way, Illarion's just arrived."

Illarion Antakov was Reliqueree's principal (well, only) investor. His varied business interests led to him keeping a low social profile and he'd been noncommittal when I'd invited him to the grand opening, but it was gratifying he'd shown up. Illarion was a tall man and dressed in his usual expensive white suit and silk tie, he stood out among the attendees. He saw me as I stood surveying the crowd and nodded and smiled.

"Excellent." I continued looking out at the store floor and did some press spotting. After a few seconds, I identified Kevin Roose, a Times technology columnist, who'd written several uncomplimentary articles about Reliqueree and the uLivv. He'd somehow managed to get his hands on some early interior photos of the store and had referred to the Into the Blue Bistro as the "Sepulcher Strip." To my tremendous joy, he was skulking around with a uLivv draped around his neck. Not that he had a choice. The grand opening units had been placed in a special case with a metal loop to which we locked the attendees' ID lanyards. Security was under strict instructions to toss out anyone not wearing the ensemble. We'd unlock the units at the end of the ceremony.

I pulled out my phone and snapped a couple of pictures of Roose before he could hide behind someone. Sheridan would post the pictures on our corporate blog, Facebook, Instagram, and Pinterest before the day was over. PR gold such as this is only valuable when it's mined instantly.

The clock showed 1 pm and the Mayor stepped up to the mike and began to talk. I didn't pay any attention to the brief speech, just watched the store's digital display and waited for His Honor to relinquish the floor. At 1:08 pm he was done and I stepped up to the microphone.

"Thank you, Your Honor. First, let me say what a privilege it is to have you appear and speak. I grew up in Riverdale and if you'd told me when I was a kid that one day I'd be welcoming New York's Mayor to the grand opening of Reliqueree's first retail store, I'd have said you were dreaming."

I paused a second to allow everyone to chuckle politely at this standard banality, then continued.

"As you all know, Reliqueree is built around a singular passion, a new vision of remembrance, connectivity, and interactivity with those who have departed and moved on to the post life. Some in the media and blogosphere have criticized our vision, but today the market is speaking with a different voice. Why? We believe the answer is found in a question every one of us has asked, first as small children to our parents, later to the universe at large as adults. This query is 'When we depart this world, is that all there is? Will we one day be forgotten and vanish forever into time?'

"Prior to Reliqueree, millions have found the answers provided by current systems and processes dispiriting and unsatisfactory. There is a tremendous desire for new technologies and better answers.

Reliqueree's success is proof we are satisfying that desire and providing those better answers."

Out of the corner of my eye, I glimpsed Boris, our chief programmer, at the rear of the room. Ignacio was standing next to him, using his phone to stream live video out to his social network. Boris had a faint smile on his face and looked more relaxed than I'd seen him in weeks. Angie and Sheridan were seated in the front row to my left, with other Reliqueree employees scattered around the store and in the audience. I looked for Boris again, but he'd moved and I'd lost him. For a second, I contemplated asking him to step up to the microphone or at least give him a call out, but decided against it. We were on a tight schedule. I glanced back down at the iPad and resumed.

"The uLivv has been described by some as an extended monument to Steve Jobs, but that's a cramped and narrow view. Our goal is to honor one of history's great entrepreneurial spirits and open up new channels of communication and companionship with anyone who has touched your life. We were fortunate to be able to take advantage of a unique opportunity to bring Steve directly back into the lives and hearts of millions of people worldwide. Doing this has been an immense privilege.

"But this is only the beginning. Today, I'm happy to report that over 100 thousand subscribers have signed up for our new TransLivvient 'Into the Blue' service. These sales reflect our passion and commitment, the same type of passion and commitment that inspired Steve Jobs to build iPods, iPhones, and tablets thousands of people were willing to line up for days in advance to purchase at **full retail** regardless of cold, snow, and rain. The same type of passion enabling me to tell you that since the uLivv first went on sale only three month ago, the Reliqueree Team has sold over **eight million** units."

I paused to allow the crowd to react to the applause line, and looked up. Boris was now standing directly in front of me, smiling broadly. He reached into his jacket, pulled out a small pistol, pointed it at me and fired. There was a loud **bang** and I felt the bullet plow into my left shoulder with a wet splatting sound. Stunned, I took a couple of steps back. Several women screamed. Simultaneously, every member of the press stampeded towards the door or dived for the cover of the counters. Ignacio disappeared under the tide heading for the exit. Angie tried to run towards me, but tripped over Sheridan, who was scrambling madly over the back of her chair in an attempt to escape the mayhem.

Bois pulled the trigger again but the gun misfired. I stared at him in disbelief.

"Boris," I said. My voice was a croak. "What are you doing? You're ruining the grand opening. I thought you believed in Reliqueree."

"I do believe in it," he said. "That is why I am doing this. You are demons. Steve Jobs has ordered me to kill you all." He aimed at me again, but before he could pull the trigger, Michael, trapped in place by the press horde struggling to escape, grabbed one of the faux marble busts of Steve Jobs we'd placed around the store and launched it at Boris.

Michael's aim was true, but as the statue caromed off my attacker's hairy head, I realized I'd fallen short of the master. Jobs had always incorporated first-class materials into his products and business operations. Who could forget his heroic insistence on using magnesium for the case of the first NeXT when anyone else would have settled for steel? The MacBook's solid aluminum chassis? The stunning glass walls of the Apple stores?

Several pounds of highly-polished crystallized ancient sea bed impacting against Boris' skull would have knocked him out, but when buying the busts, I'd opted for the terra cotta model over Gruezén's vehement opposition, and the best a cheap ceramic could do was stun him for a moment. (In my defense, the busts had looked **exactly** like marble and we were over budget and running out of time.) He wobbled in place and turned towards Angie, who had struggled to a sitting position and was looking up at him in shocked disbelief, her arms wrapped protectively (well, not around — her wingspan couldn't encompass the circumference, but the tips of the fingers of each hand definitely touched) in front of her stomach.

I'd read some time ago that when someone you love is threatened, time freezes and you see past, present, and future with perfect clarity. This is true. As Boris raised his gun at Angie, the past and present flashed bright neon signs in my forebrain. They weren't terribly relevant to the situation, so I skipped past them to the future.

It was disorienting. I seemed to be writhing slowly on a white expanse stretching out around me to the horizon. The lower part of my body felt as if it was on fire, while my head was cool, though I kept gasping for air. As I considered my predicament, the scowling face of Uncle Tony Song loomed above me. Reaching down with a pair of chopsticks, he tore a chunk of fried flesh from my lower body and ate it in front me with evident relish. I realized what was happening. Somehow, Uncle Tony, via Chinese black magic, had transformed me into a *ying yang yu*, a dish consisting of a fish whose bottom half is fried alive for consumption while the head lives on for as long as half an hour. I was receiving a strong spiritual warning my and Angie's continued survival were interlinked.

And besides, the petite Chinese snow globe about to be assassinated **was** carrying my son. That counted for **something**.

I threw myself on my knees in front of Angie. Boris pulled the trigger. I felt a huge hammer hit my chest, and then I didn't feel anything at all.

EIGHT MONTHS
EARLIER...

CHAPTER 1

NOT TOO TOGETHER

ERROR: The password you entered for Natep@thetogether-hood.com is incorrect. Lost your password?

Username: Natep@thetogetherhood.com
Password: ********

ERROR: The password you entered for Natep@thetogeth-erhood.com is incorrect. Lost your password?

Huh? I tried it again. Same thing. Odd. I checked my keyboard for the caps lock. Not on. Stuck key? No. One more login and the system would lock me out until a brightstart admin let me back in. Time to request a password reminder. Had Ignacio changed the PW for some reason?

Please enter your username or email address. You will receive a link to create a new password via email.

Get New Password

Username or email: Natep@thetogetherhood.com

ERROR: The email address you have entered is not in our database. Please reenter your email address.

Son of a... I pulled out my phone and messaged Ignacio.

Did you change the accnt pw?

No. didnt change anything

Can you login?

Hold on.

No, cant what's going on?

Dont know. will find out

I received another message on my phone.

Nate need to talk to u

Angie. My girlfriend. She could wait.

I messaged Shelley, brightstart's admin, and asked her to unlock the account. After five minutes, no response. A half hour later, still nothing. I was becoming annoyed. Let's try email. I wrote a quick note and hit send. A second later I received:

554: Sender Address rejected.

I thought about Twitter and Facebook, but decided to go directly to the phone. But I didn't have Shelley's number. She refused to give it out and insisted we message or send email.

Blocked on FB

Really? Have shelley phone num?

Yes. 415.445.8752

Tks

I dialed Shelley. She picked up.

"Hi, Shelley. This is Nate. I can't login to our account. Can you please have Bobby or someone in IT fix?"

"How did you get this number?" she said. "It's my personal number. I haven't given it out to anyone here."

"I tried to call the brightstart number. No one answered." This was a lie, but true. No one ever answered the brightstart number. It went to a voice mailbox no one listened to. Including Shelley.

"You should use the brightstart number."

"I would, Shelley, if anyone ever picked it up. I don't even know where it rings through to."

"I still want to know how you obtained this number. I only give it out to friends."

"Ignacio gave it to me, Shelley. I assume you two are friends. He likes you."

"Ignacio? We're not friends."

"I'm sorry to hear that. I know he finds you attractive."

This was Ignacio's opinion. Shelley was tall, anorexic, and possessed features so sharp that if you picked her up by the ankles and swung her, you could chop wood. Ignacio found her fascinating. I, myself, would sooner have dated a straight razor.

"I still want to know..."

"Shelley, can we can discuss this later? You know Ignacio. If it's on the web, he'll find it. In the meantime, I need account access. Can you tell Bobby to let us back in?" Bobby was brightstart's IT guru. "I've already wasted half the day on this."

"He can't."

"Why?"

"Because Seth said close the account."

"Why?"

"I don't know. He didn't tell me."

"When did he do this?

"I don't know. Could be last night."

"And do you know where Seth is today, by any chance?"

"He said he probably won't be in for the rest of the week. He has a meeting up in Seattle."

"Did he tell you how to reach him?"

"You can reach him on his phone. Everyone in brightstart has his number."

"Shelley, he never answers that number."

"You can text message him."

"He never replies to text messages. What's the number he **does** answer?"

"I don't have it. And I still want to know how Ignacio got my..."

I hung up on her. I didn't need to speak to Minnie Mouse when my prey was King Rat.

Another message. Angie.

Nate really need to talk to u

Not now.

Where is seth?

Hold on

The creamery, 685 4th st 5 mins away

OK, tks

Seth spotted me immediately and watched with dismay as I walked into the nearly empty cafe and strolled up to his table. His iPhone and MacBook Air were set up next to a couple of empty plates which held the remnants of his lunch. I sat down across from him.

"Hi, Seth. How are things?" I said.

"Hi, Nate. It's been a busy morning." He glanced at his Apple Watch. "I'd like to talk, but I have to run now."

Seth had taken over the position of San Francisco's best known technology incubator as its "bright sherpa" after he'd cashed out on two startups and moved into the venture community. His first company had created a payment app infrastructure for interactive vending machines. Your Butterfinger could now reach out and ask you to eat it. He'd repeated the play with an IoT (Internet of Things) flexible screen technology marrying your kitchen appliances with the Cloud. Your coffee maker could now implore you to buy better beans while your toaster oven nagged you to purchase expensive whole wheat bread instead of cheap white.

As my bright sherpa, Seth had mainly assisted theTogetherHood and the other startups by spending minimal time at brightstart. Instead, he focused on discussing the value of mentoring, collaboration, and providing practical business advice to entrepreneurs at the numerous seminars, conferences and events running on a 24/7 cycle in the Valley. When he'd first come on board, I'd asked him about the qualifications I should look for in a CFO. Seth hadn't had time to answer, but did suggest I attend a Silicon Valley Meetup Group talk he was giving next month where he was covering the topic. He **had** been nice enough to give me one of the "Make Mistakes" T-shirts he sometimes brought to the office.

Seth smiled at me nervously, closed his laptop, and started to stand up. I smiled back, reached across the table, grabbed him on both sides of his face by his startup-executive-laser-graded-length beard and guided my Sherpa back to his seat. Seth's 6'3" and I'm 5'10," but he's licorice-stick thin and I bench press 275. He sat back down.

"Ow. Let go of me, Nate. That's assault!"

"Shh, Seth," I said in a soothing voice. "I'm not assaulting you. We're communicating directly, without any digital smog." I gave his beard a friendly tug and he winced. "I just want to know what's going on, that's all. Then we can resolve this amicably and you won't have to go back to brightstart looking like wolverines ate your face."

His eyes widened, then he relaxed. "OK, OK. Let go and I'll tell you. How did you find me?"

"Seth, for a man who's managed two companies to successful monetization events, I'm surprised you don't know more about the capabilities of that marvelous Cupertino technology you own." I nodded towards the iPhone. "Carrying one of those is like painting a GPS locator beacon on your chest in neon pink glow paint. You can be found anywhere."

I released his face, cocked my head, and gave him by best friendly-puppy look. "So? What's going on?"

"Last week one of your beta customers contacted us. They're threatening to sue brightstart."

"About what?"

"About theTogetherHood's 'functionality.'"

"Seth, tTH is a community management and empowerment system."

"Uh, huh. I remember your original pitch. But you neglected to mention some things."

"Nothing about the system has changed. theTogetherHood is a risk management system for municipalities enabling them to manage a wide range of potential liabilities while protecting and enhancing revenues."

"Yes, Nate. I've heard the spiel and went to your demo. But you didn't spend much time showcasing tTH's nuts and bolts. Most community management systems don't track and calculate median mortality and liability ratios for multiple types of homicides and accidents such as car crashes, drug overdoses, municipal pool drownings and several dozen others I can't recall. Let's not forget the municipal incidents database. The first selectman falls in love with the head of the PTA and they fly off to Venezuela with the school fund? The chief of police is caught raiding lobsters from a local seafood restaurant?"

"So? Ripped from today's headlines," I said. "Seth, this is a dangerous world we live in. Your brother's a lawyer. Wasn't he the one who filed suit against Sausalito last summer? When those kids boat-jacked a 30-footer, got drunk, and a girl went over the side and drowned? What was the cause of action? Oh, yes. The location of the on-board life preservers wasn't properly marked. In the system as well."

"That's not the issue. The 'Community Risk Heuristics and Hedging' feature **is**."

"What's the problem with it?" I said "It's easy to use and set up."

"It is. The interface is a triumph of responsive design. The problem is what your software **does**. It runs ghoul pools."

"I'm offended by that," I said. "It does no such thing. tTH enables your community to take advantage of the power and flexibility of hedge funds to protect and enhance local revenues. The beauty of hedging is that you can invest in basically anything — land, stocks, currencies, and even your town's local events and activities in order to generate additional funds."

"So I've found out," he said. "Last week, one of your beta customers called us up and threatened to sue brightstart. It seems several months ago, some of the town's IT admins were configuring the system and stumbled across the Pet Incident Tracking feature. The one that allows you to record how often Rover is hit by a Ford or Felix meets a fisher cat?"

"Yes?"

"They used tTH to establish a fund for the kiddies they called 'HeartFriend.' The children could invest in a 'pool' that paid a monthly cash award based on how well the local fur balls avoided mortality based upon your software's metrics. The system was pitched as a way to encourage families to practice responsible pet ownership and fund local animal shelters. It was very popular and the town's veterinarians and pet stores all pitched in with financial support and advertising."

"It sounds wonderful," I said. "We need to write this up as a case study. What's the problem?"

"The problem is a couple of weeks ago dogs and cats all over town started mysteriously going missing. Apparently, some budding young speculator figured out you can increase your chances of winning by 'adjusting' the pet population downward and 'investing' accordingly."

"What makes you think it's a 'someone.' Haven't you read about the comeback of the coyote in America's urban landscape?"

"They believe they know who the culprit is."

"I don't see how tTH can be held responsible for any of this. But you're missing the beauty of hedge systems. They can generate revenue no matter how a market moves via longs and shorts.

"Let's stay with pets. This example should help. Everyone in your town thinks Prince the Pit Bull is misunderstood and lets him roam freely. So hedge Prince. Allow people to invest in the quality of your community's leadership and good sense. Short is Prince meets Cary the Coyote and the hedge pays off. Long is Prince is a lucky predator and remains unmolested. Pay off on that. Regardless, your local coffers are generating revenue no matter what the outcome.

"Then one day Prince is out on a jaunt and decides Timmy the Toddler is too tasty to ignore. Goodbye Tim, but in the meantime you've built a monetary reserve against the inevitable lawsuit and expenses. Want to avoid this? Pass a leash and muzzle law for potentially dangerous dogs, enforce it, and Prince and Timmy both live to a ripe old age. It's a win-win all around."

"I'm not sure I understand that, but it gets worse," he said. "Your system allows you to set up these 'hedges' for anyone or any event. Granny in the nursing home. Your spouse. A church fire. This is the most insidious piece of technology I've ever seen. You are literally monetizing municipal evil. The PR ramifications for brightstart are enormous."

"That's ridiculous," I said. My voice was stiff. "theTogetherHood is built around well-established theories of market dynamics. Towns and cities are implementing programs and making decisions all the time. Some of these are good, others bad. Depending on the intelligence of the local citizenry, the ratio of bad to good can differ sharply."

I looked directly at Seth. "theTogetherHood does not monetize evil. It simply allows you to short goodness."

Seth shook his head. "I can't believe how you've twisted this all about. Oh, and before I forget, can you tell me more about tTH's relationship with The Royal Grand Cayman Bank of Budapest?"

"The Royal Grand Cayman Bank of Budapest is a respected financial institution providing contingency funding for a variety of institutions as well as full banking services," I said. "theTogetherHood receives a five percent referral fee when municipalities wishing to expand their risk management coverage to take advantage of the bank's services. Our subscribers pay nothing. It's part of our monetization model. We were introduced to Grand Cayman via one of the investment firms you invited to the demos."

"Yes, I know. I spent the weekend reading through all your documentation. The Russians set up the house bank, rake off service fees, and share the take with you on the backend. Ingenious."

"If you don't like Russians, I suggest you contact the *San Jose Mercury News* and tell them brightstart is not interested in Eastern European investments," I said. Poles, Latvians, Estonians, etc.

He shook his head again. "Nice try. I'm sorry, but brightstart can't be involved with this type of thing. You're out."

I eyed his whiskers and he blanched.

"It's not just me. The board is unanimous." He reached into his laptop case and extracted a portable hard drive.

"Here's your complete environment. I was going to mail this to you. All your repositories, code, documentation, everything. It's all packaged up in a virtual box. If you can find someone to host you,

you can be up and running in a few days. And we're relinquishing our equity stake in the company. We want a clean break."

I stared at him.

"And we'll take of care of Dead BFF Village as well. We're throwing them some cash to keep this quiet. We're being as fair as we can. But tTH must go away from brightstart."

Seth stood up and while watching me warily, shoved his Mac and everything else into his carry case in a jumble, dropped $40 on the table for a bill I estimated came to $20, and left The Creamery at a skip/run without waiting for the change.

My phone vibrated. A Twitter message from Angie. I ignored it.

My phone rang. It was Ignacio.

I took the call.

CHAPTER 2

TWO MINDS AS ONE

Ignacio and I talked briefly and decided to rendezvous at the Buena Vista in an hour. We'd first met in a cab we shared from Las Vegas International Airport to the Aladdin hotel, where we were both staying for CES, the Consumer Electronics Show. CES is a mega event drawing a 100 thousand plus attendees across its five full days and displays to a wondering world the latest and greatest games, consoles, music systems, wearables, etc. If it makes noise or wastes time, you can see it at CES.

We ran into each other again on the show's first day as we worked our way through the massive crowd filling the Las Vegas Convention Center's cavernous halls. Our respective journeys ended at two mid-sized booths set up directly across the aisle from each other in the show's music section.

I was attending because I was a product manager (PM) for Creative Labs' family of MP3 players. The company was Singapore-based and its ZEN line briefly enjoyed moderate sales success. Unfortunately, ZENs looked like they'd been designed by the same people who brought you North Korean apartment block housing and the Pontiac Aztek. When Steve Jobs introduced the iPod, gym lunks who'd previously looked cool working out with ZENs topping their biceps were depressed to discover the only girls now paying attention to them sported silky coverings on their upper lips and excess cellulite. The hot chicks followed the iPods.

As a result of this social upheaval, I spent most of CES enduring pitying looks from the major retail chain buyers, who refused to enter our booth even to collect the "bribe bags" stuffed with merchandise and goodies, the normal quid pro quo for a business card or agreement to sit through a product demo.

The show was a trial for Ignacio as well. He'd been sent as a PM by a Taiwanese startup to extoll the virtues of a new series of incredibly sleek and light speakers designed to be wall mounted or placed near your computer. The units looked superb, but sonically reminded people of Rosie Perez singing through a helium balloon. For the next five days, our aisle provided a contrapuntal of my device, which no one wanted to use to listen **to** music, with Ignacio's, which no one could stand to listen to music **through**.

As the event dragged interminably on, Ignacio and I whined, swapped demo horror stories, mocked passing attendees, and tried to end the show on a high note by persuading two Booth Babes from a nearby exhibit to accompany us out for dinner, drinks, and hopefully a visit to Ignacio's suite for further fun activities. They devoured our food and alcohol, but extended our losing streak by declining any further engagement. We finished off the show in my room, morosely sharing a liter of Scotch I'd picked up earlier in the evening, which helped us review the week with increasing equanimity as the bottle's contents steadily decreased.

On the way back to the airport the next day we shared roiled stomachs, bloodshot eyes, and that special bond felt by men who have endured the hard glare of defeat and catastrophe, yet survived. I imagine the heroes of The Battle of the Bulge felt the same way. As the slot machines tinkled around us in the main terminal, we exchanged business cards and promised to keep in touch before flying out.

To our mild surprise, we kept that promise. Fate played a hand. In high technology, the role of product manager is an unusual one. PMs are entrusted with a product's success, but have no authority to hire, fire, or directly manage the work of the various people who create said product (architects, programmers, designers, etc.). Their job function consists of encouraging, empowering, and incentivizing their "team members" to create excellent products and services the market will be unable to resist. In other industries, this function is called "cheerleading" and you carry a pom-pom.

A critical difference between the two roles is that when, say, the New York Jets lose a game, the cheerleaders are not fired. This is a sharp contrast to the fate suffered by a PM. When a product craters, regardless of who the actual culprit(s) are, the PM's job is placed on an altar and ritually slaughtered in an attempt to expiate the sales gods and propitiate upper management. There is no evidence this works, but high technology is surprisingly reactionary in certain areas.

As ZEN sales buckled before the iPod onslaught, I decided to leave Creative before the sharpened knife was drawn across my employment's throat. After inspecting the industry landscape and trends, I decided software was the place to be. My next job was as at Friendster, a hot social media company connecting you and your friends, family, and business contacts within a community framework connecting to other people's frameworks, eventually resulting in your being connected to hundreds of millions of people with whom you had nothing in common except for their ability to receive hundreds of millions of ads from Friendster's servers.

Simultaneously, Ignacio landed a job with Myspace, a hot social media company connecting you and your friends, family, and business contacts within a community framework connecting to other people's frameworks, which...well, you get the idea.

Both of us thought we had landed in technology's current sweetest spot, and we began to meet periodically at local San Francisco bars and in particular the Buena Vista, known nationwide for its Irish Coffee (we were fans) in the spirit of friendly rivalry. Each of us was confident our horse was destined to win this particular business race. And even if it only placed, how bad could that be when your target market was the planet? Then Mark Zuckerberg and Facebook appeared.

Zuckerberg was not as innovative as the Friendster and Myspace founders, but he was a better coder. After compensating for the imagination deficit by stealing the idea for Facebook from the Harvard-attending Winklevoss twins (yes, Winklevoss), Zuckerberg proceeded to create a social media platform which outperformed Friendster and Myspace in connecting hundreds of millions people together to receive Facebook ads. And to show he was no slouch at the innovation game, in the event you actually **had** many friends, family, acquaintances and business contacts, Zuckerberg figured out how to charge you to ensure those people were able to read and see your posts and pictures, turning **your** friends, family, and business contacts into **his** friends, family acquaintances and business contacts.

Ignacio and I both decamped from our respective hotshot social media companies just ahead of the bloodletting and decided hardware wasn't a bad place to be after all. Ignacio's next job was as a senior product manager at Sony for a hot phone running the latest version of Windows Mobile, Microsoft's increasingly popular smartphone operating system. In the meantime, I scored a sweet gig at Samsung as the senior product manager for **their** hot new phone running Windows Mobile. When Ignacio and I met at the Buena Vista to swap war stories and rib each other over Irish coffees in the spirit of friendly competition, we did so secure in the knowledge we'd this time both made the smart-money career choice. Who'd ever lost betting on Microsoft operating systems?

The crimson tide was lapping about our ankles as we sprinted out of our respective jobs just inches ahead of the baying mob, Windows Mobile gurgling behind us horribly as it was throttled to death by Steve Jobs and his touchy/feely buddy, iOS. Disconsolate, we met at the Buena Vista to commiserate and try to understand what had gone so wrong with our jobs and careers.

The answer came in a mutual burst of inspiration.

The problem was we hadn't been true to ourselves. We'd moved to the West Coast to take our places as princes in a glittering world of technological change and entrepreneurial transformation. I'd graduated from New York's CUNY with a business degree and a minor in computer science. Ignacio, a Pittsburgh native, was a Carnegie Mellon graduate with a degree in electrical engineering. He'd proven to be an indifferent engineer, but had a knack for building bridges between the marketing and development sides of technology companies and had eventually moved into product management. He'd also discovered he possessed a natural talent for programming in languages such as JavaScript and PHP, but decided he didn't want to become a professional coder and exercised these skills privately.

But by settling for product management jobs, we'd become mere men-at-arms. We'd stifled our natural creativity in return for the illusory safety of steady paychecks and mid-level technology prestige. We needed to combine our complementary skills, trend-spotting abilities, industry-insider perspectives, and grab hold of our own destinies. And we both knew where opportunity's path led to.

Mobile applications.

Apple's launch of the App Store was remaking the software industry. Thousands of new business opportunities were springing to life every day, from the Angry Birds gaming phenomena to Yelp. Both of us were brimming with ideas.

The first thing we did was establish our new company's core principles over drinks and dinner. Before you can define markets, you have to define yourself. We finally narrowed it down to three fundamentals:

Our products would address mass markets.
Our products would fulfill fundamental needs and goals.
Our products would push technology to its limits. We would move and disrupt.

And thus was born GateIconic.com. We developed the name by submitting Nate and Ignacio to an online anagram generator that spit out

"Gate an Iconic" and dropped the "an." We felt it expressed the spirit of innovation we meant to dominate every aspect of our business. And the domain was available.

We incorporated and I took a job working as a manufacturer's rep for a second-tier firm hawking phone and gadget accessories. Ignacio went to work as a contract programmer developing kiosk software. To save money, we rented a tiny ratty apartment in the urban dystopia known as Oakland, lived on fast food, and for the next 11 months mind-melded and built our first product, "GLT." Things became more complicated when Angie showed up, but the infusion of capital she brought with her was much appreciated.

GLT was short for "Get Lucky Tonight," the flagship of a new software line we positioned as "Romance Acquisition." We were self-funded. I came up with the original concept, product specifications, and headed the team. Ignacio did most of the coding with outsource help. Angie pitched in on the website and marketing.

GLT integrated real-time body language and voice analysis to continually report on the likelihood of a date or similar encounter ending with a romantic outcome. It was possibly ahead of its time. The first version targeted a male audience, though a female version, GLTP ("Pink") was in development but never made it to market.

I feel to this day GLT adhered to our core company principles, despite many unfair criticisms. The product certainly addressed both a mass market and fundamental human goal. However, the first release was probably too feature-rich and overly complex. The criticism the user spent too much time interacting with the app instead of participating in such dating activities as talking, eating, and drinking had some validity. However, this was a 1.0 product and the second version would have been faster and the UI less "busy." Still, GLT may have pushed the technology too far. It's one thing for your reach to exceed your grasp, another to throw your shoulder out of joint.

To be fair, I'm sympathetic to the observation certain women would find the prospect of someone continually pointing an iPhone at them during a meal or while at the movies "creepy" and "disconcerting." However, a miniature Bluetooth camera Ignacio and I evaluated would have overcome this objection. The device's resolution was excellent, its power requirements small, and its tiny size made it possible for it to be concealed practically anywhere.

GLT's initial reviews were less favorable than we'd hoped and claims the product advanced privacy violation hurtful. One female blogger wrote the app was "the worse thing to happen to dating since 'the moist guy who won't stop talking about his ex.'" Sale were poor and it was clear we had misfired.

Ignacio and I learned valuable lessons from this experience and after the initial disappointment, prepared to fail upwards and resume growth hacking our way to success. Angie was perturbed by our financial losses, but recovered. After all, Steve Jobs had botched the launch of the original Macintosh, then burned through millions with NeXT. What had saved him and Apple was the iMac, a frothy, fun, translucent little computer screaming "engage with me." Ignacio and I both decided to take our inspiration from Apple's supreme visionary and build a frothy, fun little app that also screamed engagement. Literally.

Thus, **StartleSnap!**

StartleSnap! was inspired by the fact that many of the best pictures you'll ever take are when someone is surprised or not expecting a camera to go off. Everyone has heard of Candid Camera or seen one of those "America's Funniest Videos" shows. Who's not been delighted and charmed by the antics and stunts recorded and sent in regularly to online video sites and producers?

StartleSnap! transformed all that good natured fun into an iPhone experience. The development and funding cycle followed the same path as GLT, (though Angie was at first reluctant to kick in more cash). The product worked by first entering a "Startle" phrase into the app such as "Surprise!" or "Happy Birthday!" You then placed the phone in the location of your choice or on a stand or similar accessory. Next, you needed to lure your target into camera range and trigger a

StartleSnap! via a "Snap Command" such as "take picture" or "shoot." A nice feature enabled you to use another iPhone or tablet as a remote. The device would play the Startle phrase via the phone's internal or an external speaker, then took a StartleSnap! For more sophisticated users, you could string Startles together or even use your own sound recordings.

Initial sales were strong until people began to abuse the app. Word spread of Startles with extended sequences including "You've been fired. Go see HR," "The coffee is poisoned, spit it out," and "An airliner just hit the building," followed by a rumbling sound. Most of these pranks were good-natured in spirit, but some people were offended. The rumors of heart incidents were unfounded.

As a result of the negative feedback, Apple pulled the product from the App Store and GateIconic had suffered its second failure.

Despite this, we remained optimistic and full of energy. We'd learned another important lesson. The market for consumer apps was fickle and subject to unexpected whims and vagaries. A business product, on the other hand, was a more predictable beast. It might not enjoy an Angry Birds' or Yelp's viral growth, but once sales began to scale, the company's increases in revenue and profitability would be more stable and forecastable.

The idea for theTogetherHood came to me after reading a series of articles about how California towns Stockton, San Jose, Newport, San Bernardino and others were bankrupting themselves by paying lifeguards $200 thousand annual salaries and granting police and fire personnel pensions equal to 100 percent of their pay after only 25 years on the job. The problem wasn't limited to California. The entire state of Illinois is insolvent and hundreds of thousands of residents have fled the resultant taxopalypse. Detroit's government is transforming the place back to prairie land.

Similar situations can be found in hundreds of other locales throughout the country. It didn't take much research to uncover cowardly politicians, bad policies, indifferent citizenries, and entrenched bureaucracies are plentiful commodities in modern urban and municipal life. And commodities can be traded.

Ignacio and I both realized this represented a huge opportunity. In the stock market and other exchanges, almost all the public focus is on the upside, but a great deal of money is made on the down. There was no reason the same model couldn't be applied to public affairs and politics. Understood properly, tTH provided a means for local communities to recoup from and monetize their own idiocy. Both Ignacio and I thought the model's revenue potential was almost limitless.

Our next move was to apply for a slot in brightstart. We positioned the product as an innovative way for local communities to manage risk and enhance revenues. To our joy, we'd been accepted and had happily handed over the incubator's standard seven percent equity cut. Our first demo to potential investors had impressed the group and we'd raised north of $600 thousand from multiple sources. Early response from our beta customers was enthusiastic and I was sure we'd hit the entrepreneurial and innovation bull's-eye dead on this time.

Now this.

I arrived first and took a seat at the nearly empty bar. As I waited for theTogetherHood's co-founder to join me, I ignored another message from Angie and ordered an Anchor Steam. After a few minutes, I saw Ignacio enter the restaurant. I pointed to the seat next to me and he hurried over. "What happened with Seth?" he said. "What's going on?"

I glanced over and down at him. Ignacio is about two inches shorter than me, round, and possesses soft puppy-dog eyes to which he owes his occasional romantic success. People who first meet him always assume he's Hispanic, but his father was of German-Jewish origin (hence his last name of "Loehman") while his mother was Italian and had attended a Jesuit high school (thus "Ignacio Loyola").

"We've been thrown out of brightstart." I reached into my pocket, pulled out the hard drive, and handed it to him. "Here. Seth said the entire system is on this."

"Jesus." He took the drive and stared at it. "Did he say why? What's the problem?"

"They don't like our business model. They said it's evil."

"What do you mean 'evil.' It's brilliant. Once the risk hedges and pools are established, a town can sit back and watch the money flow in. The software pays for itself almost immediately. Hell, with the deal we struck with that Russian bank, we'll be able to give subscriber seats away and monetize."

"You don't have to tell me. I came up with the idea."

"Why now? We've been in beta for nine months."

"One of our betas called to complain a few furry disease vectors in their suburban utopia had gone missing and blamed it on theTogetherHood. If we had any money, I'd hire a lawyer and sue the bastards."

"I've just checked the site," Ignacio said. "We're completely down. No home page, not even a 404 error. We've been absorbed into the ether. What do we do?"

"I'm not sure. How long will it take to restore off the drive and get us back up?"

"Best case, a week. But are we going to have any customers when this is all over? And the server space won't be that cheap. We only paid those low prices because of brightstart. I don't know about you, but I'm tapped out. I placed almost all my savings into theTogetherHood. I know we've run through most of our funding. We were supposed to reload at the next series of demos using our beta feedback as incentive. How are you for money?"

"Same position as you. But, I'll talk to Angie. We're so close to breaking through. Even if her personal piggy bank is somewhat thin, she has serious ties in Shenzen. And theTogetherHood has great appeal to the Chinese market. Highly entrepreneurial."

Ignacio looked at me. "I don't know. Angie's been waiting to become a bride longer than is healthy in most relationships. Didn't she almost leave you when you hit her up for tTH money?"

"I was offering an equity stake. I'll worry about her. In the meantime, you worry about shaving time off our back-on-line schedule."

"I will."

We spent the next hour or so planning our comeback and laughing at brightstart's lack of vision. While we talked, my phone vibrated several times, but I ignored it.

When we'd finished outlining our recovery plan over a napkin, I picked up the check and headed home to set the stage for theTogetherHood's rebirth.

CHAPTER 3

FATHERHOOD

The rebirth was abortive.

"I'm late," was the first thing Angie said when I walked through the door of our apartment. "I kept trying to contact you. Why didn't you answer your phone? Or at least message me back?"

"I had the ringer and notifications off and didn't check my phone. And what do you mean you're 'late?' We don't have anything on our calendar."

"I thought you said you didn't check your phone," she said.

"I checked it in the morning. Early. What are we late for?"

"Not you. **Me**." She pointed to her stomach.

Oh. Oh. Uh, oh. She was "late."

"Do you mean..."

"Five weeks." There was a long, significant pause. "Daddy."

I felt the blood begin to drain from my head and my cheeks whiten. Of all the times for her to pull a stunt like this.

"Aren't you happy?" she said.

Under these circumstances, this is the most dangerous question a man can be asked. An answer other than "Yes" courts homicide.

"Of course I'm happy, tim sam, but I'm a bit surprised." Tim sam means "darling" in Cantonese. If you date a girl from Shenzen, you must learn this word.) "Aren't we on birth control? How did this happen?"

"**We** are not on birth control. You don't like to use condoms. I'm the one who's been on the pill. It makes me feel fat. As for how it happened, I can buy you a picture book if you need. Well?"

"Well, then, I'm not sure how **you** became pregnant."

"The pill failed. Well?"

Right. The birth control "failed." The pill doesn't "fail." What had failed was Angie's patience. A wave of indignation swept over me. What an underhanded thing to do to a man.

"Well, I'm happy, but the timing is bad. brightstart shut down the TogetherHood today. As of this moment, we're out of business."

"What?? What happened?"

I narrated the day's events. When I was finished, I told her, "But the news isn't all bad."

"What's not bad about any of this? This is your third failure, I'm pregnant, and the baby and I need money. I have to eat properly if our son is going to have a proper start in life."

"Why do you say it's a boy? Isn't it too early to know?"

"It's a boy," she said. Angie was mainland Chinese. After several years in the U.S., she was fairly Americanized and had grown up learning English as a second language from U.K. tutors hired in Hong Kong. She spoke as well as I did, and I thought the light British accent and occasional mix-up of American and English idioms cute. But she wasn't **that** acculturated. In China, it's still a boy's world. Yes, the powers that be have relaxed the one child regime (the program had led to a serious shortage of brides for China's Brave Young Men to marry), but no one trusted the government on this one. And god-forbid you had **two** daughters. The cost of buying a shot at that son was too high to bear thinking about.

I went on. "Here's what's not so bad. Ignacio can restore the site in a few days. Other than the one unhappy beta, feedback on the system is positive. If you can talk to your uncle and the right contacts in Shenzen and tell them about the opportunity, I bet they'll be willing to help us out with an investment. And Ignacio and I both think the Chinese market will be open to the value proposition of theTogeth..."

"No," she said.

"It would be nice if you'd let me finish my sentence. And what do you mean 'no?' You're pregnant, must eat to grow a better male, and we need money. Our **son** needs the money. And we're so close to turning theTogetherHood into a major success. I've been through the numbers with Ignacio."

"I mean 'No.' You need to find a job." She put her hand on her stomach. "We need money."

"And I'm trying to make it. We're so close that..."

"No. theTogetherHood is dead. How are you going to explain to your betas why you dropped offline so suddenly? And why brightstart withdrew funding? Within a few days, the entire Valley will know you were tossed out. You're lepers. I've met Seth. He has a big mouth and I'll bet he's already added theTogtherHood to one of those 'Lessons I've Learned' slides he's always bringing to Meetup groups."

"He said brightstart wanted to keep this quiet."

"It won't matter what anyone thinks about brightstart. You need to find a job."

"I have a job. I'm the CEO of GateIconic."

"You're an ex-CEO. Go find a job as a product manager. I can help you there. My uncle says a Chinese company is opening an office in South San Francisco. A new line of battery accessories for the iPhone and Android. A Shenzen company is the prime contractor."

I groaned. "Those accessory companies don't have real product managers. What they do is hire a few Americans to go to tradeshows as demo dollies and try to close sales."

"Isn't that what you did?"

"I inspired a product team. In Chinese firms, American management is a front for tax purposes. The company stuffs the back office with their mainland friends and relatives who want to work in or live in America."

"My uncle said the CEO is an American."

"They always hire an American to be the 'CEO.' The CFO is Chinese, right?"

"Yes."

"Good to know who the CEO really is. I'm not interested."

"Then you need to find a job on your own. When are we getting married?"

"Angie, how can I discuss marriage when I've just lost my company and you won't help me?"

"I can discuss it because I invested in all three of your startups, have no expectations of seeing any return, am pregnant with your son, and am not turning 30 with a child and no husband. I'm sorry about what happened with tTH, but we've been discussing our marriage forever. You'll find a job, we'll marry, I won't lose face in front of my family, and we'll climb back on our feet financially. And I still have my job with the bank. After the baby is born, let's move to Shenzen. Uncle Tony will hire you. Your Cantonese isn't any good, but you can learn. Then Mandarin. When are we getting married?"

Right. Move to China. We've all heard the statement, marry the girl, marry the family, but the Chinese **mean** it. Angie's parents were dead, but she had a brother and plenty of leftover cousins, aunt, uncles, and at least two grandparents extant, a substantial number of whom would inevitably be moving in with us. I was **not** moving to China. That's the equivalent of an American mallard visiting Chinatown's Hakksan restaurant to announce it's there for the Peking Duck.

"Angie, give me time to process what just happened today. I'm going through a great deal. No job, now fatherhood. And I need to think about how my mother is going to take all this."

"Your mother won't be happy. Your mother hates me because I'm Chinese."

"That's not true." Actually, it **was** true. Mom was old-school New York. In the neighborhood she grew up in, Italians ran the fruit stores, the Irish were the cops and firemen, and the doctors were Jews and

Germans. Puerto Ricans were the superintendents. The Chinese role was to staff laundries and serve spare ribs, not marry her son.

My mother had met Angie once, when she accompanied me back to New York for my father's funeral after he dropped dead one day from a heart attack. Mother had been barely polite to my girlfriend, and I'd watched her closely to make sure she didn't hand Angie her dress blouses with instructions to add extra starch. To her credit, Angie kept control of her temper, though she extracted revenge by commenting loudly enough so that Mom could hear it on the attractiveness of the two middle-aged women who came to Dad's wake to dab tears from their eyes as they gazed down mournfully at him in his casket. Neither woman introduced themselves.

The rest of the evening and the next few days were grim. Angie's prediction about the fate of theTogetherHood turned out to be the wisdom of the East. Calls made to our beta customers elicited skeptical questions about why we were off line and open speculation about our viability. The retail prices we were quoted for server space made Ignacio and I gulp. Our Columbian outsource team apologized, but ceased work. None of our investors responded to our attempts to contact them. I contacted Seth a couple of times, but he didn't answer either.

After a couple of weeks of this, Ignacio and I were forced to accept the truth. We were dead.

In the meantime, Angie initiated a modern, psychological version of the venerable Chinese water torture. Every time I sat down at our computer, a web page discussing topics such as why mothers-to-be required security, needed to be pampered, and should consume brain-building foods dominated the desktop. The questions about the date of our nuptials increased in frequency and became more edged.

Unfortunately for her, I'm not someone who bends easily to unfair pressure and coercion. When a man marries, it needs to be at the right time, for the right reason, to the right person. The first two factors of this equation weren't in place and I was becoming unsure of the third.

To escape the drip, drip, drip, I started to take long walks in the Presidio while contemplating my future. I was in the park and had just passed by the military cemetery when my phone rang. I looked down and saw Michael Song's ID. I hesitated for a second, then connected. Angie's younger brother had just completed his residency at Stanford, preparatory to moving on to an oncology specialty. We'd never had much use for each other, but we did have Angie and the fact we were both a little afraid of her in common. This call was undoubtedly a ploy to ratchet up the pressure even higher.

"So, my sister tells me she's expecting and you're reluctant to marry the Daughter of Fu Manchu?" he said without preamble.

"Isn't that racist?"

"I'm Chinese. I'm allowed to make those observations. You're white and your last name is 'Pennington.' You're not allowed to make fun of anybody. Regardless, is there a good reason why you're not taking responsibility and doing the right thing?"

"I'm not sure this is the right thing to do," I said. "I'm out of work and can't support a child. Angie was supposed to be on the pill and now she's pregnant. That's unfair."

"That's clueless. The birth control she's on has a 90 percent prevention rate. You've been living with Angie for four years and it's not unlikely there could have been a failure. Besides, what does it matter? She's going to turn 29 in a couple of months and you know how Chinese women are about turning 30 without a husband and no family prospects. Consider yourself lucky. On the mainland, she'd have had Uncle Tony truss you up and delivered in your blue dragon robe for the temple ceremony before she turned 25."

"It just doesn't feel right."

"It apparently felt right enough for you two to make a baby together. And you weren't even engaged."

"I want to be financially viable before I take responsibility for a child."

"I bet Angie feels the same way. I imagine that's why she helped fund your startups. She just informed me. She must truly love you. Not many Chinese women would tap their personal savings three times for their boyfriend. In China, it's the other way around.

"Look, I know Angie's not the easiest woman to live with," he said. "And since my uncle has two sons and has treated Angie like a daughter since my parents died, she's also your typical Chinese princess. A bossy, opinionated control freak who desperately wants to be married and have a child. But you already know this. You could have ended the relationship years ago. Nothing stopped you. And I can tell you Uncle Tony is not dying to have a white barbarian nephew. Why did you stay with her?"

It was a good question. But given Michael's sibling relationship with Angie, answering him didn't make me feel comfortable. And Uncle Tony would hear the answer and that didn't make me feel safe.

The reason I had stayed with Angie is she is the closest thing to sexual paradise I will ever experience on this earth. (And I'd needed capital.)

Don't misunderstand me. Angie was smart, for a Chinese had a good sense of humor, and was beautiful. But in bed, she was the goddess of Eros. I have often thought that if China wanted to revive Chairman Mao, all they need do is let Angie spend a night with the corpse. In the morning, they would find the Great Helmsman revived, all banners flying, and ready to leap forward and kill another 45 million Chinese.

I'd first met Angie on a trip to Shenzen, China's answer to Silicon Valley. Early samples of the American version of the Samsung phone I was managing had suffered from poor reception and dropped signals. The problem had been traced back to a manufacturing defect in the case. I'd flown to Hong Kong and taken the 30-mile cab ride north to Shenzen to visit SongTech, LLC, the case contractor. My task was to ensure the problem had been resolved and check on quality control and related issues.

The deal represented a major opportunity for SongTech. The firm's founder and resident emperor, Tony Song, had accorded me VIP treatment. This included a personal tour of the facilities by his niece, Angie. She was a recent MBA graduate from Hong Kong's School of Business, charming, and highly knowledgeable about her uncle's operations. She began to flirt as she guided me by the different production and assembly lines, and I was happy to reciprocate. If Get Lucky Tonight had existed back then, its predictive infographics would have been flashing green by the tour's end.

That evening, Tony held a dinner in my honor at one of Shenzen's best restaurants. Angie was seated next to me and as the meal progressed, we began teasing each other until I looked up to see SongTech's CEO looking at me with a sour mien. I immediately went into full running-dog-of-capitalism-here-to-do-sell-rope sales mode and Tony relaxed. I didn't see Angie again for the rest of the visit.

Our paths crossed a year later at the Hong Kong Electronics Fair, the region's largest. I'd been sent to get a jump on CES and spy out new gadgets and gizmos with the potential to tickle the fancies of the U.S. market. On the show's second day, I was cruising through the peripherals section when I heard a voice call out my name. I turned around and there was Angie. SongTech was exhibiting and she'd come to help staff the booth and provide English translation assistance.

Angie had not gone into the family business, but instead had been hired by the Industrial and Commercial Bank of China, one of the Mainland's big four lenders. We exchanged business cards, I asked her out to dinner, and she accepted. Dinner was wonderful, we went to the hotel bar for after-dinner drinks, and later that evening in my hotel room I discovered that bliss **does** exist on this earth.

Angie and I repeated our first night's experience till the show's end. I left for the U.S. with a handful of product leads and a vague regret my employer didn't have an overseas office in Hong Kong. Over the next year, we stayed in touch and continued to flirt online. I **do** remember she mentioned she might be visiting the U.S. in the near future and I replied we'd have to meet while she was in the States. It's possible I may have used the words "love to see you" or even "I love you" or words to that affect. It may have been my fault Angie over-interpreted my response.

Regardless, after Ignacio and I had decamped to the city across the Bay where there's no there there, the doorbell to our apartment rang and there stood Angie.

Once I'd scraped my lower jaw off the pavement, I discovered she'd wrangled a staff job at one of her bank's San Francisco locations. Possibly a gift from Uncle Tony, who swung weight in Chinese political circles. U.S. commercial postings are highly coveted in China, and obtaining one is often a matter of who you know.

I also learned Angie now categorized me as her boyfriend. A tad presumptuous, but since Ignacio and I had quit our day jobs to work on GLT full time and were running on financial fumes, her willingness to help fund the venture decided the issue.

Angie had no intention of living in Oakland and invited me to move into her apartment in San Francisco on Gough Street. I put up zero resistance, anxious to escape Oakland and Ignacio's snore. Ignacio, likewise anxious to return to civilization, rented an illegal basement "apartment" from a couple in the Mission district and GLT's launch stormed ahead.

From a personal standpoint, life was grand. Gough Street was heaven compared to my previous abode, my sex life was wonderful, and I was relieved of the burden of having to kick in for the monthly rent. Ignacio and I could focus solely on GateIconic's success.

There **was** a fly in the ointment. This fly was named "Angie." Several months after I'd moved in, she began to hint about marriage. I refused to take the hint. She then began to **talk** about marriage. I countered by observing that in the U.S., most couples date or live together at least two or three years before tying the knot. Angie responded by telling me that's not how things were done in China. I riposted by noting that when in Rome, you must do as the Romans do. She didn't appreciate the cultural comparison, but I avoided a nuclear conflagration by telling her marriage was on the horizon, but currently my time was limited and I had to focus on business success and product monetization. Once these were achieved, the wedding could be something more impressive than a quick trip down to City Hall.

"Nate? You still there?" Michael's voice broke my reverie.

"Yes. Michael, I need time to sort this all out. I'm going to do the right thing, but I need to figure out what that is."

"Angie thinks the answer is obvious."

"I know, Michael." I didn't say anything else.

After a second he cleared his throat. "Well, I've said everything I can. I'll let you two work it out. My uncle is not going to be happy. Oh, one thing. Angie asked me to give you this message. She said to tell you she read Isaacson's book on Steve Jobs too."

"I understand." Actually, I had no clue. I spent more time on the Presidio's quiet pathways puzzling over the obscure message, then returned home.

I found my clothing, tablet, laptop, and a few other belongings packed neatly into a stack of boxes in front of the apartment. The locks had been changed. She didn't answer my knocks nor entreaties through the door of "Tim sam, let's talk about this."

Outside the door, I remembered. Steve Jobs hadn't married Laurene Powell until she was three months pregnant.

CHAPTER 4

MEETING MOTHER CABRINI

After absorbing that I'd been kicked out, I called Ignacio. He showed up in half an hour with an Uber ride and we took my boxes over to his place.

"You can stay with me for a few days, but it won't work out long term," he said. He was apologetic, but I understood. His 'apartment' was maybe 400 square feet. "Let's go to the Buena Vista."

Inside we ordered Irish coffees and lunch. It was a quiet meal for the most part. There wasn't much to say. We'd taken three swings at entrepreneurial success and had three whiffs to show for it. Towards the end of the meal, Ignacio looked up at me.

"What are your plans? What about Angie and the baby?"

"I'm not sure about my plans. The one thing I know is I don't want to become a father right now."

"I don't think you have a choice anymore. And I do suggest you not mention abortion to Angie."

"I don't intend to. Uncle Tony would send the Tong to kill me." I didn't think I was kidding.

The waiter came over to ask if we wanted anything else. We shook our heads no, and he returned with the bill. Ignacio swiped and when I offered to pay my half, shook his head. "It's on me."

"Thanks," I said. I looked at him and a thought crossed my mind. Ever since we'd met, I'd noticed no matter how tight things became financially, Ignacio always seemed to have funds in reserve.

"Could I ask? How are you doing for money?"

"I'm doing OK. I have a website I've been running for several years that provides me a steady little side income. I'm not going to retire on it, but it's nice to have. I wasn't holding out on you, by the way. I put in money I generated from the site into the company."

"What's the content? Anything we could tie into for another app?"

He looked embarrassed. "I don't think so. I've always been into horror movies, particularly zombie films. You know that."

I **did** know that. A few years ago, Ignacio had made me sit through an awful film called "Dead Snow," a **Norwegian** slasher flick about Nazi zombies chasing skiers. Midway through the film, I found myself pining for a chainsaw with which to kill Ignacio. Our partnership almost came to an end then and there.

"I set up a fan site for hard-core horror movie buffs," he said. "You know, a portal where you could discuss the latest vampire flick, argue about whether 'Suspiria' is scarier than 'The Bird with the Crystal Plumage,' catch up on your zombie gossip, that type of thing."

"I wouldn't think zombie gossip would be very interesting," I said. "What's new in the typical zombie's life? Die, eat brains, eat brains the next day. What's the name of the site? Why didn't you tell me about it? How do you make any money?"

"I didn't tell you because you made it abundantly clear you don't care for horror. The site's called Deadland.com. I make money via advertising. I'll admit it's not a high-class clientele. Viagra hawkers, click farmers, porn sites. But the money's been steady for years and I don't have to do much. Just occasionally post up fresh, well, new, content."

I reached for my phone and typed in the URL. A picture of a decapitated head popped up on my screen. Underneath it was a review for "Dead Snow 2: Red vs. Dead."

"Ugh, Ignacio."

"Sorry. The gore draws the eyeballs. I wish more people would focus on the artistry of zombie film making."

"The world is full of Philistines." I shut the URL down. I was depressed enough without looking at **that**.

That night I slept in Ignacio's basement and tried to make myself as comfortable as possible, with limited success. It was cramped and he snored. The next day, I called Angie in the hope she'd be reasonable and let me regain Gough Street rooming privileges. She refused to answer. There wasn't anything I could do. Her name was on the apartment lease, not mine.

After a few more days rooming with Ignacio, a desperate look appeared on his face and the landlord began to dish out fisheyes. I'd been too depressed to look for a job and had a feeling it would be a waste of time. Every significant company in the Valley would have heard about the tTH debacle. From an employer perspective, I was radioactive and unsure when the local do-not-hire employment Geiger counters would stop clicking.

I finally surrendered to the inevitable and called my Mom to tell her I was flying back East for a visit. I guess I was going home. It was the place where, when you have to go there, they have to take you in. At least when Mom is in a good mood.

The day of my flight I took BART to SFO for a redeye back to New York. On the train and in the terminal, large signs advertising Body Worlds were everywhere. I've always found the Corpse on Parade concept grisly, though it was tame compared to Ignacio's ongoing horror festival. Waiting to board, I read more about the event. It was mildly interesting. The first Body World had debuted in1995, and over 43 million people have attended an exhibit, making it a bigger touring show than the circus. But the public has always been interested in this sort of thing. Go to any museum with an Ancient Egypt display and people will be lined up to mummy-gaze.

The plane began boarding and I tucked my phone away. When I touched down,I called Mom and left a message on her answering machine telling her I'd arrived. My cab pulled up to her apartment late in the morning. I paid the fare, retrieved my luggage, key-coded into the main entrance, and took the elevator up to her floor.

My mother lives in Riverdale in a spacious three bedroom apartment built in the 40s with a view of the Hudson River. Riverdale is located in The Bronx's northwest corner and is an anomaly, a bucolic, hilly place with large homes, gracious apartments, and forest copses. The area never suffered the burnings and despoliation that plagued the only part of New York City attached to the mainland, and people who live in Riverdale **never** acknowledge it's part of The Bronx. It remains one of the great joys of people who live in other sections of the borough to remind Riverdalians that it **is**.

I'd grown up here and used to visit my parents at least once a year. However, after Dad's death, Mom had initiated a gravesite ritual which she insisted I participate in when I was in town. It provided me maximum incentive to stay on the West Coast.

I stepped off the elevator with my luggage, walked down the quiet corridor to Mom's apartment, and rang her bell. I'd had a key, but lost track of it after my last visit. My mother was not a technology fan and never used the feature phone I'd bought her. Her answering machine still used tape cassettes. After a minute, I called her landline and the machine picked up. I rang the bell again. No response. I called out in the hallway "Mom, it's Nate. Please open the door." Silence. I began to hear the metallic swish of peepholes opening in doors up and down the corridor and started to feel the pressure of unseen eyes peering at me. In a few seconds, the 911 calls would begin.

I rang again and finally heard Mom's peephole slide up, then slide down. There was a fumbling sound at the lock and she opened the door. The pressure ceased and the phantoms returned to their lives.

"Oh. It's you," Mom said. "Why didn't you use your key?"

"Good to see you too, Mom. I lost the key." She presented her cheek. I bent down and kissed it, then rolled my luggage into the apartment. Scott, her large, muted-calico cat, strolled out from behind the living room sofa, raised his tail to comma station, then came over to rub his head against my ankle. I was his again. When I was growing up, Mom had never permitted me to own so much as a parakeet, but soon after my Dad's death she'd adopted a kitten being hawked by one of her bridge club friends who'd found an abandoned litter outside the building.

"I have a spare somewhere. I'll give it you."

"Thanks, Mom."

"So, where's your girlfriend Annie?"

"Angie, Mom. She's back in San Francisco. We're going through a rough patch."

"What's the problem? Is she double-creasing your trousers?"

"Mom, this is the 21st century, not 1960. The world is changing. Angie does not work in a dry cleaners. She's on staff at a San Francisco branch of one of China's largest banks."

"That's nice. The laundries need to get their loans from somewhere. Do you want breakfast?"

"Yes, Mom. That would be nice. How are you feeling?"

"I'm feeling wonderful. Every day I wake up, breathe the fresh air, see the sun, enjoy the sight of the Hudson through my window, and remind myself your father is still dead."

"Yes, Mom. How's the Bridge Club?"

After Dad's death, Mom's social life had revolved around the building's bridge club, a group of older women and a couple of token men who met almost daily in the recreation hall to play Bridge, Pinochle, Rummy, and so on while discussing at relentless lengths their marriages, deceased spouses if applicable, grandchildren, etc.

"They're fine. I've been on a losing streak recently. I can't seem to make contract."

It was relatively quiet at home for the next couple of days. In my other visits, Mom had cooked breakfast and dinner for me, but these had been replaced with an assortment of microwave dinners. I couldn't blame her. It's no fun cooking for one.

A day after I arrived, I did tell Mom a little about my latest entrepreneurial setback. I don't think she understood much of my story, but she came to full alert when I mentioned we were monetarily tapped out.

"I hope you're not here to ask me for money," she said. "I'm a widow living on a fixed income. I don't have a dime to spare. You'll get it all when I die, but I plan to stick around a good long time so don't get your hopes up anytime soon."

"No, Mom, I didn't come here to ask for a loan." I knew better. My father had left Mom well provided for, but she was extremely 'thrifty.' I had doubts about her longevity boasts, though. In contrast to my previous visits, the apartment seemed to be in an increased state of disorder. This morning, I found she'd left her toothbrush by the kitchen sink. The large mahogany table dominating the dining room was marred by water rings from coffee cups and soda cans left to condense on the once highly-polished, immaculate surface. The apartment windows needed to be cleaned, and Scott's litterbox was overburdened. Mom did have a cleaning lady come in once a week, but the Mrs. Janine Pennington I'd known as a boy would never have allowed this level of disorder to enter her home.

In the evening I sent Angie a short text, which she ignored. Fine. She was the one with the belly on the way, not me.

After settling in, I decided to revisit a few local haunts. After strolling around Riverdale a while, I headed over to Broadway and boarded the Number 1 train to Dyckman Street, got off, and headed to The Cloisters.

The Cloisters is officially part of New York's Metropolitan Museum, the big downtown fortress on Fifth Avenue, and is located in Fort Tryon Park. It's mostly a native New Yorker secret. It was built in the 30s and the exhibits, with only a few temporary exceptions, focus on medieval European art and sculpture.

My mother had taken me to the place periodically when I was a boy, though at the time I hadn't shown much appreciation for my extended cultural education. I'd found the museum tedious and dull. Like every other kid, I wanted to go the Museum of Natural History and see the dinosaurs. However, as I grew older, I developed a new appreciation for the institution, especially after I discovered it was a cheap place to take a girl for a date and bestowed upon you a patina of cultural credibility. Girls like that. And there are excellent make out sections if you know the park's terrain.

I reached the museum and entered. There are always visitors, but unless there's a special exhibit, The Cloisters lacks the Grand Central Station feel of the Met, particularly on weekdays. For the next couple of hours I wandered through the halls and galleries, looking at the multiple pictures, reliefs, and statues, all with their stiff, passionate gazes focused on a spectral realm beyond the reach of human cares and concerns. A place similar to the one where my entrepreneurial career now resided.

I left feeling thoroughly depressed and wandered further south out of Fort Tyron and onto Fort Washington Avenue, a pleasant, tree-lined street. After strolling a few more blocks, I came upon a small crowd of people standing on the sidewalk handing out flyers to passers-by calling for federal immigration reform. I took one and looked over at the building they were gathered in front of. It was the Mother Cabrini Shrine, home of New York's only above ground saint. I'd heard of the place, but had never visited. I hesitated a second, then walked inside.

I pulled out my phone as I entered the building, a chapel of modest size, and did a quick search on the Mother. Saint Francis Xavier Cabrini was born in in 1850 in Italy and died in New York City in 1917. A nun who knew how to organize, she founded The Missionary Sisters of the Sacred Heart of Jesus and functioned as its CEO, err, "Superior General" until she died. Impressive. Every entrepreneur knows how hard it can be to hold onto executive control of a company you've founded. During her tenure, she managed a nationwide expansion of her order to 67 branches. Originally, she'd wanted to be a missionary in China, but went to the U.S. instead, a much better market. This was a smart, savvy nun.

During her life, she managed the "Do You Want to Be a Saint?" checklist perfectly. Founded orphanages? Yes. Education for the kids? Ditto. Services for the sick and elderly? Why even ask. **She even managed to die while preparing Christmas candy for the local urchins**. Add PR Master to her accomplishments.

Her managerial talent paid off after her death. In 1931, she was disinterred and her corpse was found to be in good enough shape to make it to beatification, sainthood's minor leagues. After only a few years, Mother Cabrini performed the two requisite miracles and went to the majors, becoming a saint in 1938. She is the patron saint of immigrants, hence the flyers on the sidewalk. More PR genius. She may have been dead for a century, but this woman still had her heavenly hand on the current political pulse.

I walked to the chapel's front to take a closer look at the Mother. Her body is displayed in repose in a glass case. The wall behind her features a large mural celebrating her life's work. As I gazed down at her, a middle-aged woman wearing a dark jacket and a simple head dress came up and stood next to me. "I see you find our foundress of great interest," she said.

"Yes," I said. "I grew up not far from here, but never came to the Shrine before. I'm glad I did. I've never understood why Catholics display saints in this way, though. Forgive me Sister, but it seems, I don't know, atavistic? Primitive? Don't most Christian religions believe in a life after this? That we one day exist in a perfect heavenly body? I'm sorry, I don't mean to be insulting. By the way, my name's Nate Pennington."

"I'm Sister Mary Gael." She smiled at me. "Don't worry about it. You're by no means the first person to make that observation. But while God eventually escorts us to a spiritual world, He created matter as well and loves it. You and I are proof.

"And the Church is by no means the only organization or group of people who venerate relics. Have you ever been to Ford's Theater Museum? It displays a collection of things associated with President Lincoln, including the blood-stained pillow on which his head rested as he lay dying through the night. The pillow is a relic of a dark and terrible moment in our country's history, yet no one has ever suggested it be cleaned or discarded. Most people would call it 'sacrilege' if it was."

"You have a point." I looked back down at Mother Cabrini. "Her face has an interesting cast after all these years. Almost like wax."

"It **is** wax," she said.

"Excuse me?"

"After she became a saint, her head was taken to the Vatican, her heart to Italy, and her arm to Chicago. A piece of her finger is in Colorado at an orphanage she founded."

"You distributed Mother Cabrini?"

"We Catholics like to share our saints. We think it helps spread the holiness. Over a billion Catholics can't be wrong. And it's not only bodies we venerate." She tapped a small silver locket she wore above her crucifix and I leaned closer to take a look. The front of the locket was clear and inside was a small black square against a white background.

"What is it?"

"A second-class relic. A first-class relic is the body or a part of the body of a blessed or a saint. A second-class item is something once owned by them. A secular example is a Lincoln letter. This relic is from a piece of clothing once owned by the Blessed Mother. It enables me to keep a small part of Mother Cabrini close to my heart."

"Where did you buy it from? The Vatican?"

"E-bay." She smiled at me again, then moved away to talk to a group who'd entered the chapel holding bundles of leaflets. I took a last look at most of Mother Cabrini, stuck a five dollar bill in the contribution box, left the chapel, and walked to the subway for the ride back to Riverdale.

CHAPTER 5

VISITING DAD

The next day, the moment I'd been dreading since my return to Riverdale arrived.

"We're going to see your Father today," Mom said over breakfast. "Call a cab to take us to Woodlawn."

I groaned. "Mom, must we? The last time we went it was not a pleasant experience. For either of us."

"We are going to see your Father. Dress nicely and shave."

"Mom..."

"Get dressed and call the cab. Or you can pack your bags and fly back to San Francisco."

I surrendered to the unavoidable. "Yes, Mom." I finished my breakfast and Ubered a ride. "They'll be here in 30 minutes."

"Good. Go get ready."

I went into the extra bathroom, took a quick shower, and started shaving. As I drew the razor across my chin, Scott sprung into the room and batted something across the floor. He crouched, relocated his prey, and swatted again. Something bright and shiny skittered by my feet. I bent over and picked it up. Scott sat down and looked up at me, his tail swishing rhythmically over the tiles as he waited for the return of his toy.

His prey was a ring made of white gold or possibly platinum, with a large, clear, emerald-cut diamond in the setting. I looked at it a second, then remembered where I'd seen it. It was my Granma's engagement ring. She'd died when I was five and I possessed only a few clear memories of her, but I'd seen this ring in a couple of old family portraits. Mom was an only child and I guessed she'd inherited it when Granma had passed.

"Nate, are you ready?" Mom said. "The cab should be here in a few minutes. I want to wait in front. I don't want to miss them."

"Yes, Mom." I stuck the ring in my pajama pocket and resumed shaving. Scott stared up at me hopefully for a minute, then stalked away in disgust when it became clear I wasn't returning his prize.

"Nate, are you ready yet?"

"Almost, Mom. No rush. They won't be here for another 20 minutes." I finished shaving and went into my bedroom to dress.

"Nate, are you ready...?"

"In a second, Mother."

I finished dressing and we went downstairs. The cab pulled up in 15 minutes and we headed off. Mom was dressed in her Going-to-Visit-Dad outfit, a dark grey dress, jacket, black pumps, and her pearls. On her head she wore what I called her widow's peak, a fedora-like confection complete with pull down veil in front.

Dad was interred in Woodlawn Cemetery, about a 15-minute drive from Riverdale. We weren't visiting an actual grave. Woodlawn is a historic landmark and you need to be very wealthy to grab a plot of real dirt in the place. After his funeral, Dad was cremated and interred in a mausoleum niche with his name, date of birth and death, and the inscription "Beloved Husband and Father." Well, **I'd** liked him.

My parents' marriage had not been happy. Dad had been a district salesman and manager for Scott Paper Corporation. His best friends called him "Pistol." His territory ran east to Hartford, CT, west and south to Allentown, PA, and as far north as Albany, NY. The job required he spend about 50 percent of his working time on the road and Dad, according to Mom, had followed the maxim that when the cat's away, the cat will cat around. My mother was sure Dad had a girlfriend in every town, village, and city located in his sales purview and became increasingly embittered as the years went by.

The Pistol **was** a good looking fellow, but I always thought Mom's groupie estimates were far out of alignment for someone whose chief claim to glamor was his ability to provide deep discounts on pallets of extra-soft toilet paper. But there's no doubt Dad presided over a successful extramarital fan club during his time at Scott. He never made much effort to hide the signs.

The cab dropped us off at the Sunset Chapel and we walked over to the wall holding Dad's urn. As we drew nearer, Mom began to fidget and mutter under her breath. The closer we drew, the more agitated she became and the clearer her commentary.

"Hi, Frank. I'm back to visit and keep you company. You know what I like about this whole you being dead thing, 'Pistol?' We're both at peace. You're stuck in that wall and I don't have to worry about what floozy you're screwing in Allentown, or listen to your lies about how your car broke down on the Taconic so you'll be away for a couple of more days, or worry about what filthy disease you're going to be bringing home in your trousers, Frank. These days, you keep it in your pants. You know why? Because it's burned **off**."

Mother's voice had steadily risen during her soliloquy, and other mourners at the wall were beginning to stare. The Widow continued, gathering both force and volume.

"How about I bring you up to date on some of your accounts. Remember Sylvia? Your buyer in East Hartford? She's gotten fat, Frank. So fat that when she's walking around, people wonder how they missed the weather balloon landing. And Terry? The store manager in Poughkeepsie? The one with the rack? All gone, Frank. A double mastectomy. She's flatter than a treadmill. If you'd spent more time on one of those instead of that tramp, you might still be here, Frank."

I looked around. Several people were staring at us openly. I smiled apologetically and tried to divert The Widow Pennington. "Uh, Mother, how do you know about these women?"

"Robin in the Bridge Club uses something on her phone called 'Facehead.' I had her look them up."

"I see." I made a note to have a talk with Robin before my visit was over. Some people should not have access to technology. I put my arm around Mom's shoulder and tried to lead her away. "Well, we've visited with Dad enough, Mom. Why don't we leave and go home. Tell you what. I'll take you out to lunch and..."

She pushed my arm away. "I'm not leaving yet." She took a step closer to the wall. "By the way, Frank, your son's here to visit you as well. Too bad I had to wait till I was almost 40 to have him. You know why that is, Frank? Because while you were out screwing everything from Albany to Riverdale, you weren't able to perform your duties as a man at home. Do you remember how big he was at birth? Nine pounds, six ounces. Do you know what it's like to give birth to a monster like that when you're almost forty, Frank? You nearly **killed** me, you bastard."

Mom's voice had risen to a near shriek and she was sobbing as well. Everyone had by now retreated a safe distance from the erupting widow. Then I saw a gentleman walk out the front of the Sunset Chapel and head over to us with a purposeful stride. It was time to leave.

"Let's go, Mother." This time she didn't knock my arm away. We walked a short distance from the building and sat down on a bench. She reached into her purse for a tissue and began to dry her tear-stained face and blot up her runny makeup. I called for a ride to come pick us up.

"Mother, I don't understand why you do this. OK, you hated Dad. He's gone. Why do you come here and torture yourself? Drag it all up? Why not let it go?"

She glared at me, and I noticed for the first time her eyes were rheumy. Was it age? Anger? Grief? Or all three?

"Let me tell you something, Nate. You can only truly hate something you love. And only the people who love you can make you hate. That's the power of love. Once you've given someone that power over you, it's an iron collar riveted around your neck. You can never take it off or unlock it. And when they betray you, the collar tightens and you can never breathe easily again."

I sighed. I'd heard a variation of this speech several times already. It had sounded profound the first time, but the novelty had worn off.

"Why not hate him in the privacy of your apartment? Why make a spectacle of yourself in public?"

"I can't. He's here, in that damn wall. I should never have sealed him up in this place. He should be home, where I can keep an eye on him. All the time. I deserve at least that much."

"But it's what Dad wanted. You two made your arrangements years ago."

"I don't care." She swayed back and forth on the bench. "It was a mistake. I want him out of that wall. Take him out for me, Nate."

"I'll look into it, Mom." I had no intention of doing this. Given Mom's condition, I was sure Dad would end up as carpet additive soon after his "return" home. He was much safer where he was.

"Mom, I want to ask you a question. You two fought for years. Why did you stay together? You were beautiful. You could have found someone."

"Because the marriage vows said for better or worse," she said. "And you came along so late. I wasn't going to raise you by myself. I warned your father that if he left me, I'd take everything."

When I was 16, after listening in my bedroom to yet another knock-down, drag out between my parents, I'd asked my Dad very much the same question. He'd smiled at me, but there'd been a slight hint of resentment in his answer. "Nate, it's a hard thing to leave home when you have a child."

"I'm so lonely without him," she said. "You're on the other side of the country. I have no grandchildren. I want your father home."

I thought about it for a second, then decided to tell her about Angie. It might make her feel better.

"Mom, I have good news. You don't have to worry about being a grandmother. Angie's pregnant. She's due in about eight months and sure it's a boy. So life **does** go on. You have something to look forward to. A bridge to the future."

She was silent. The seconds dragged by. "So, what do you think?" I said. "Are you happy for me? Looking forward to being able to spoil your first grandchild?"

She sniffed. "Oh, of course. This is what I've lived for my entire life. So I can visit Chinatown with the Bridge Club, go into a restaurant, sit down with all my friends, point to a table, and say 'See the waiter in the corner? The one wearing the uniform and serving those people dim sum? That's **my** grandson."

"You're a princess of diversity, Mom."

"I believe in diversity. I like Chinese food. People should marry their own kind."

The ride rolled up and we returned home.

CHAPTER 6

ILLARION

I was out running on Palisade Ave when I noticed a limo following me. I'd first spotted the long black Lincoln sitting in front of Mom's building when I'd left at 10 am for Riverdale Park and its quiet jogging trails. I stopped. The car stopped. I resumed running. The car resumed following.

I stopped again and the Lincoln again halted. I stood and contemplated it for a moment. It couldn't be the Mafia. The closest I'd ever come to organized crime was watching *Goodfellas*" on Netflix. I hadn't even seen *The Godfather*. Had Angie's uncle unleashed a Chinatown tong on me? Unlikely. I didn't think his influence reached as far as Riverdale. Besides, it was too early to put the arm on me to marry Angie. She wasn't even showing. And I hadn't said I **wouldn't** marry her. I just needed time to think things over. Heck, Steve Jobs took two years after Lisa Brennan-Jobs' birth to even acknowledge she was his daughter.

I decided to cut the Gordian knot and walked over to the Lincoln. The left rear tinted window rolled down. I looked inside and saw a handsome middle-aged man with silver hair wearing an expensive white suit. He looked at me and smiled. Other than his driver, the car was empty.

"Excuse me," I said. "Is there something I can help you with?"

"No, no," the man said. He had a distinct Russian accent. "I am looking for Nate Pennington. I am sorry to have alarmed you. I was not sure it was you, so I had my driver follow while I examined your picture. You are Nate Pennington?"

"May I ask who's asking?"

He reached into his pocket, took out a business card, and handed it to me through the window.

Illarion Antakov, CEO
Sunrize Technology Investments, LLC
Moscow New York Austin San Francisco

"Oh, yes," I said. "We were going to be working with you guys. The person we met with was Vasily, Vasily...uh...Lilov?"

"Limonov."

"Yes, sorry, 'Limonov.' It's a pleasure to meet you Mr. Antakov. Could I ask how you found me?"

"Your partner Ignacio informed us you were visiting your mother, so here I am. Would you like to step into the car? I'm interested in finding out more about theTogetherHood."

"I don't think you were one of the investors. Wasn'tthat...uh...Sunrise? The person we dealt with was Gennady Dubrovsky."

"Yes. He handed me another card through the windows.

Illarion Antakov, CEO
Sunrize Technology Investments, LLC
Moscow New York Austin San Francisco

Please, step into the car. I and my associates are curious to know what happened. The incubator refused to say why you left. Gennady was impressed with your technology and business plan." The driver stepped out of the car and opened the rear door for me.

Let us talk. Perhaps there is something to be done about the situation?"

I had a sudden flare of hope. Perhaps theTogetherHood could be resurrected? We didn't need much money to restart operations.

I climbed into the soft leather seat opposite Illarion and we pulled away from the curb. "What do you want to know?"

"Tell me the whole story. Do not leave anything out."

"My pleasure. I took out my phone, pulled up our slides, spreadsheets, and infographic charts and provided the best financial overview I could on such short notice. I concluded with a competitive analysis and list of potential threats.

"Unfortunately, the one threat we didn't anticipate was being kicked out of brightstart at a critical moment in our company's development," I said. "By the way, I'll be glad to send you these files and our complete business plan any time."

He waved his hand. "It is not necessary. We wanted to understand what had happened. When Gennady called brightstart, they were most uninformative. We decided to talk to you directly to discover why we could not anticipate receiving a return on the $100 thousand dollars we invested in theTogetherHood. By our standards, it was not much money, but still. In Russia, we have an old saying —'If the hen stops laying eggs, you can still have a meal to eat.'"

This sounded vaguely ominous. "Is that an actual Russian proverb?" I said.

"No. But it illuminates. I am sure one day it will be."

"I can assure you everything about theTogetherHood was completely on the up and up. Ignacio and I are still committed to the business model."

"I believe you. When Gennady sat through the demo of the product, he was quite taken with your original thinking. He called me the next day and said, 'Na to i shchuka v more , chtoby karas' ne dremal.'"

"Excuse me? I'm sorry, I don't speak Russian."

"My apologies. It is another Russian proverb. It is not an improvisation on my part. It is hard to translate. Literally, it means 'The pike in the sea is there to make the crucian stay alert.' A crucian is a type of, how do you say it in English...'carp.' The fish."

"I've heard of carp. Let me improvise a proverb on behalf of my company and its product. I still believe theTogetherHood is a valid, viable business concept. That was not bad money you threw at us. theTogetherHood enables any municipality to protect their revenues against poor planning and life's constant misfortunes.

"In other words, providing additional funding for theTogetherHood would be an act of throwing good money after good money. Of course, we'd be willing to discuss an extended equity position for Sunrize if you make the smart decision to further invest."

He slapped his thigh and laughed. "You are just as Gennady described you. Incredibly persuasive and all without the assistance of a Makarov."

"Makarov?"

"A pistol. It was popular with the KGB. But, I'm sorry, no. We have done our due diligence and believe theTogetherHood is irretrievable. There are too many rumors and speculations about your shutdown. The VC community presently views you as the equivalent of Ebola."

"What about the Russian market?"

"Russia currently takes its cues from the U.S. It would be hard to make a strong business case to fund a product in local markets from a failed American startup. Though, give it two or three years and it might be possible." He barked out something in Russian to the driver and the car stopped. The driver got out and came over to my side of the Lincoln. The presentation was over.

"I would like to apologize for my intrusion into your day. While I do not believe theTogetherHood presently represents a good business proposition, both Gennady and I are impressed with you and your partner's innovative spirit." He handed me a third business card. This one had only his name, a phone number, and an email address.

"If you have other ideas or concepts, I invite you to contact me via the information on this card. I will respond. I do not often hand this card out and request you not distribute it or share the information it contains with any third parties. My best wishes for your continued success." The driver opened the door and I stepped out. The Lincoln resumed its course on Palisade, then turned onto a side street and out of sight.

I tucked the card carefully into my wallet and headed back to Mom's apartment. My run for the day was over.

That night, after I'd downed a Swanson's Zesty Beef and Rice Skillet dinner, Ignacio called me.

CHAPTER 7

ITEM FOR SALE

"Hi. What's up?" I said.

"I wanted to let you know. Someone from one of our investors is probably going to be contacting you. They kicked in for the demo rounds. Gennady was the one we dealt with directly. A VC firm called 'Sunrise.' With a 'z.'"

"Yes, I met with a gentleman named Illarion today. He runs Sunrize and several other things."

"That was fast. And?"

"And I think that if he'd thought we'd ripped him off, I'd currently be swimming with the Hudson River sturgeons."

"Sturgeons? I thought they only lived in Russia."

"The Hudson River sturgeons beg to differ."

"Oh. Are they still interested in investing?"

"Doesn't look like it. At the moment, we're as popular as a Microsoft Surface in Cupertino."

"Oh. Too bad."

"Yes," I said. "Anything else?"

"As a matter of fact, there is. I received a strange email this afternoon and wanted to discuss it with you."

"What was it?"

"Ah...hmmm. I need to set the stage. I received an email at the contact address on Deadland.com yesterday from 'L' telling me he had a business proposition for me.

"L?"

"L. I have no idea if it's a man or a woman, though 90 percent of my site traffic is male."

"Somehow, I guessed."

"Yeah. Anyway, I receive that sort of stuff almost daily, but L has spent serious time on the site. For instance, he's read the *Deadsnow 2* review carefully and spotted several inaccuracies in the zombies' Nazi uniforms. For instance, in one scene the zombie Nazi SS officer's hat has the Death's Head emblem looking to the **left**, but it actually always looked **right**. I hadn't even noticed. It's the attention to detail separating the poseurs from the true fans."

"How true. It might be a good idea if for *Deadsnow 3*, the producers use one of those WWII reenactment groups as a reference source to ensure the historical accuracy of zombie Nazi uniforms."

"That **is** an idea. In any event, I emailed him back suggesting he text me and we began to discuss his proposal.

"Ignacio, this sounds like an elaborate spamming campaign or a scam."

"Could be. But hold on. The story gets better. So we begin to text back and forth. L asks me if I'm the guy who actually runs the site. I tell him I am. We discuss the site. L then asks me questions about my background and I realize I'm being vetted. I apparently pass.

"Were you able to track his location?"

"No. He was using one of those send and vanish services. In any event, while we're talking, he asks me if I'm interested in 'rare collectibles' of a 'physical' nature. I tell him it depends on the collectible. Then L asks if the collectible was a one-of-a-kind object and had played an important role in the history of high tech, would I be more interested. I tell L yes, but if he's referring to an Apple I, Altair, or similar item, I can't afford it and couldn't properly store it in any event. L says the collectible is much, much rarer and can be easily stored for long periods of time at minimal cost. So I ask L what the collectible is."

Ignacio paused and the line was silent for several seconds.

"OK," I said. "You've set the hook and I'll bite. What is the collectible?"

"Steve Jobs' liver."

"Excuse me?"

"Steve Jobs' liver."

"I'm sorry. Steve Jobs is dead. He's been dead since 2011. If his grave had been desecrated, it would make national news. Anyone associated with grave-robbing would be facing serious jail time. And after more than a decade, I don't think there's much left of Steve Jobs to recover. Not that I have the slightest interest in doing this."

"I'm not talking about the 2.0 version of his liver. I'm talking the 1.0 version. The original."

"Oh." I remembered. In 2009, Jobs had undergone a liver transplant because the cancer that eventually killed him had spread to the organ.

"So what do you think?" he said.

"I don't know. How could this person have gotten hold of Steve Jobs' liver? Doesn't Steve Jobs still own his liver?"

"Steve Jobs is dead. I don't think he can own anything."

"What about his family?"

"I'm not sure. Have you ever heard of anyone taking home their diseased liver? Or a failed kidney? A ruptured spleen? People sometimes take home their relative's ashes, but that's not the same thing."

"No, it's not." I thought for a moment. A puzzle was assembling itself in my head, but I didn't quite know how the pieces fit or what it would look like when completed. But a small voice whispered to me the puzzle might be worth finishing.

"Nate?" Ignacio's voice broke my train of thought. "What do you think? Is this strange or what? Do you think there's anything here worth pursuing, or should I just tell this ghoul to get lost?"

"I'm not sure. Let me ask you. Did L mention a price? Describe how he intended to...uh...deliver the liver?"

"We didn't go that far. I told L I needed to consult with a colleague on the matter and would follow up."

"Uh, huh. What do **you** think?" I said.

"I don't know. I mean, we **are** discussing Steve Jobs' liver. He's on every top 100 influential-people-of all-time list I've seen recently. The guy's a Valley saint. I know people who still won't sell their iPods and become choked up every time they're applying scratch polish. It has to have **some** value."

"You would imagine," I said. "Another thing. How do we know this is the real thing? That L isn't a cannibal? Or he didn't buy a liver on E-bay from someone in Bangladesh or New Jersey?"

"I don't think they let you sell human organs on E-bay."

"What about Amazon?"

"Not sure. I've heard the buyers there will sell their mothers to get best price. Don't think it's the same thing. The moms are still alive. Probably."

"Yes," I said. "Well, before we could even consider it, we'd have to be sure we're not being conned. We'd need proof of liver, so to speak."

"Yeah, you're right. So?"

"When are you supposed to talk to L again?"

"No set time. Soon."

"I understand. I'm going to do some research. I'll get back to you in a bit."

"Talk to you then." He disconnected.

I walked over to my MacAir lying on the old desk I'd studied at as a boy and began to surf. It wasn't hard to find links to articles on Jobs' health and treatment in 2009. He'd first been diagnosed with pancreatic cancer in 2003. It's a vicious killer and most people die from it within a few months. Jobs had a less aggressive form of the cancer, and after pausing to take a typical California detour into quack medicine, launched a full-fledged battle against his disease. This included being one of the first people in the world to have his cancer's genome fully sequenced (at a cost of $100 thousand). The work was carried out at Stanford and MIT.

Unfortunately, by 2009 it seemed as if the battle was over. The cancer spread into his liver and it appeared Jobs had weeks to live without a transplant.

At this juncture, despite having previously displayed no previous affinity for Nashville, country music, Elvis Presley, Jack Daniels, and the Old Confederacy, Jobs vacated his CEO position for six months and decamped for Tennessee, where the waiting list for a donor liver was much shorter than California's. In April of 2009, he underwent a transplant at Methodist University Hospital Transplant Institute in Memphis, Tennessee. The operation was carried out by Dr. James Eason, one of the field's leading specialists.

The surgery is credited with prolonging Jobs' life for an additional two-and-a-half years. He finally succumbed to his illness in October of 2011. None of the accounts of the surgery made any mention of the fate of the diseased liver.

When I was done, I sat back in my chair and entered a fugue state, again scanning the puzzle pieces in my head, turning them over, and attempting to fit them together. After a few minutes, I called Ignacio.

"Yeah? What do you want me to do?" he said.

"Tell L we're interested. Are you calling or texting tomorrow?"

"Texting."

"Tell him we'd like to arrange for a three-way call between him, you and me. How about 1 pm tomorrow? Use a Bluetooth headphone so we can sidetext."

"Care to share what you're thinking?" he said.

"I haven't worked it out yet. There's something missing, but I can't put my finger on it. Let's talk to Mr. L, then discuss."

"Got it. If nothing else, it should be an interesting conversation. See you tomorrow."

I went to bed early, but around 1 am found myself staring at the ceiling as my thoughts chased each other inside my head. I got up, walked over to my desk, and tapped the Mac's touchpad. The flickering blue palantir managing all our lives glowed to life in the dark room and I resumed surfing. After entering a series of keywords and phrases, I pulled up this LA Times article:

Steve Jobs' Virtual DNA to Be Fostered in Apple University

To survive its late founder, Apple and Steve Jobs planned a training program in which company executives will be taught to think like him, in 'a forum to impart that DNA to future generations.' Key to this effort is Joel Podolny, former Yale Business School dean.

Reporting from San Francisco - Apple Inc. now has to get down to the business of surviving its founder.

It's something that Apple - and Steve Jobs himself - had been painstakingly planning for years.

Deep inside its sprawling Cupertino, Calif., campus, one of the world's most successful and secretive companies has had a team of experts hard at work on a closely guarded project.

But it isn't a cool new gadget. It's an executive training program called Apple University that Jobs considered vital to the company's future: Teaching Apple executives to think like him.

"Steve was looking to his legacy. The idea was to take what is unique about Apple and create a forum that can impart that DNA to future generations of Apple employees," said a former Apple executive who spoke on the condition of anonymity to preserve his relationship with the company.

D.N.A.

The pieces clicked together. The puzzle took shape. I returned to my bed exalted, tired, and refreshed. As I dropped off to sleep, I imagined I was feeling the same sense of excitement that Steve Jobs must have felt when, silent in a building in Palo Alto, he stared at a Xerox workstation and was filled with a wild surmise he needed to copy it as soon as possible.

CHAPTER 8

INNOVATIVE THINKING

Ignacio made arrangements for the call. He wanted to discuss my plan for the liver, but I asked him to wait until after our conversation with L. Despite my previous night's excitement, there was no use wasting too much time and energy on what might be a wild goose chase.

L called Ignacio at 1 pm and I joined in.

"So, you boys are interested in my little collectible?" The sound coming from the phone was distorted. L was using a voice-obfuscation system, but he was a man and only Southerners call grown men "boys."

Ignacio replied. "Yes. My colleague Nate is on the line as we discussed. But we have a few questions."

"Glad to help you fellows out. What do you want to know?"

"I have two questions," I said. "How do we know it's real and how much?"

"Y'all like to get to the point, don't you?"

"Yes. If we can't agree on those issues, there's no need to talk further."

"Well, let's take the first one. The proof's in the pudding. You're welcome to inspect the item before taking delivery. You pay in cash."

"I'm not an expert, but I don't think the item we're discussing comes with a stamp of origin," I said. "How do we know the, uh, 'collectible' is accurately sourced?"

"There are tests I'll be pleased to let you carry out before we finalize our transaction. You can look up them up online. You can do them yourselves or bring along someone who can."

"I have an alternate proposal. Why don't you send us a sample and we'll do the tests at our location? That way..."

"No." His voice was emphatic. "It's proof of origin, then cash and carry. And even if I send you a sample, you'll still want to test the entire collectible. After all, as you rightly observed, there's no FDA stamp. You come here, test, pay, and leave with the collectible. What you do with it later is your business."

"Point taken. Let's circle back to those details later. How much?"

"Fifty thousand dollars."

"No. Too high. Ten thousand."

Ignacio began to sidetext me.

Isn't it early to talk money?

"I'll do 40 thousand. LBF."

No

"Too high. Be realistic. The item's rare, but there's a limited market and verifying it is difficult. Otherwise, you would have sold it years ago. We're your market. Fifteen thousand. And we'll pay cash. I bet you'll like the feel of all those greenbacks running through your fingers. Cash is a wonderful thing. No credit card companies snooping on your purchases. No IRS sniffing through your affairs."

But only have 15k in bank. no more

Have about 15k also. Raise advert rates on deadland. Im ready to go all in. u?

"Thirty thousand."

"Twenty five. LBF. Cash. That's all we have."

OMG

We hav a fundng source. Maybe.

Maybe?!

"You're a hard Yankee."

"We have a deal?"

"You two boys have a deal."

"Great. What's the next step?'

"I'll be in touch in the next couple of days. I'll give you contact info and a date and time to pick up the collectible."

OMG, OMG

Its ok

"We'll be ready," I said. He disconnected.

Ignacio was still on the line. "I can't believe you did that," he said. "Twenty-five thousand dollars! For what?"

"For Steve Jobs' liver. And stop whining. You called me. How did you think this was going to end up?"

"Not at $25 thousand! And we don't even know where the damn thing is. Or if he's telling us the truth."

"If he's telling us the truth, the liver's probably in Memphis. Or nearby."

"How do you know?"

"I don't know it. I'm guessing it because a hospital in Memphis is where they took Jobs' liver out. I don't think the organ relocated itself back to Silicon Valley. Whoever has it must have been involved in the operation or the disposal process. So they worked at or were associated with the hospital. Probably doing only 'middling' well, as they like to say down south of the Mason-Dixon. And therefore they're probably still close to Memphis."

"Why?"

"Because if you were rich, is brokering diseased human organs the business model you'd pursue? If not, where are the jobs going to be around there? In and around Memphis."

"How do we know he has the liver?"

"We don't. This could be a scam. But think about it. There's a nationwide market for methamphetamine, but not for Steve Jobs' liver. Our grave rat has been working on his monetization model for years. I don't think destroying his customer base is part of his business strategy.

"In any event, the next move is up to him. If he doesn't get back to us, nothing ventured, nothing gained. But he's going to get back to us."

"You sound sure."

"I am."

"Well, we can always change our minds," he said. "We haven't signed a contract. But I need to know why you think we should pay $25 thousand for Steve Jobs' liver."

"You said it yourself. Steve Jobs is the closest thing that exists right now to a secular saint in this world. The books, movies, articles and hagiography just keep on coming. And his appeal is worldwide. They've put statues up of him in Russia and Budapest, of all places."

"I agree about Jobs, but I don't think people want to buy his liver or read a book about it."

"You're wrong," I said. "I've done a little research. There are 1.2 billion Roman Catholics, one billion Hindus, 300 million Eastern Orthodox, and 500 million Buddhists on this planet, as well as dozens of other religions and sects that venerate, worship, collect, and sell relics. I bet at least half the planetary population of seven billion believes in some form of relic worship and collection. A huge potential market. I visited the Mother Cabrini Shrine the other day. She's a local Roman Catholic saint. I talked with a nun who purchased a piece of clothing owned by her on E-bay."

"I've never heard of Saint Cabrini," he said.

"Local institution. I'll take you by her place when we get a chance. In any event, there's another angle on this. Humans never want to accept the finality of death. Even secularists. Why do you think people buy millions of Ouija boards every year, watch those silly shot-innight-vision ghost hunter shows, and fork over good money to watch atrocities such as *Deadsnow* again and again?"

"*Deadsnow* was **not** an atrocity. It was wonderful example of the genre and a fascinating..."

I cut him off. "We'll discuss your terrible esthetics later. But it illustrates the market's desire to maintain an active relationship with the departed, even if said relationship consists of them dining on your cerebellum.

"The fascination is universal. Everyone lining up to see King Tut's mummy wonders what he looked like, how he sounded, what he thought about the world. Ditto for the show time cadavers at Body Worlds. I visited my Father's urn the other day at Woodlawn cemetery and my Mother asked me to take it home with us so she could keep an 'eye' on him."

"Does she expect your father to go somewhere?"

"Given their history together, possibly."

"And Steve Jobs' liver fits into this how?"

I sent him the LA Times link. "Look at this."

It was silent for several seconds as he read. Then "Huh. How much DNA do you estimate is in the liver?" he said.

"A lot. I'm still researching the issue, but at least 100 million units. Possibly many more. That's the relic side of the business model. Technology can provide the interaction, AI new vistas."

The discussion sparked a productive mind-meld between us for the next hour or so and when we'd finished, Ignacio had bought into my vision of the challenge and opportunity awaiting us.

"You said we had a funding source. Who is it?"

"The Russian gentleman you referred to me a few days ago. He said he'd be interested in hearing from us about new business ideas and concepts. Well, we have one. How soon can you fly out here? We need to put together an early numbers overview and a presentation."

"Where will I stay?"

"You can stay at my Mom's place with me. We have plenty of room and I'm sure she'll love you."

"I'll book the flight and send you my itinerary."

"Good. In the meantime, I'm going to contact the Russian. By the way, have you heard from Angie?"

"Err, yes. She called me today. She wanted to know if I'd heard from you. You know Nate, I don't think it's fair to put me the middle of this. Hell, I don't even have my own girlfriend, and I'm supposed to play Cupid for you two? And besides, we both know what you need to do."

That had become clear last night. The new business model wouldn't work without Angie.

"I agree with you. I'm going to do the right thing."

"You are? Great!" I could hear the relief in his voice. "And congratulations."

"On what?"

"On becoming a father."

"Oh, right. Thank you."

"Do you want me to say anything to Angie? Or you'll contact her directly."

"Ignacio, for the next several days we're going to need to focus on our new venture. And Angie has refused to speak to me since she threw me out. If she calls you, tell her I'm planning to return to the West Coast the week after next and will be in touch shortly."

"Got it." He disconnected and I dialed Illarion at his 'special' number. He picked up.

"Ah, Mr. Pennington. I thought I would hear from you soon, though not quite **this** soon."

"You said I should contact you if we had a new concept or business idea to discuss. We do. Ignacio and I are creating a truly unique opportunity and we'd like to meet with you and discuss your participation."

"I am leaving for the West Coast and will be back in New York and available to meet next Tuesday. I can spare you half an hour, from 10 to 10:30 am. My office is 200 Park Ave. The Met Life building, 72nd floor. Please be on time and prepared."

"We'll be there on time and prepared. You'll be impressed."

"We will see. Next Tuesday, then."

CHAPTER 9

CROSSING THE YANGTZE

Ignacio took a redeye out of SFO and was in Riverdale by the next day. Mom had been less than thrilled when I'd informed her he'd be visiting with us, but I appeased her by taking her out to her favorite diner, **Greek Express** on Riverdale Avenue, for lunch with all the trimmings and then giving the apartment a thorough cleaning.

It didn't hurt that when Ignacio showed up, he immediately showered Mom with numerous compliments on her looks, charm and graciousness. He was rewarded with smiles, simpers, an invitation to kiss her cheek, and assurances he was welcome to stay as long as he liked. I was rewarded with the statement that at least this particular acquaintance of mine didn't look like he should be working the local Peking Garden's takeout counter.

We set up shop on Mom's dining room table and spent the next five days working on our presentation and business plan for Sunrize and Illarion. Thursday and Friday were spent brainstorming and solidifying our ideas and concepts. Saturday and Sunday were devoted to building our presentation and an early business plan.

Monday was dedicated to refining the deck, challenging our assumptions, and working on timing. Our actual presentation wouldn't run more than 20 minutes. Newbies pitching to investors believe success is measured by presenting past your allotted time and talking more. This is a mistake. The goal of a successful pitch is to ensure when you've finished talking, the investor wants to continue. Then the discussion is serious.

We also made a decision to rebrand the company. We felt a twinge of regret, but GateIconic had been an unlucky moniker. The right name seemed to just pop into my head while we were online domain searching and browsing the WHOIS database and Ignacio agreed. Besides, the dot-com was available.

That afternoon, as we were practicing, my phone vibrated. I looked down. It was Angie.

Nate, u there?

Ignacio looked over at me. "Who is it?"

"Angie."

He stood up and stretched. "I need a break and you need to talk to her."

"Yes."

He walked out of the room.

Im here

We need to talk

Yes. how are u?

Feeling bit sick in morning

Oh

You going to be responsible?

Yes

When back in SF?

Week after next. Am still locked out?

Do right thing?

Yes

Come home

Love you

I hesitated. A romantic Rubicon had been reached. I remembered a *Forbes* article by Alan Hall I'd read a few years ago.

"Sacrifice is a key characteristic of successful entrepreneurs."

I love u too. Will send schedule when flite booked

Bye

Bye

The Yangtze had been crossed.

"Ignacio?" I called out. "I've done the right thing. Let's get back to work."

CHAPTER 10

PRESENTATION

We called it a night and went to bed in accordance with the EEE/RRR rule. Early to bed, early to rise, early to arrive so you show up refreshed, relaxed and ready. We were at Illarion's office a couple of minutes early and a receptionist escorted us into a small conference room where I placed my Mac on the table. At 10:00 am sharp, Illarion stepped through the door.

"I am ready," he said.

"Thank you. You told me we had 30 minutes. We'll finish the deck in 20 and answer any questions in the remaining time. Of course, feel free to break in at any time." I handed Illarion the first cut of the business plan. "This document contains early financial numbers." He placed the papers on the conference table without looking at them. "By the way, GateIconic is now Reliqueree."

"Please, go ahead," he said.

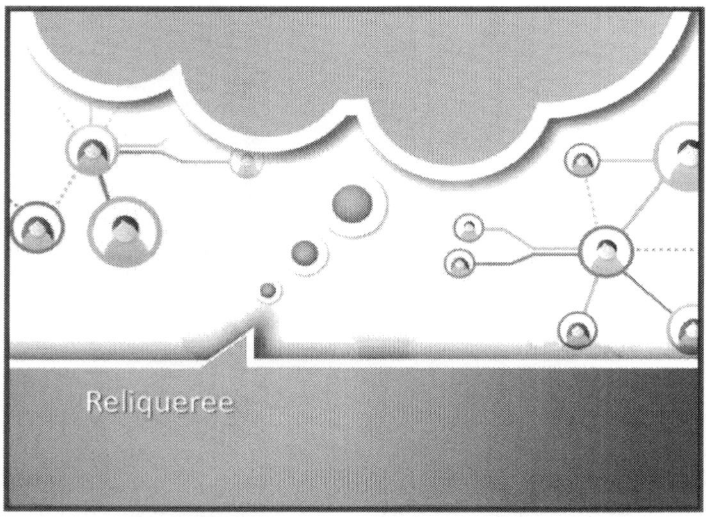

I brought up the cover slide, then moved to the next.

"Just a fast note about our company values. This philosophy has guided us in our previous projects and endeavors. It's who we are. We think you'll agree our new venture adheres to all of them.

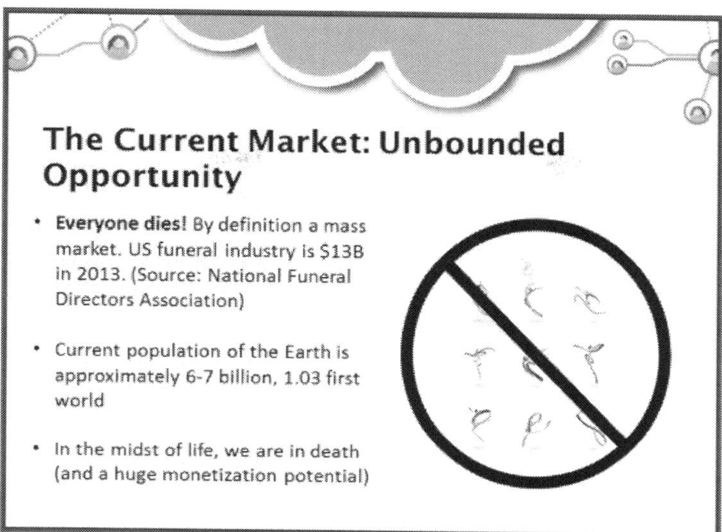

"A quick market overview. Our new enterprise is built around the inescapable reality that everyone dies. It's an unpleasant truth people prefer not to dwell on, but we believe it's this ubiquity that opens paths to major new markets and revenue opportunities.

"The downside of death is, obviously, dying. The upside is it's a universally shared experience creating a huge set of expectations and shared challenges across every country, culture and market. Steve Jobs himself recognized and spoke to this issue directly at his famous commencement address at Stanford in 2005. You can watch the entire speech on YouTube. It's extremely moving.

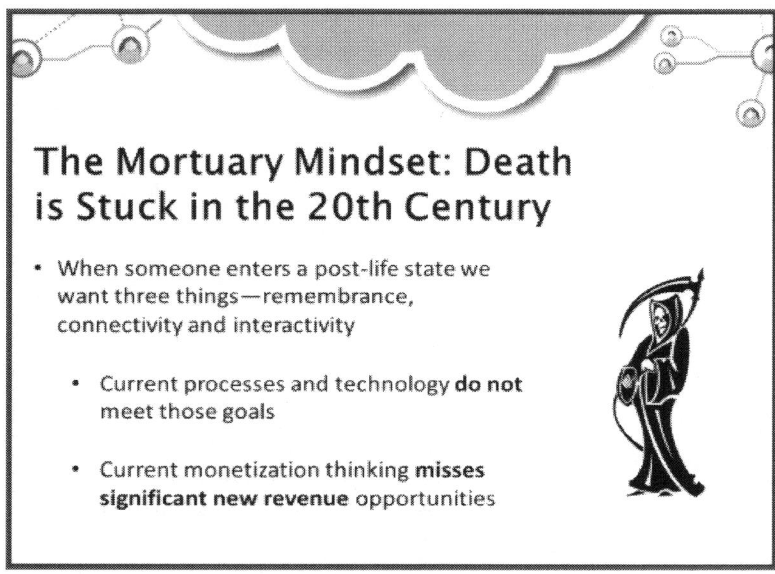

"The challenge facing the U.S. market is how to explore death's incredible growth potential. However, today's 'funeral' industries no longer innovate. Instead, they recycle outdated concepts and processes, what we label the 'mortuary mindset.' But technology today offers new opportunities **for remembrance, connectivity, and interactivity**, or 'RCI,' with loved ones who have departed and move onto the post-life."

"Go on," he said.

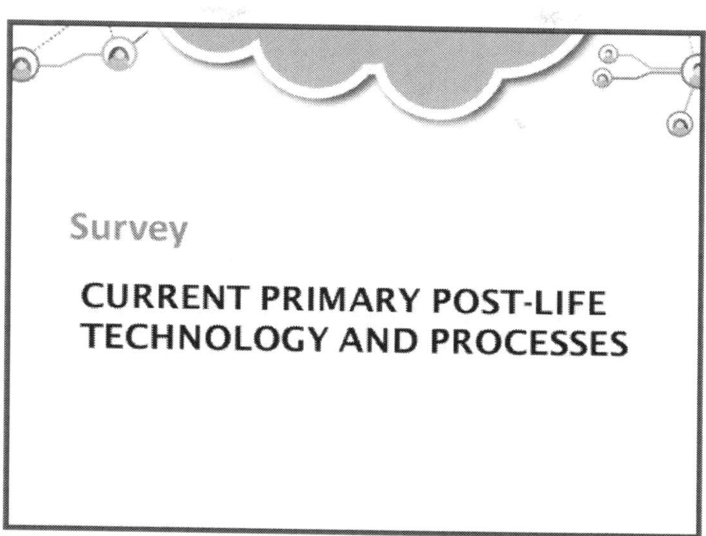

"Let's quickly review the current mortuary approaches dominating post-life thinking and examine how they fail to meet today's needs and expectations.

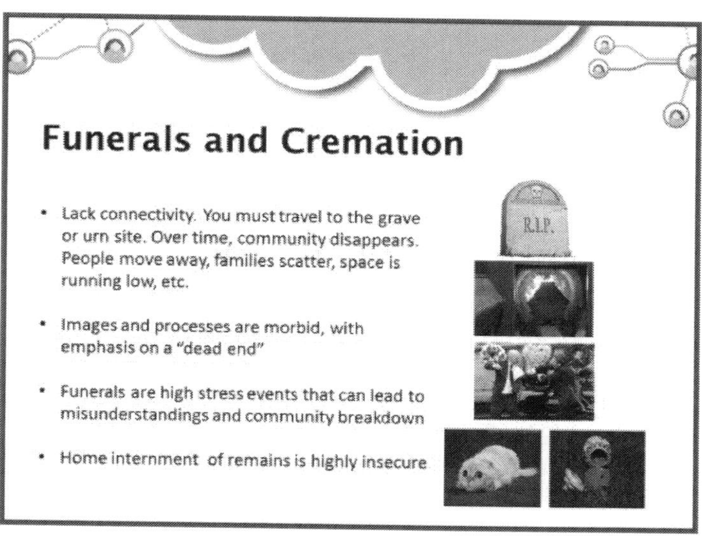

"Cemeteries tend to depress attendees, and people often die in inconvenient places or times. And Americans are always on the move, leading to situations where the departed may be interred hundreds or thousands of miles away from you. And we're running out of space to stack the bodies. Clearly, not a satisfactory solution. Cremation faces the same issues, though in the quest for connectivity, some choose to keep funeral ashes at home. It's almost a cliché to observe the possibility of an unfortunate and tragic accident is often only a cat leap or slip of the hand away.

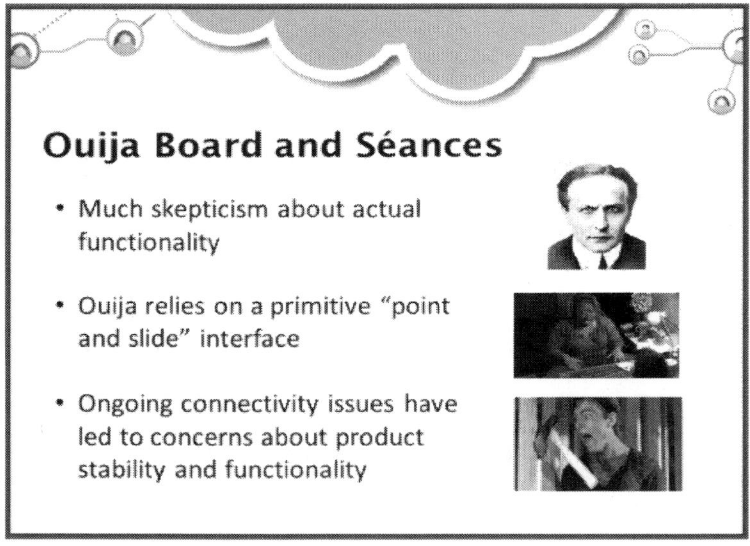

"This takes us to systems that **do** offer different types of RCI. Some are popular and generate significant revenue. However, as we all know, many people doubt their functionality. Others feel their interactivity relies on dubious or insecure connections, including Hell, demons, evil spirits, angry ghosts, etc. These questions and issues disqualify all of these approaches.

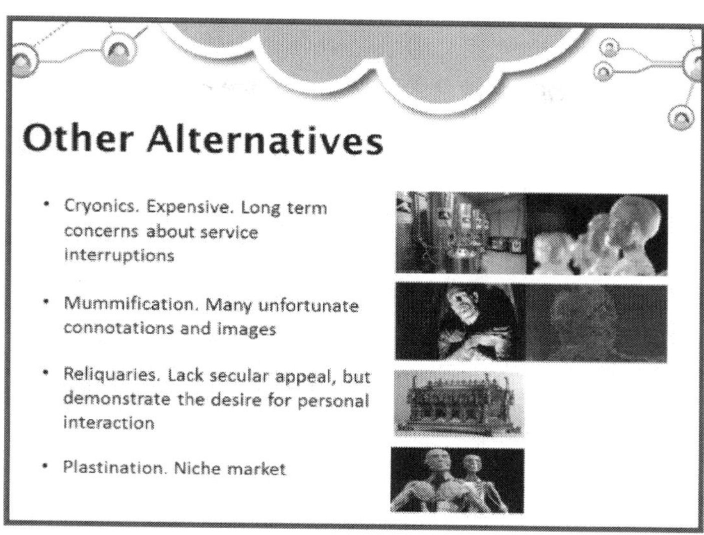

"I don't need to spend too much time on any of these. The problems associated with cryonics, mummification, plastination and so on are well understood. However, we believe the billions in direct and indirect income the Catholic Church generates on the exhibit and possession of relics provides a window into Reliqueree's revenue growth potential.

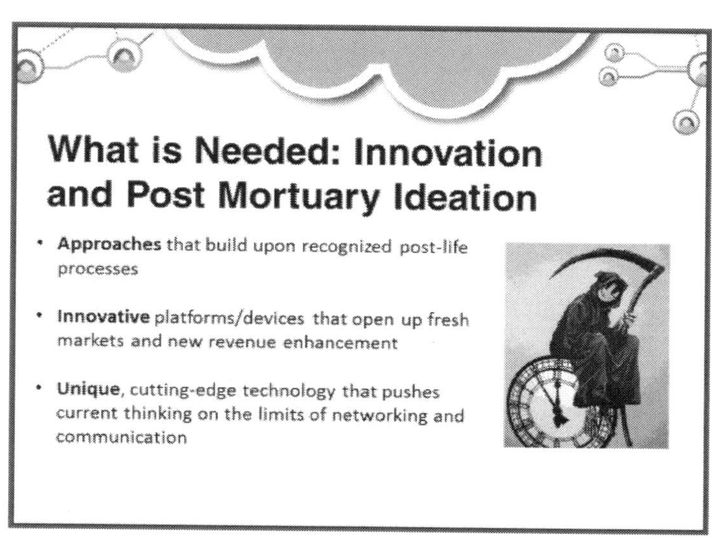

"This brings us to the critical question — What are the change agents? What new concepts and disruptive technologies must be developed to meet the demand for enhanced RCI?

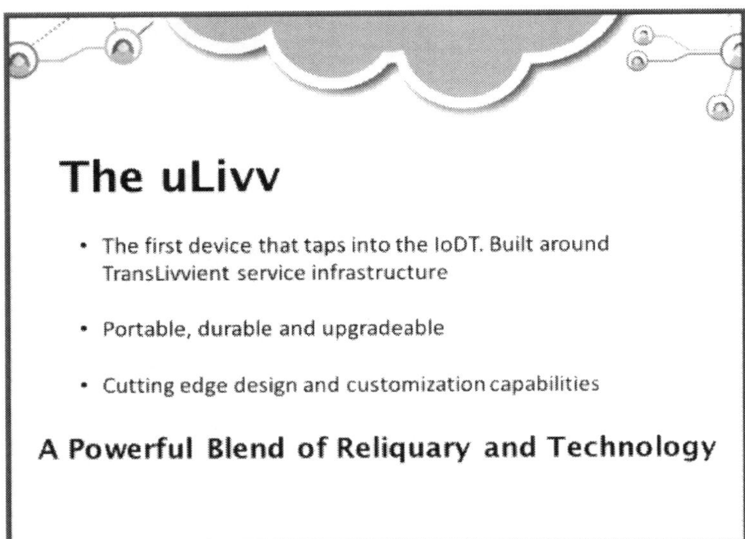

"Change's vanguard is the uLivv. Built around our ChipLivv technology, the uLivv is sleek, powerful, and upgradeable. The device plays a dual role. First, it functions as a modern version of the traditional reliquary, the container used to store relics. Second, it serves as the gateway to new Cloud-based services."

"What do mean by the uLivv acting as a 'reliquary?'" Illarion said. "What relic will it hold?"

"Thank you for asking. This leads directly to our next slide. Every first release uLivv will include a complete and verified sample of Steve Jobs' actual DNA, as well as his entire genome."

"Is this a joke?" Illarion said.

"No. We're dead serious."

"Jobs is not dead?"

"Oh, he's dead," Ignacio said. "He passed away in 2011."

A Compelling and Unique Go-to-Market Value Proposition

- Every initial uLivv will ship with an integrated, verified, and complete sample of Steve Jobs' DNA
- Owners will possess a physical memento of the man who made us all "Think Different" about technology and will do it again with the Post-Life
- Every uLivv purchaser will be able to explore the IoDT via TransLivvient and the genome of technology's most revered entrepreneur

"Has his grave been robbed?"

"Not by us," I said firmly. "And not by anyone else. Steve Jobs is lying undisturbed and intact in California."

"Ah. I do not understand. While I am not a scientist, I am not a fool." Illarion was staring directly at me with no hint of a smile on this face. "Please do not insult my intelligence with jibber-jabber about cloning and similar nonsense. We have an old saying in Russia. 'A chicken that offers a worm to a hungry bear is missing the point.'"

"We have no intention of discussing cloning, a magical breakthrough in stem cell research, or the discovery of Steve Jobs' long-lost identical twin," I said. "But we have located an alternate source of DNA, enough for us to be confident we can meet any short or medium-term promotional requirements. Once the Reliqueree business and services models are established, we won't need this resource except for special promotional programs."

"Yes?" Illarion was looking at his phone. The room was quiet for a couple of minutes while he read. He looked up and the hostile look was gone. "Ah, I see. Fascinating. You do not think you are being tricked? Does your pitch incorporate a need for funds to purchase this 'resource?'"

I shook my head. "No. Purchasing and transportation is our skin in the game. Obviously, we'll be prepared to validate its bona fides.

"We know the value we'll be offering the market is irresistible. Steve Jobs is technology's closest thing to a holy man, a market naturally attracted to innovation and disruption. Hundreds of millions of people still remember Jobs and mourn his loss, with the possible exception of Microsoft, some former members of the Apple board, and probably Google."

"You believe people will be willing to pay to carry a piece of Steve Jobs' DNA around their necks?"

"Or in their pocket," Ignacio said. "Hundreds of millions of Catholics, Russian Orthodox, Buddhists, and Hindus already pay to possess remnants of saints and seers. The good news is Jobs crosses sectarian lines."

"This is true," Illarion said.

"And it's not just the DNA they'll be purchasing," I said. "They'll also have full access to Jobs' completely sequenced genome. They'll be

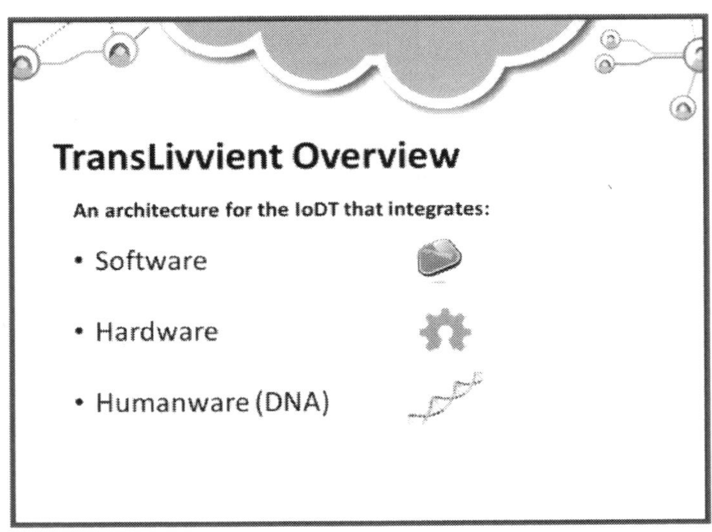

able to hold in their hands his essential information foundation, both virtually and physically." I moved to the next slide.

"Reliqueree's vision incorporates more than just a device. It also extends to building a new services architecture, TransLivvient, on top of a platform we define as the **IoDT,** the Internet of Departed Things. We define the IoDT as Cloud-enabled data and personal remnants of your family and friends. Over time, we believe these services will be more important to our long term growth and revenue generation than the uLivv.

"TransLivvient integrates software, hardware, and 'Humanware,' in other words, DNA, to extend the IoDT in ways encouraging innovation and incents visionaries to provide new RCI opportunities.

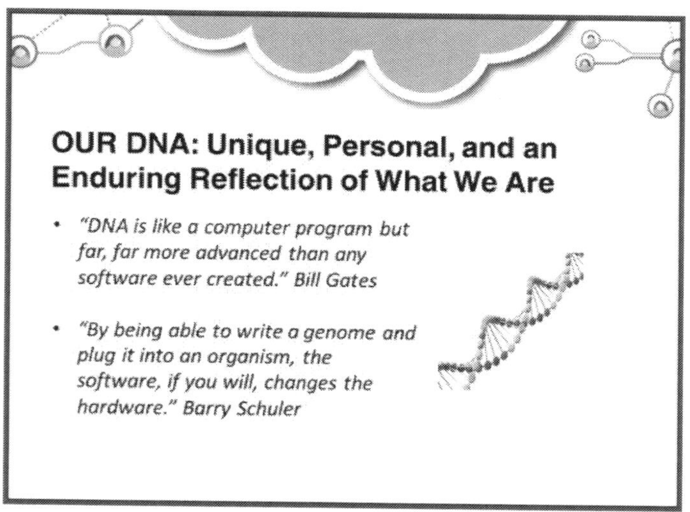

"DNA is the amazing molecule underlying all life on Earth and makes each of us different. Every strand of a person's DNA encodes approximately one gigabyte of storage or 300 MP3 songs. This may not seem large, but that's enough information to build a species that painted the Mona Lisa, constructed the Pyramids, and nurtured Steve Jobs.

"Unfortunately, almost no thought is given to the inherent value of our DNA. When we die, it's usually buried, burned, or otherwise discarded. But this is changing.

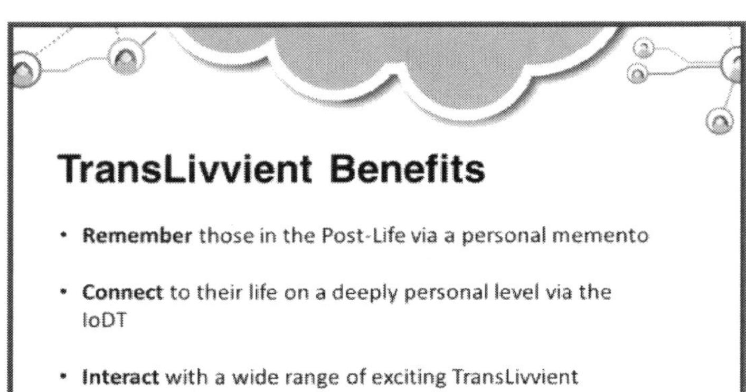

"TransLivvient and the uLivv organize change's infrastructure. They enable anyone to possess a physical memento of the departed, remain connected to them in positive and new ways, and access a wide range of exciting services that enhance your interactivity with their life and times.

"The combination of the uLivv and TransLivvient opens up major new revenue sources beyond sales of devices. An example is our 'transfer to the IoDT' TransLivvient service. Subscribers will be able to submit a DNA sample from a loved one for genomic sequencing. The data and DNA sample will then be integrated into the uLivv. As of today, the cost of a complete sequencing is approximately $500, but by partnering with leading firms, we believe the price will drop to under $200 and maybe even lower. Reliqueree will receive a referral fee on every order.

"To sum up, Reliqueree is positioning itself to disrupt and dominate a market encrusted with obsolete concepts and technology and entrenched in the past. When grasping the potential of the uLivv and TransLivvient, Steve Jobs says it best," I said.

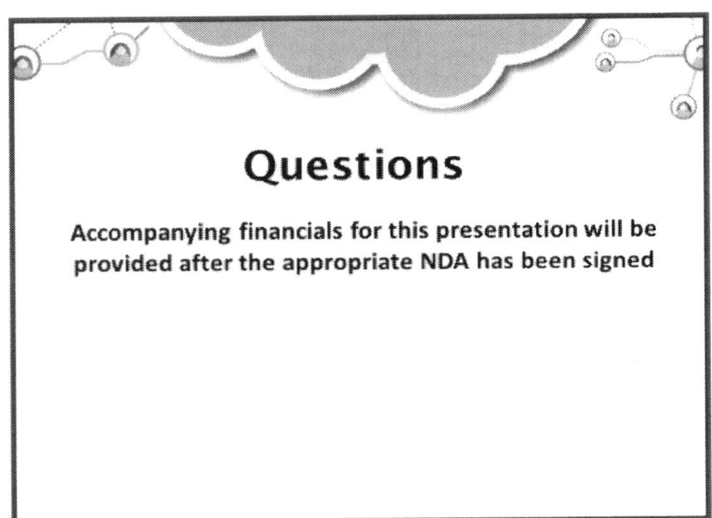

"Questions?"

"Your concepts are truly unique," Illarion said. "I'm not even sure 'innovation' is the right word to describe what I have just seen."

"Thank you," I said. "I'm pleased we've been able to convey our vision of a new market offering vast growth and revenue possibilities. We're offering you a ground floor opportunity to invest. Are you interested?"

"The concept is fascinating. I attended the funeral of a cousin the other day. It was at Cyprus Hill in Brooklyn. So crowded." He shuddered. "He and I were good friends, but I do not wish to go back to that place." He picked up the business plan and began to scan it. The time was 10:30 am. We were officially serious.

CHAPTER 11

THE BIG APPLE MANDATE

We left Illarion's office with a handshake agreement on an initial $6.5M investment, contingent on our taking delivery of the liver. He declined to discuss the equity position.

"No, no, not yet," he said. "I am only taking you semi-seriously at this time. I will believe this is truly real when I see this Steve Jobs leftover in my office with my own eyes. If you can deliver, we will discuss equity. If you cannot, you have probably been swindled. But this is the most entertaining business proposal I have ever considered, and I am willing to examine other details. Let us move ahead."

We discussed our estimated startup expenses, the bulk of which would be dedicated to R&D and quickly building up our patent portfolio. There was little disagreement on these areas, but he pushed back against our initial monetary evaluation of the company.

"To execute this plan, you must build something, no?" Illarion said. He looked at the business plan. "It says you plan to launch in October. How can you have enough units ready for market by October? It is not the same thing as software. It takes considerably more time to design and build a device."

"We're not going to design or build anything. Just assemble something and ship it."

"Assemble?"

"Yes. For the first generation uLivv, we're going to use an off-the-shelf design and parts. We don't need cutting edge hardware when you're leveraging the DNA of the man who helped create some of the industry's most cutting-edge hardware."

"This sounds like something your Bill Gates would say."

"Gates was pretty successful in his own right when he was in the industry. You can't argue his model of ripping off Apple after Apple ripped off Xerox wasn't hugely successful. It's the beauty of the IoDT concept and Steve Jobs' DNA that's going to make Reliqueree a huge success."

"Where is this 'shelf' you refer to?"

"In Shenzen. We have a major manufacturing contact. The company builds and assembles a wide variety of devices for companies including Samsung, Huwaei, Sony and half a dozen others. There's always an overage somewhere in the market. Someone miscalculated the number of phones they'd sell or demand for an accessory. Or a contract was broken and all of sudden there are palettes full of different parts but no device to put them into.

"We'll scavenge the Shenzen parts bin and contract to assemble something. We need a CPU, memory, and a display. That's not hard to find. There are multiple ways to get the DNA sample into the device. I already have a couple of ideas. Our target cost of goods per unit is $50 dollars. Applying the normal metric, at retail we charge six times and sell for $299. However, this is Steve Jobs' DNA we're offering. That buys us a premium. We should be able to go out the door at $399."

After more back and forth, we eventually arrived at an evaluation satisfactory to Illarion. We then discussed a personnel issue.

"I see the plan calls for you to hire another programmer? An 'embedded systems specialist?' Could you tell me more?"

"Sure," I said. "Ignacio will take the lead on architecting the uLivv's software apps and manage development. Portions of the work will be handled by a Columbian development house we've outsourced work to previously. But it's vital to find a firmware expert, someone who knows how to integrate software with hardware. World class people in this area are not easy to recruit."

"I know someone who can do this. He is highly world class," Illarion said.

"He has to be," Ignacio said. "This work is critical path. It's one thing if a utility or app moves from 'launch' to 'available for the next release' status. We're dead if the device won't boot or bricks five minutes into operation."

"Who is the person you're recommending?" I said.

"My nephew Boris. My sister's boy. I have no children. He is like a son to me. He is talented at math, at...uh...how do you say it...the calculus. Advanced math. He was always at the top finisher levels at the Moscow State University programming contests. He is also excellent with hardware. Perhaps too good."

"Is he in the U.S.?" I said.

"He is coming to the U.S. next week. His English is acceptable."

"Can he handle embedded systems?"

"He has an affinity for working with, what did you call it? Ah, yes. 'Firmware.'"

"Does he have an H-1B?" I said.

"He has a green card."

"What kind of work has he done?" Ignacio said.

"He has done interesting work with hard drives. Reprogramming them. Among other things. As I said, he has much talent, but is sometimes misled. He is passionate about his work. One of his recent projects caused too much excitement in Moscow and it is best if he works in the U.S. for a while."

"Is he wanted?" I said.

"In the U.S.? No."

"Uh, in Russia?" Ignacio said.

"Not officially." Illarion smiled at me affably but I noted a certain look in his eyes and I recalled an old Russian proverb. It goes, "If Boris Badenov's uncle is funding Moose and Squirrel's shiny new startup and wants Moose and Squirrel to hire Boris Badenov, hire Bois Badenov." Even if the kid turned out to be useless, we were well ahead of the game. And if this was a case of an investor placing a proxy in the company to keep an eye on his interests, that was nothing new. We could handle it.

"We'll set up an interview once we're at contract," I said. "We're going to move quickly and he's going to need to hit the ground running. Ignacio and I look forward to meeting him."

The only real area of contention was where we'd be headquartered.

"You should establish your main office in New York," Illarion said.

Ignacio and I looked at each other. New York may bill itself as the Big Apple, but it's a high-tech kumquat. If you want to write a book or sing on Broadway, move to New York. If you want to introduce an innovative new software/hardware platform to the world, that's what Silicon Valley is for.

"The Valley is the logical place for Reliqueree to be, Illarion," I said. "It's the industry hub. Access to programing talent, movers and shakers, reputation management, it all flows out of the Valley. And it's easier to fly to China from the West Coast and we're going to need to make several trips."

"Yes, but I need to fly to Moscow far more frequently than I travel to California. You mentioned 'reputation.' Presently, you **do** have a reputation in the Valley and it is not a good one. In New York, there will be less gossip and attention paid to your new venture. I believe this is a healthy thing. I am sure you both know there are potential issues that may arise from your special 'resource.' These issues are best dealt with in New York. You have family here, your mother. It would be good to be close to her. A son needs to look out for his mother. And you, Ignacio. You are from Pittsburgh? It is far easier to fly home to visit from New York than from San Francisco or San Jose."

I had to admit he was right about Valley gossip, though being closer to Mom wasn't much of a draw. On the other hand, there were definite positives to having Angie on the West Coast for the next several months while I brought Reliqueree to life. She could focus on her pregnancy while I was focusing on my startup. In the age of the Cloud, creating meaningful, at-a-distance communications between couples is much easier.

"Illarion, these are good points. Do you mind if we..."

"Then it is settled. It is New York. I will be able to assist you in finding space for the company."

It was settled. It was New York.

When we walked out of the building, we stopped in the middle of the sidewalk, turned, and hugged each other.

I can't believe it," Ignacio said. "We are in business."

"We're almost in business," I said. "But we need the liver."

As the words left my mouth, Ignacio's phone buzzed. He pulled it out of his pocket, looked at the screen, and mouthed '"L." The type of coincidence that makes you believe there **is** a God. He connected, listened for a second, then replied.

"Yes," he said. "We're still interested. Yes, the offer still stands. Twenty five thousand cash. We're serious. You tell us where and when and we'll be there. This Sunday? Where? Got it. Let me check with my colleague, he's right here." He hit "hold."

"This Sunday, 6 pm. Memphis. You were right. He'll meet us at the airport."

"Tell him there'll be three of us. You, me, and a person to verify."

"We're bringing someone with us to test the item," Ignacio said into the phone. "Yes. No, I can assure you there will be no problems. See you Sunday." He disconnected and looked at me. "He wants to be paid in fifties. What next?"

"What's next is we go back to Mom's place while you book us a cheap flight back to San Francisco ASAP."

"Why not just stay here and fly out to Memphis?"

"Two reasons. One is you heard me mention our contact in Shenzen. That relationship needs immediate managing to ensure its continued usefulness."

"I understand why Angie loves you. Mr. Romantic."

"We're entrepreneurs, Ignacio. This is the time to be in love with commitment, excellence and success."

"Well, I'm not pregnant with your child so I'll shut up. What's the other reason?"

"We need to slot in our verification resource."

"Huh?"

"Who do we know who has a medical degree and is a cancer specialist?"

"I don't know...oh. Him."

"Yes, him."

"I'll track down a flight immediately. I'll book the trip for the three of us to Memphis while I'm at it. I strongly suggest you be especially sweet to Angie. Bring her something extra nice. If you're short of cash, I'll spring for it."

"I have it covered."

That night on the ride to the airport, I texted Angie.

U there?

Yes

On way to airport

Yes?

Great news. we're back in biz

Really?

Yes. new venture

Out of money

Have funding. Don't need ur money. need u

Really?

Yes, really

What time flite in

10 am

Will meet u at airport ok?

Ok

CHAPTER 12

ENGAGEMENT

The flight back West was quiet and as I passed through security, I spotted Angie waiting for me. She ran towards me with her arms open, but stopped short in surprise when I suddenly dropped to one knee, grasped her left hand, and slipped Granma's ring on her finger.

"Tim sam," I said in front of the smiling crowd and a gaping Ignacio, who was behind me and had nearly tripped when I'd performed my proposal dive, "will you marry me?"

I have to admit I'd had a slight qualm or two when I'd remembered after the funding meeting I'd left the ring in my pajama pocket instead of handing it back over to Mom. But I realized this was the right thing to do. Angie wanted a ring and this one was undoubtedly safer on her hand than back in Riverdale performing the role of cat toy. In her present state of mind, Mom wouldn't miss it and I was sure Granma would have wanted me to have it. And I was happy I wouldn't be rooming with Ignacio and his snore and that the Shenzen connection was secured. A win all around.

After a few moments of stunned silence, Angie stammered "Yes." I picked her up, gave her my best happiest-man-in-the-world hug, endured Ignacio pounding on my back while saying over and over again "Congratulations man!" and finished up the sequence by staring meaningfully into my official fiancée's eyes for several seconds before moving everyone along out of the terminal and into Angie's car. Forty minutes later we dropped Reliqueree's co-founder off at his Mission abode and Angie and I continued over to Gough Street, where I anticipated a reunion with the apartment's king-sized bed, firm, comfortable mattress, and hopefully an even more enjoyable encounter with something softer.

The bed was just as I remembered it, but Angie's amatory mood wasn't. Morning sickness. Oh well. Her nausea didn't stop her from thoroughly grilling me about Illarion and Reliqueree's business plan, though. Her eyes widened when Steve Jobs' liver came up.

"You have to buy his liver before the Russian company will provide the funds?"

"Yes. It's going to cost $25 thousand. The liver is in Tennessee. Ignacio and I are flying out Sunday to complete the transaction and pick it up."

"I don't have any money."

I walked over and stared deeply into her almond eyes. "Tim sam, I don't need your money. I came back here for you. Because I need you. Ignacio and I are funding this part of the operation on our own."

"Is this legal?"

"Once the liver was removed, it became a case of 'finders keepers.'"

"Do you really think this Russian is going to fund the company based on your retrieving a dead man's liver?"

"Yes. He invested in us once. There's no reason for him to waste his time on this idea unless he believed in it. Illarion is a man who recognizes innovation and forward thinking. He proved it by investing in theTogetherHood.

"And this isn't any dead guy, Angie. This is Steve Jobs. America's greatest business icon. A man who before his death taught the world how to sell consumer electronics at 70 percent profit margins. Made us care about touch screens and gesturing. Proselytized to fast food workers on how to make the perfect smoothie and remove the pulp from fresh-squeezed orange juice. Who suffered his own personal Calvary at the

the hands of people such as Mike Markkula, John Sculley, and yes, even Bill Gates. People who didn't understand why the one-button mouse was important. Why swiping was necessary. Why charging $1 dollar per download for pop music was right. He gave the world so much, Angie. He was a generous man, a great spirit."

"I've never heard he contributed much to charity."

"I don't think a dime. Anyone can hand out money. Or write an industry-standard BASIC. Bill Gates has shown us that. But there's more to giving than just money. Steve sold us all dreams, inspiration, the iPod, iPad, iPhone, and Woody and Buzz. Beautiful things delighting us all and transforming Apple into the world's most valuable company. That's true greatness. Would you like to see the business plan and presentation that describes how we're leveraging it?"

"Immediately."

I ran through the deck. When I reached the end, I could see she was impressed.

"The numbers look good," she said. "But how do you plan to build the units?"

"Your uncle. I'm going to be flying out to Shenzen shortly to discuss hardware options. And yes, I do expect him to show his nephew-in-law extra consideration."

"'Future' nephew-in-law."

Successful entrepreneurs learn to not avoid problems, but instead seize the terms of the debate so as to dictate the outcome.

"You're completely right. We need to discuss setting a date. But the business plan is aggressive. Why don't we head down to city hall and take care of this? We'll only have time for a big wedding after the launch and it's not fair to you. Let's get married now."

Angie hesitated, torn. Chinese girls love big weddings.

"When after the launch?"

"You pick the date," I said.

"I want doves."

"Excuse me?"

"My cousin Li Yan had doves released at her wedding a few years ago. It was beautiful. The late afternoon blue sky, she and her husband deeply in love. I'll never forget the sight of the white birds swirling above them, then flying into the distance."

The doves probably had incentive. Chinese cuisine is very inclusive.

"We'll have doves. But short term, we need to fly to Shenzen and decide on our hardware. Do you think you can persuade the bank to give you a few days off?"

Angie smiled at me, then reached down and touched her stomach. Pregnant women love to do that. "It won't be a problem. I'll call my uncle tonight. I haven't told him we're expecting."

I had a strong feeling Michael had, but never mind. And that reminded me.

"Tim sam, speaking of Michael, there's something he can do for us."

"What?"

"We need someone to fly out with us to Tennessee to authenticate the liver. Michael is the perfect person. Can you talk to him? It's important for the future of the company. For **our** future."

"I'll call him."

She took out her phone and a minute later I was listening to an increasingly heated conversation in Cantonese. At its crescendo, Angie pulled the phone from her ear and handed it to me.

"He wants to talk to you." She walked into the bedroom.

"Hi, Michael," I said. "Actually, shouldn't I start calling you 'bro?'"

"You bastard. What are you up to?"

"Michael, my Cantonese is poor, but I don't think the word for 'brother-in-law' translates to 'bastard.' As for what I'm trying to do, I'm working on providing a safe and secure future for your sister and nephew. I hope I'm not going over the line."

I heard muffled Cantonese, then a moment of silence. "What do you want me to do?"

"Ignacio and I are flying out to Memphis on Sunday to take delivery of Steve Jobs' liver. Angie already told you."

"Yes, she did. This is insane."

"No, it isn't Michael. The liver was removed from Jobs in Memphis. As we both know. I want you to fly out with us and test for authenticity."

"What makes you think I can?"

"I have a list. First on it is that Stanford contributed to the 2009 genome work. His information is all over every oncologist's computer at your temple of learning. It's the most famous cancer of all time. I need you to bring a data sample for testing purposes.

"Second is Google says Stanford has purchased several of those U.C. Berkeley portable DNA extraction kits and I bet you can lay your hands on one. That enables us to test on location.

"The third item is a potentially huge financial payoff awaits you.

"The fourth is what are you worried about? Jobs is dead. There's nothing illegal about testing a dead man's liver.

"And here's bullet 4.5. Imagine what Angie will do to you if you help screw this up."

There was a long pause on the line. "What time do we fly out?" he said.

"Ignacio will send you the itinerary. We'll meet you at the airport. Angie's seeing us all off."

"Sunday." The line went dead.

Angie came out of the bedroom. "What did Michael say?"

"He's looking forward to helping out."

CHAPTER 13

TO THE LAND OF THE KING

After Angie dropped Ignacio and me off, we met Michael at our flight's departure gate. He looked extremely unhappy and continually muttered to himself in Cantonese as we waited to board. Ignacio and I were going to have to put up with him cross country, so I tried calming him down.

"Michael, why so jumpy? Relax. It'll be fine."

"I can't believe I'm here. I can't believe I let Angie bully me into this. I didn't just complete a residency at Stanford to become a grave robber."

"We're not 'robbing' anything. Jobs gave up possession of his liver willingly. In fact, he was glad to get rid of it. And we both know what Angie wants, Angie gets. That's why I'm engaged to your sister."

"You know what I mean. This is ghoulish. Flying out to Hillbilly Heaven to test the DNA of a man who died years ago. Of all the blue-eyed devils in the world she had to pick, why did it have to be you?"

"My eyes are brown."

"I was speaking metaphorically. Though not about the 'devil' part."

My conversational strategy didn't seem to be working, so I changed gears.

"Do you have the sequencer?"

"Yes." He jostled one of his carry-ons. "It's in there."

"I didn't realize it was going to be so compact. Impressive."

"It is. And it's fast and flexible. With the previous units, you had to sequence the entire genome. It took several days. This unit enables me to set up on a small table and sequence selected sections. Since I have Jobs' data, I should be able to complete the analysis in a couple of hours. Maybe one. And then I'm done with this."

"Your choice. You may want to reconsider once you've thought about it."

Michael looked at me closely. "Angie says you didn't ask for any money for this new 'venture.'"

"I didn't. We're paying for this part of the operation. Your flight and all travel expenses. The transaction. I haven't asked Angie for a dime. In fact, I just gave her a diamond ring."

"I have to confess you hit a home run there. She took it in to be appraised the other day for insurance purposes and they quoted her $75 thousand. It may be an emerald cut, but it's over two carats and a quality stone. Nice chunk of platinum as well. You are not only her fiancée, you are now her hero."

Seventy-five thousand dollars! Holy God! If I'd realized it was worth that much, I could have sold it, bought Angie a nice ring for half the price, and pocketed the difference. For a second, I thought I felt Granma glaring down at me, but remembered I was usually an atheist and the feeling went away. But there was nothing I could do.

"It's even better," I said. "You know we've been offered funding? Contingent on this all going smoothly, which I'm sure it will."

He looked doubtful, but at least had calmed down and was no longer muttering when we boarded the plane and departed for Memphis, home of Graceland and the capital of Elvis Presley Nation.

The flight was quiet and we landed on time at 6:00 pm. We'd provided Mr. L with a basic description of our group and he'd told Ignacio he'd pick us up at the terminal. By 6:20 he hadn't shown and Ignacio and Michael were becoming edgy. I was more sanguine. I thought he was nearby and checking us out for safety's sake. My guess was confirmed when after another five minutes, a tall skinny fellow wearing a Tennessee Titans' cap unfolded himself from a nearby chair and walked over to us.

"You boys are looking for me? I'm supposed to be meeting two white guys and a Chinaman and you fit the bill," he said.

"I'm Chinese," Michael said.

"Yes, you are," the man said.

"You're Mr. L?" I said. Our "host" possessed pale blue eyes and regular features marred by a few old acne scars.

"I am indeed. But you can call me Landon. And you're Nate and I believe that's Ignacio." He smiled widely at the webmaster of Deadland.com. "It is surely a pleasure to meet y'all. I don't have the pleasure of knowing your name, though," he said, looking at Michael.

"I'm Michael. I'm here to test the item."

"Good. Gentlemen, if you'd follow me to the parking lot and we'll get this pow-wow underway. Are you fellows hungry? There's a good barbecue place not far from where we're going where you can chow down on some ribs and enjoy a few cold ones."

I, personally, was starving after the long flight and standard inedible airplane food. I looked over at Ignacio and Michael and they both nodded "yes." Besides, it wasn't a bad idea for the group to be seen together in public. I hadn't been overly concerned about this being an elaborate con or robbery attempt. Landon had to figure someone knew where we'd flown to and why. Our smartphones would enable anyone to track where we'd been while away. And we were being recorded as we headed towards the terminal exit. Still, a public sit-down nearby Landon's place of business made it even less likely there'd be problems later on.

"Sounds great, Landon. We could all do with some good food and beer," I said.

"I figured you might. Where you boys staying?"

"The downtown Sheraton."

"Why'd you pick there?"

"It's near the medical district. We thought it might be convenient."

"Uh, huh."

Memphis International is not a large airport and we walked to Landon's car, a rusty Ford four-door pickup. The interior was only somewhat clean. We climbed in and a minute later were on 51 North. It's a short ride to the city and everyone was quiet. We were soon pulling into a parking lot and in front of an unassuming building with a red-and-white checked roof and a sign out in front proclaiming "Central Barbecue."

Landon stepped out of the car. "Gentlemen, please follow me. It's not fancy inside, but they serve authentic Memphis barbecue. Y'all are due for a treat."

I'm not an expert on regional barbecues, but he spoke the truth. The food was excellent. By unspoken consent, no one talked about the business reasons for our trip. Instead, the conversation soon devolved into a passionate discussion between Ignacio and Landon on the respective artistic and technical merits of zombie movies. The discussion slowly grew more heated.

"The problem is the entire industry is on the verge of self-parody, Ignacio. The other night I was looking at the list on your site of the most popular zombie films of the last several years and I almost cried. *Zombeavers*? *The Co-ed and the Zombie Stoner*? *Samurai of the Dead*? That last film almost made me just want to give up. The film was a sacrilege against everything a true zombie enthusiast believes in." Landon looked over at Michael. "Nothing personal, mind you."

"Don't worry about it. I'm Chinese. Take the movie up with Japan," Michael said.

"Right. But I'm saying, Ignacio. The spirit of George Romero is dead in today's auteurs. A revival is needed. Zombie movies need to return to their roots and shed all this camp and sniggering disrespect for the genre. It just has to happen."

"Landon, I can understand your viewpoint, but I can't endorse it." Ignacio's tone was stern. "The zombie movie must evolve. Many of these films have taken the zombie to places none of us expected. *Warm Bodies*, for example. Read the comments on the board. About how the movie explores the zombie's emotional world in fresh new ways. Another referred to it as the best love story since *Love Story*."

"Love story?" Michael said. "Don't zombies want to eat their dates? I just don't see that as romantic. *In Romeo and Juliet*, when Romeo dies, Juliet doesn't treat him as a snack. Besides, if zombies are so wonderful, why haven't they done one with your local hero, Elvis?"

"They have," Ignacio said.

"*Bubba Ho Tep*. A classic," said Landon.

"Excuse me," I said. "Just to give my friend here some support, I don't understand how zombie movies can 'evolve.' I mean, zombies are dead, right? Their whole goal is to **not** evolve."

Ignacio shook his head sadly. "Nate, you need to expand your horizons. America has embraced the zombie. *The Walking Dead* proved the point. How many zombie movies have you seen? Other than *Dead Snow*? How can you criticize something you haven't experienced?"

"Ignacio, I haven't experienced going to International Falls in the middle of winter and licking an aluminum lamp post with my tongue, either. Something a zombie could do with zero discomfort, even if they left their tongue stuck to the pole."

"A striking image," Landon said.

"Thank you," I said. "Is everyone finished? If so, it's time we proceed to business."

CHAPTER 14

THE TRANSACTION

Landon's place was five minutes from Central Barbecue. We passed by the Memphis medical district and Methodist University Hospital on the way. I'd guessed right again. He stopped in front of a two-story house with two entrances and led us through the one on the left and up to the second-floor apartment. We waited on the stairs behind him as he used separate keys to throw the bolts of the three locks securing his front door.

Landon pushed it open, flicked a light switch, and pointed us inside to a round, worn vinyl table sitting in a dining space next to the kitchen.

"If you boys don't mind, I'll ask you to sit here while I go check my email. I don't much care for reading it on my phone. I'll just be a minute."

I sat down in the chair opposite the kitchen. After a second or so, I realized I was being watched. The observer was a bright green eye fixing me with a straight, unwavering stare. I blinked for a second and shook my head. The eye was still there, accompanied by what I assumed was its optic nerve. It was floating in a sealed jar on a counter separating the dining room from the kitchen. After a second, I realized the eye was flanked by two other organs, also in jars. The one on the left looked like a heart. The one on the right I had no idea.

Michael looked around, spotted the eye, froze, then began murmuring under his breath in Cantonese.

A second later Ignacio also spotted the eye and paled mildly, but otherwise seemed less affected, though he began lightly drumming his fingers on the table. I was far more concerned about Michael, who looked like he was about to bolt.

"Michael, stop carrying on. You're going to cause a problem."

"He has an eeyyee," he said in a low tone. "In his kitchen."

"And you have two in your head, which puts you ahead of that eye's original owner. Cut it out. You're a doctor for God's sake. You've seen human remains in jars hundreds of times. Hell, you had to dissect a corpse in medical school."

"No, I didn't. We used a virtual corpse. It was plastic. Why is an eye on the counter? And a heart?"

"Private collections of human remains are nothing new. The heart's there to keep the eye company."

"I feel like it's staring at me."

"Fine." There was a napkin holder in the middle of the table. I picked it up and placed it in front of the eye.

"There. Better?"

"Yes. Thank you."

"You're welcome. And get hold of yourself."

Landon came back and walked into the kitchen. "You boys want a cold one? It's on the house."

"Yes," I said. "Me, too," said Ignacio. Michael just stared ahead and said nothing.

"What's wrong with him?" Landon said

"Nothing. Jet lag catching up."

"I can understand. When I flew out to California a few years ago, I felt like crap. You hang in there, Michael."

Angie's brother smiled weakly. Landon walked to his refrigerator and extracted three Budweisers, then a Tupperware container from the freezer section. He handed each of us a beer and placed the container in the middle of the table. Ignacio and I twisted the caps off our bottles and took a deep swig of brew, our eyes never leaving the box. Landon glanced down and frowned. He looked behind him, picked up the napkin holder, and placed it back on the table. Michael shuddered and looked up at the ceiling.

"Gentlemen," Landon said, "I want y'all to meet Steve Jobs' entire liver."

There was a moment of dead silence as the three of us contemplated the final resting place of approximately two to four percent of Steve Jobs.

"Do you mind if I open it?" I said to Landon.

"Go right ahead. But don't take too long. You don't want it to defrost."

I pried the cover open. Inside, the liver was wrapped in a protective plastic wrap. I looked at Landon.

"Yeah," he said. "Hold on a sec."

He went into the kitchen and came back with a small knife and sliced open the covering. The liver lay bare in front of us.

I reached out reverently and brought the box closer to me. The human liver is not the world's most beautiful organ, but at the moment I thought this one was lovelier than a Van Gogh and certainly more monetizable. And the events this liver had experienced! Metabolizing copious amounts of LSD while visiting India with Daniel Kottke. Processing dozens of fad diets while Steve Wozniak designed and built the Apple I and Apple II computers. And undoubtedly filling with bile when Jobs was tossed out of his own company by John Sculley.

"What are those white sections?" I said.

"Those are the metastases caused by the spread of his pancreatic neuroendocrine tumor," Michael said. He was studying the liver closely and looked better. "I'd estimate about 25 percent of the total mass is cancerous. He certainly needed that transplant."

"Are you ready to take a sample and verify?" I said.

"Yes. Landon, do you have a place where I can set up my equipment?"

"How about there?" he said, pointing to an unlit space next to the dining area. "The living room."

"Do you have a table I can use?" Michael said.

"I have a card table I set up for poker nights. Will that do?"

"That should be fine."

"Just don't get any mess on it."

"I'll be careful. I'll be ready to start once I biopsy the organ," Michael said. He left the kitchen with his sequencer while Landon assembled the table. Coming back in, Michael extracted a sample from the liver with a small needle and went to work.

Landon placed the liver back in the freezer and sat back down at the table. No one said anything and the silence began to stretch. Abruptly, he reached back and placed the jar with the eye in front of me.

"I imagine y'all are interested in my little collection here," he said.

"Oh, we don't want to pry," I said. I had no desire to dig any depth at all into this grave rat's life and career. "A man's hobbies are his own business."

"I'm interested," Ignacio said. I kicked him under the table, but he ignored me. "What's with the eye?"

"Well, some background is called for. I have a friend, you see, who's involved with a company that handles what the state likes to call medical 'waste.' That includes cultures, specimens, discarded needles, whatever. And human organs.

"Here in Tennessee, most of this stuff is normally packaged up specially and tossed in landfills or incinerated. Take this here eye. This belonged to a fellow who loved gunning his motorcycle down side streets in town at over 100 mph and waking folks up after midnight. Took the mufflers off the engine. Had kind of a regular route, which included this neighborhood. One night he was roaring down this very street and wouldn't you know it? He went over an oil patch in the middle of the road, went airborne off the bike, and hit his head against a lamppost. Autopsy doc at the hospital said he estimated he was doing 90 MPH or so on impact. He was flying so fast his eye popped clear out of his skull. When they brought him into the ER, he was a sight to behold. Or so my friend says."

"That's, um, fascinating," I said. "But what's the eye doing here? Wouldn't the hospital have tried to recover the cornea?"

"The eye was too messed up. It was due to be packed up and thrown out. What an awful waste."

I knew I shouldn't ask, but I couldn't resist. "Why?"

"Because my friend had discovered there's a market for body parts that have separated from their previous owners on a permanent basis. He and I talked it over and realized there was an opportunity to make some extra cash on the side via private disposal of these items. Particularly parts with an interesting history, like our acquaintance here."

"What kind of market?" I just couldn't help myself. "If the parts can't be used for transplants, what good are they?"

"What good is Steve Jobs' liver?"

"Research," I said. "Jobs' liver cancer was a rare type and his DNA possessed interesting mutations along its, uh, base pairs. The scientific community wants to learn more."

"Whatever you say, friend. I don't mean to pry either. This here is a cash-and-carry endeavor and as you said, our hobbies are our own affairs.

"To answer your question, they're all kinds of people out there who are interested in items like this. Some customers are medical establishments who want specimens for various reasons and aren't overly picky about how they get them. You may know something about that. Others just like collecting these things.

"Some customers want the parts for various religious and spiritual reasons. You know, witch doctors, Wiccans, the occasional Satanist, those kind of folks. Apparently, the magic just doesn't work so well unless you've got the right human part to help lubricate the spiritual gears, so to speak."

"So why haven't you sold the liver already?" Ignacio said. "I mean, you and your friend. Jobs underwent the transplant in 2009."

"Well, I have to confess my friend's acquisition of the liver was something of a spur of the moment decision. The opportunity presented itself as the organ was being disposed of and he just took it. But it might have caused problems if the word had gone out the liver was for sale when its original owner was still alive and kicking. It seemed the smart thing to do was just sit on it and let the situation cool down.

"Then my friend found out celebrity parts is a more difficult market than he'd thought. People want to stay away from controversy. It limits your opportunities. And we were asking a premium for something truly rare and a real part of history. A lot of people are still emotional about this fella, but not enough to fork over a fair price to own an actual piece of him.

"On the other hand, the organs of everyday folks who've died violently or in unusual circumstances are always in demand. As I said, to have thrown this eye away would have been purely a waste. And from what my friend heard about his character, I don't think the eye's former owner would mind participating in casting a few curses or trying to contact an axe murderer in the hereafter."

"Did anyone ever find out how the oil slick ended up on the road?" Ignacio asked.

"They did not. Everyone just chalked it up to someone's oil pan cracked at an inconvenient time."

"Tragic," I said.

"Now," Landon said, grabbing the jar holding the organ I'd been unable to identify and placing it next to the eye, "this here's a uterus. My friend remembers the girl it came from. She was a pretty young thing, all blue-eyed and blonde hair. There's quite a story behind this item. I bet you boys would like to hear it."

"Oh, no, no," Ignacio and I said. "That's quite OK," I said. "I'm superstitious, actually. I believe discussing too much bad luck generates more of the same. And I'm starting to feel the effects of jet lag myself. Why don't you check on how Michael is doing?"

Landon looked disappointed, but let the matter drop and walked into the dining room. I could hear the two of them chatting as the testing continued. After a half hour had passed, both of them returned to the kitchen. Michael looked at me and gave me a thumbs-up.

"That was fast," I said. "Less than an hour."

"The machine is state of the art and the sample was in excellent shape. The organ has been well preserved. I told you earlier, we didn't need to do a full sequence. It's Steve Jobs' liver."

"Excellent," I said to Landon. Ignacio and I stood up and removed the money belts we'd used to carry the cash and counted out the $25 thousand. "It's in fifties per your request," I said. He waited till we were done, then recounted the stacks.

"Are we finished?" I said.

"Hold on." He reached into the stacked bills, pulled out four at random, and removed a thick pen from his pants pocket. One end held a UV light which he used to scan each bill's security strip. He replaced them in the stacks, pulled out an additional four, and scratched a small "X" on each with the other side of the pen. After a second, he returned them to the stacks as well.

"Gentlemen, you are now the proud owners of Steve Jobs' liver," he said. "Congratulations." He took the organ out of the freezer.

"Here it is. It's all yours."

"Thanks." I pried the box open again and looked inside. The liver was there, the wrap still pulled aside where it had been cut. I could see the small marks Michael's biopsy needle had made. It would have been a pity to head home with Bossie the Cow's liver instead of Steve Jobs'.

"Ignacio, Uber us a car. Let's head over to the hotel."

Landon didn't offer to drive us back and I wouldn't have accepted anyway. During transactions of this nature, the customer and purchaser should limit their engagement. It helps avoid unexpected problems and friction.

"You boys understand it needs to be kept frozen?"

"We do. We've made preparations. Landon, we've taken too much of your time already. We'll wait outside for our ride. I want to thank you for reaching out to us." I stuck out my hand and we shook. I made a mental note to not touch my face until I'd thoroughly scrubbed my hand clean back at the hotel. Preferably with antibiotic soap.

"No problem. It was a pleasure doing business with you. And who knows? We may be doing business again sometime in the future. Me and my friend."

I thought this unlikely, but it's foolish to end a relationship prematurely. "Who knows?"

CHAPTER 15

THE TOAST

When we arrived at the hotel, the three of us agreed to meet down in the lobby in an hour for a nightcap. I stopped at the front desk to pick up the special package I'd shipped to the hotel ahead of our trip. Inside were Tecni-ICE packs stored in a small insulated box. Airlines regulations allow passengers to bring frozen food on board, but it has to be stored in an appropriately-sized container.

Up in my room, I placed the liver in the freezer section of the mini-fridge, changed into fresh clothes, and messaged Angie.

U there?

Yes

Its done. we own item

Any problem?

No. went smooth

How's michael?

Wants to go back to china

Ha ha

He did good. How are you feeling

Ok. A little sick

Im sorry. Will be home soon

OK. miss u. Luv u

Miss u. Luv u

Bye

Ignacio and Michael were already sitting at a table in the lounge when I walked in.

"Gentlemen, have you ordered yet?" I said.

"No," Ignacio said. "We were waiting for you. In the meantime, I've been explaining our growth plans to Michael." He gestured to the waiter, who came over and took our orders.

I looked at Michael. "What do you think?"

"Is this legal? I'm not a permanent resident yet."

"Is what legal? Asking you to test the DNA of an organ whose possessor paid millions to have it removed from his body and has died?"

"It still feels like grave robbing."

"The liver was never in the grave. But to answer your question directly, no, this is not about grave robbing. This is about the opportunity to bring Steve Jobs back to us in a deeply personal way. It's about rethinking death and reopening connections between the departed and the living. We're not ghouls, Michael. We're using technology to bring new ideas and options to an out of touch, exhausted market."

"To be honest, I'm more a Bill Gates kind of guy," he said. "I sort of like Windows."

"Long term, I'm not sure the prognosis for Windows is much better than Steve Jobs in 2009," I said. "But don't worry. We're open to Microsoft opportunities as well. But we need someone with your skillset at Reliqueree. There's an important role for you to play at what's going to become a leading technology firm. And an opportunity to become so wealthy you won't need to find work at a cancer research center. You'll be able to fund your own."

Michael's eyes had gone as wide as is possible for someone with an epicanthic fold. "What is it?"

"Jobs' liver is an invaluable resource. We need someone who can ensure it's properly processed. Someone we trust."

"What do you want me to do?"

"Oversee the DNA extraction process. Optimize the yield and quality coming out of the liver. No RNA or ethanol contamination."

"Someone's been spending time on Google," he said. "Do you understand what you just told me?"

"Not really. That's why I want to hire you. Reliqueree is committed to excellence in every step of our operations. Every initial purchaser of a uLivv is going to be receiving a verified, certified, and complete sample of Steve Jobs' DNA. A purchasing experience that delights our customers and guarantees when we go to IPO, your options will convert to highly valued shares."

"By the way, Michael, how much DNA are we talking about?" Ignacio said.

"A lot," he said. "An adult human body contains about 37 trillion cells. Except for sperm and egg cells, each one contains the 46 chromosomes making up the complete genome." He paused a second. "Let's see, the human liver is about four percent of the total, so let's guesstimate around 900 million DNA strands or so. Of course, based upon a visual inspection, about 25 percent of that volume consists of cancerous cells, which contain a mutated version of Jobs' DNA. We'll need to filter it out and discard it."

"Wait a second," I said. "That seems wasteful."

"I agree," Ignacio said. "I'm not the marketing genius here, but we can do better than **that**. We could create a 'C' version."

"You're onto something." The 'Black Edition?' Or the uLivv Plus?"

"Let's think on it."

"You two are unbelievable," Michael said.

"We think so," I said. "So, do you want a slot at Reliqueree?"

"I'll give it serious consideration. When I'm back home, I'll ask Angie to run through the business plan again."

"Please do. In the meantime, it's been a long but successful day. Ignacio, I'll give you a call once I'm in New York."

"You're not flying back with us?" Michael said.

"No. I need to meet with our funding source and finalize the deal. Our headquarters is going to be located in New York and we need to find a place."

"In New York? Does Angie know about this?" Michael said.

"Uh, I'm not sure I mentioned it yet."

"She's not going to be happy. Why didn't you tell her?"

"It slipped my mind. You may have noticed we've been extremely busy recently. Besides, we don't have a choice. Our backer insisted on us setting up shop in New York."

Michael looked at Ignacio for confirmation. Ignacio shrugged his shoulders. "The money guy said New York."

"Very unhappy."

"She can cheer herself up by looking at her $12075 thousand dollar diamond ring," I said. "I'll be coming back to the West Coast periodically on visits to China. And while I'm in New York, I'll start scouting out a place for both of us.

"Gentlemen, a quick toast and I'm off to bed. Here's to Steve Jobs' liver. It's going to bring us far more luck than it did him."

Ignacio downed his glass. Michael also drank but looked skeptical. A few minutes later I was back in my room and asleep almost as soon as my head hit the pillow.

CHAPTER 16

MEETING MISS FANCY

The next morning I packed the liver carefully and placed it in the small box. The organ would stay in my possession every minute — Reliqueree's cornerstone would not be flying with the luggage. We cabbed back to Memphis, said goodbye at the airport, and I headed for my gate.

I'd been concerned the liver might attract attention going through security, but it received just a quick glance as it cleared the scanner. I reached my window seat on the small jet, placed the box on the floor underneath the space in front of me where I could keep an eye on it, and buckled in. I thought I'd be too nervous to snooze, but I've always slept well on planes and dozed off a few minutes before takeoff.

I was awakened by the sensation of someone tapping on my shoulder while a soft voice said, "Young man? Young man?" I looked to my left. The aisle seat next to me was occupied by a small, white haired woman with a cherubic smile and blue eyes. She was holding a bright red carry-on in her lap sporting an unusual decoration, a furry head. After a second, the head's eyes blinked and the mouth snarled at me.

I sat straight up and looked at the little old lady more closely. She was indeed carrying a small dog in a bag on her lap. I didn't recognize the breed. As I watched, the hound heaved and scrabbled desperately in an attempt to fight free of its diminutive prison.

"Yes, ma'am?" I said. "Can I help you?"

"Oh, I'm sorry. Did I wake you up?"

"Isn't that why you tapped me on the shoulder and talked to me while I was asleep?"

She smiled at me but her eyes stopped twinkling and another expression entered them. "Ignite," or "kindle" is perhaps the right word. Regardless, I felt a sudden chill.

"Oh, I'm so sorry. But Miss Fancy has taken quite a shine to you and just insists on meeting you."

I stared at Miss Fancy. "Really? I'm not known as a dog whisperer. Canines can normally take or leave me."

"Well, Miss Fancy is an intuitive little girl and knows what she likes."

"Really." I inspected the animal more closely. Its fur was an odd colored mélange of white, brown and black. Small dark eyes stared frantically out of a wizened little rat-like face while its oversized nose snuffled and waved in the air like a fat, black, borer bee. "I don't think I've ever seen a dog like this. What breed is she?"

"Miss Fancy is a special breed. She's a mix of a Cavalier King Charles Spaniel and a Yorkie. She's a Corkie."

"A Corkie. Is that an official breed?"

"No, not yet, but Miss Fancy and I intend to change that, don't we, Miss Fancy?" She stared down at the rodent face fondly. "When we get back to 20 East 74th, we're not going to let that stuck-up AKC ignore all our petitions and letters, are we Miss Fancy? No, no, no." She brought the dog's head up to her face and the creature briefly lathered her cheeks with drool. Miss Fancy then turned her beady eyes back to me.

I decided some in-flight diplomacy might be a good idea and reached out to pet the little monster on its head. Miss Fancy bided her time and waited till my fingers were in easy reach, then snapped at them.

"Ouch!" I jerked my hand back and examined the fresh indentations in my flesh. "I thought you said Miss Fancy liked me."

"Oh, I'm so sorry. Miss Fancy, what a naughty, naughty girl." She brought the verminous little pest back up to her face for a saliva reapplication. "I thought so too. But there's something about you that fascinates Miss Fancy."

I thought it was time for this conversation to end. I didn't fancy Miss Fancy.

"Ma'am, it's been a pleasure meeting you and Miss Fancy. And good luck with the AKC. If you don't mind, I'm going to try to sleep some more. I've been on the go for the last week and need to catch up."

I turned my face towards the window without waiting for an answer and closed my eyes. Beside me, I could hear Miss Fancy snarbling and growling. We were only 40 minutes out from New York.

The tapping on my shoulder resumed. "Young man? Young man? Can I ask you a question?"

I turned over in my seat to gaze at my tormentor. I'd thought earlier she was cherubic looking, but as I looked at those hard blue eyes and steely pursed lips painted with deep red lipstick, I realized she probably derived her looks from another locale.

"Can I ask what you have under the seat? By the way, my name is Millicent."

"Millicent, may I ask why you want to know?" I did not tell her my name.

"Because Miss Fancy is very attracted to it. When I put her in her little bag under my seat, she became so excited. She's been trying to reach your package for most of the flight. Miss Fancy has a very sensitive nose. She'd love to see what's in the case."

Oh, God. "I'm sorry, Millicent. Miss Fancy can't see what's in the case."

"Is it something dangerous?"

"No, Millicent. They don't allow dangerous things on board."

"May I ask what it is?"

At this juncture, I thought a partial strategic retreat was in order. "It's a steak, Millicent."

"A steak. Oh, that explains it. Miss Fancy loves steak."

"I'm not surprised. Miss Fancy is a dog."

"Oh, Miss Fancy is more than a dog. She's a real little person. I've been taking video and pictures of her with my iPhone ever since she was a puppy and I can tell you it was just like watching my own daughter grow up. If I had a daughter. She's a little precious."

In her arms, the precious continued its quest for **my** precious. Millicent was right in regards to the first part of her declamation. Miss Fancy was indeed more than a dog. She was a Cerberus. A mini.

"I must say, it's rare for someone to bring a single steak home and from Memphis of all places," she said. "It must be a special cut of meat."

I switched gears to a Fabian strategy of delay and misdirection. We were only 30 minutes from New York.

"Oh, it is. Millicent, are you from Tennessee?"

"Oh, no. I just connected there. I was visiting my sister in Dallas."

"Well, I bet you didn't know it, but before the Civil War, Tennessee was known as The Steakhouse of the Old South. People came from all around to eat Tennessee steaks. Chuck, filet, sirloin, you name it. Davy Crockett is reported to have said before the end at the Alamo that the only thing he regretted was not going to be able to go home and enjoy one last Tennessee tenderloin. And of course, you've heard about Memphis barbecue. Officially, Elvis is supposed to have died from a drug overdose, but unofficially it's always been rumored he choked to death on a piece of brisket. It makes sense, when you think about it."

She looked at me closely, trying to figure out if I was making fun of her or not. Miss Fancy had been quiet during my dissertation, but resumed her struggle to reach the liver.

"What kind of steak is in the case?" she said.

"A special porterhouse. Super tender."

I picked up the inflight magazine and began to read an article about the current renaissance of Newark, New Jersey. As I read through the piece about the city's exciting events, including the McDonald's Gospelfest and the Geraldine R. Dodge Poetry Festival, as well as go-to-places- to-visit such as the Newark Public Library and the historic John Ballantine House, it became apparent whoever had written the article had **actually** spent time in Newark, drank the water, and contracted lead-chromate poisoning of the brain. Almost inevitable. Newark has as much chance of undergoing a renaissance as the Bikini Atoll.

This tactic bought me about five minutes as Millicent and Miss Fancy continued to bathe me in their unwanted attention. The torture then resumed.

"Young man, do you think you could possibly put the steak away in one of the rear galleys? It might calm Miss Fancy down. It's becoming tiring holding her away from it."

"I'd prefer not to, Millicent. I can put it in the overhead compartment, if you'd like." I didn't want to do that, but I was willing to compromise if I could just make her leave me alone.

"Oh, no, that won't work," she said. "Miss Fancy will be able to smell the steak anywhere on this little plane. If you don't want to get up, I'm sure one of those nice young stewardesses will be glad to put the steak away. Just so Miss Fancy won't be tempted." A little steel had entered her tone.

I began to sweat. The last thing I needed was for Steve Jobs' liver to be manhandled by a flight attendant. What if they insisted on opening the box before sticking it in their fridge?

"I **really** don't want to do that, Millicent. But, there's something interesting I've been noting about Miss Fancy. I believe I've seen dogs almost identical to her in China and South Korea. If I'm right, this might help you to convince the AKC to recognize her as a certified Corkie."

We were 25 minutes out from New York.

"Oh, they don't say 'certified.' The correct word is 'registered.' You've been to China and Korea?"

"I have indeed. They're both fascinating places. Would you like to know more?"

"Yes. I particularly would like to hear more about the Corkies."

"Well, before I answer, can I ask you a favor? You said you have pictures and video of Miss Fancy as a puppy and a young girl? Would you mind terribly if I asked you to show them to me? It would help me compare her with the fascinating dogs I saw in China."

She dimpled up. "Oh, I wouldn't mind in the least." She pulled out her phone and swiped. "Here's a picture of my precious at three months." A video played of Miss Fancy ripping a sock to shreds and snarling. "Six months." Miss Fancy ripping a chew toy to shreds. More snarling. "Twelve months. Almost a big girl." A stuffed cat undergoing dismemberment. Snarling.

"Does that help?"

"I never realized a dog that small could salivate that much," I said. "Yes, it does. Have you ever heard of Yulin? It's a city in China. They have this amazing festival."

"No, I haven't. What is it? A dog show?"

"In a sense. You see, the Chinese have different customs than we do. Can you believe that in some cultures, people actually dine on these wonderful animals? The Chinese celebrate this aspect of their ancient heritage at the annual Yulin Dog Eating Festival. Of course, I realize the idea takes getting used to, but a culture that created gunpowder, moveable type, and the compass may have something to teach us."

I looked at Miss Fancy intently. "Now, the good news is while they're a few differences, your little girl looks almost identical to a breed often used for certain of the festival's stir fry recipes. At the moment, I feel it would be sad to eat a pooch as wonderful as Miss Fancy, but my travels have taught me to be open to new experiences and sensations." I gently licked my lips.

Millicent shuddered and yanked Miss Fancy as far away from me as the limited seating allowed. I looked out the window, but could still hear the dog carrying on. A second later, there was the sound of a sharp slap. Miss Fancy yelped, then whined and was quiet.

A few minutes later, the pilot announced we were descending for landing. On the ground, Millicent rushed out of the airplane ahead of me as quickly as the people in front of her would allow.

I arrived back at Mom's without further incident.

CHAPTER 17

BUSINESS PLAN

That afternoon, I called Illarion and arranged to meet with him at his offices.

"I want to verify the item," he said.

"No problem. When do you want me there?"

"Be at the office at 10 am. Someone will be there to handle things. I will see you at 11."

During the trip down, messages began arriving from Angie. I ignored them. This was the wrong time to argue about domestic living arrangements.

When I arrived at Illarion's, I was led to the conference room. Waiting inside was an unsmiling gentleman who looked to be in his 40's. He opened the liver's container, carefully removed and inspected it, then took out a biopsy needle and plunged it into the organ at three separate locations.

"Hey," I said. "That's original stock. It's valuable."

The man ignored me and walked out of the room. While I waited, I took out my iPad and resumed work on the project management framework I'd created after our first meeting.

At 11 am, Illarion walked into the conference room.

"Congratulations. You have Steve Jobs' liver."

"I wasn't going to show up with something from Gristedes or the meat counter at Zabars."

He shrugged. "Due diligence. You understand."

"I do. Can we review the business plan?"

"Please go ahead."

"I've updated the spreadsheets and created a project management timeline. Notice our scheduled launch is October 15th. This will be a 'preview' edition of the unit designed to generate excitement and drive holiday sales and backorders. This is highly aggressive, but it can be done if everyone executes.

"Initially, we're going to distribute direct to the public. This is a new product and concept. I'm not going to waste time chasing Best Buy, Walmart, Staples and the rest. There's no reason. A few of them, particularly Best Buy, will take a presentation and a demo, but nothing goes on a pallet until they see sales and proven demand generation. I've projected an initial run of 30 thousand units with the COG still at $50 per unit."

"Thirty thousand seems high," he said. "An initial investment of close to $2 million. Why not be more conservative and start with twenty thousand?"

"Several reasons. One is every 10 thousand units built pushes the COG lower. The second is selling out a run of 30 thousand is more impressive than twenty and will generate more market momentum. And the more people who own a uLivv, the more word of mouth and buzz we'll build for phase two of the launch.

"And phase two is?"

"Build on our momentum and make sure everyone knows about our growing mountain of backorders. We'll use our early cash flow to develop targeted web-based advertising, generate PR, obtain product reviews, engage with key influencers, and start to build out our services infrastructure. At that point we may want to talk to selected retailers about carrying the product line."

"What is your unit forecast for phase two?"

"I'm pegging it at 250 thousand. We need to be in a position to take advantage of the holiday season."

"Very aggressive. You'll need another, say, $15 million to build the necessary inventory."

"I'll be honest. I think the 250 number is conservative. If we can reach one million in orders, assuming a ridiculously low 2.5-to-1 stock evaluation against sales, we'll have a seat-of-the-pants market cap of $1 billion. That's what the industry wants to see nowadays and the news will drive more interest and revenue."

"I assume you will have enough DNA to cover anticipated demand?"

"A conservative estimate is we'll have between 200 to 300 million units available," I said. "Enough to fulfill orders for years to come.

"But remember. We're using Steve Jobs' liver as a branding exercise to establish our core values and product differentiation. For Reliqueree to grow and reach its full potential, we need to reach beyond Jobs' acolytes and admirers. We have to communicate to the world how we're reshaping the post-life experience and interaction with the departed. The first generation uLivv is the vanguard of a new paradigm."

The room was quiet as Illarion contemplated the numbers and the schedule. He reached out and pulled the liver's container in front of him. "Do you mind if I look?"

"Be my guest. Not too long, though. If the liver defrosts, the DNA will begin to degrade."

"I understand." He lifted off the cover. For a second, his face was obscured by the cloud of vapor rising off the organ. He reached out gingerly with an expensive-looking pen to lift the plastic wrap protecting the liver, looked at it a long moment, then replaced the lid.

"It is not much to see, is it."

"When I look at it, I don't see the organ," I said. "I see the beauty of Steve Jobs' DNA and how it enabled him to achieve so many extraordinary things. And that molecule's work isn't done yet. Being dead doesn't have to mean not being productive. When we launch, the world will realize Steve Jobs is not finished changing the world."

"After I met you, I began to read about Jobs' life and sayings," he said." This one is my favorite. *'Here's to the crazy ones, the misfits, the rebels, the troublemakers, the round pegs in the square holes. The ones who see things differently — they're not fond of rules.'* I myself have never been fond of rules."

"Illarion, we're of the same mind. Can we discuss our funding requirements?"

"Of course."

"The plan calls for an initial cash infusion of $3.5 million. That funds operations until the October release. Our personnel list includes a slot to hire your nephew by the way, assuming he's still interested and possesses the skills required. Is he still available?"

"He is. He is ready to meet with you anytime."

"Give me his contact info. By the way, in our last meeting you said you could help us find a reasonable commercial location downtown?"

"We own a building near the Flatiron. Silicon Alley. There are currently several vacancies. You said twenty to forty people over the next 18 months? More than enough room."

"I hope so. We're going to be expanding. In return for your initial investment, you'll receive a 20 percent equity stake. For the second round, we'll increase that to 25 percent."

"I have a counter proposal. I will give you the $3.5 million and I will take 70 percent in equity. For round two, I receive an additional 20 percent."

"No. It's not worth it. I want to become rich, not your employee."

"But I have the money."

"And I have the liver. And the team executing on it. And I'm hiring your nephew."

"But I am providing you the money to hire Boris."

"30 percent, then 15 percent."

"65 percent, then 15 percent."

In the end, we agreed on 50/50 for the first investment round, 62/38 for the second. Illarion said he'd have his lawyers draw up the paperwork and we'd incorporate in Delaware.

I thought I'd done well, though I hated losing control of my business before it started. But when Fearless Leader provides the funding, Fearless Leader ends up with the biggest pile of rubles at the end of the day. I'd done well in holding onto enough equity to insure that when the big payoff came, I'd become mega-rich.

"I'm heading back to the West Coast and then on to Shenzen," I said. "We need to make a decision on the device."

"Yes. Let me ask you something. Have you heard of a show called DEMO?"

"It's a tech showcase," I said. "Each year they invite new companies to present their products for a few minutes in front of about two thousand or so people. If you have the right product, it can be an excellent place to debut."

"Would you like to attend? This year?"

"Yes, but we would have had to apply months ago and I'm sure the slots have been filled."

"You will attend."

"Really? How?"

"They hold this DEMO in Russia. I make investments in other high-tech firms. I have done them a favor and now they owe me a favor. You will go to this DEMO."

"That sounds great. Thank you for the opportunity."

"You are welcome. Have a safe trip."

Once Steve Jobs' liver and I were back in Riverdale, I messaged Angie back.

U there?

Yes. No NYC!!!

Sorry, no choice. We're funded. money man says HQ NYC

Funded?

Yes. $3.5M. Hav job 4 michael. tell u more when back home

Not happy

We'll work it out. coming back to west coast. need to talk to your uncle. business. need u to com if u can get off wrk.

When back?

Tomorrow afternoon, will send itin

Will pick u up?

Yes.

CHAPTER 18

GREY CHINESE BLOB

Angie was waiting for me at the airport when I landed and, as promised, was not happy.

"Why didn't you tell me the company was going to be located in New York?" she said as we headed back to her apartment.

"I'm sure it was in the slide presentation or the business plan."

"I'm sure it wasn't. I rechecked."

"I'm sorry. I missed that. Illarion decided on New York. As God is my witness, we pushed for the Valley, but it was one of the conditions for our funding."

"What am I supposed to do in San Francisco while you're in New York?"

Several answers to this question crossed my mind, including "whatever you want," and "gain considerable weight." I wasn't being insensitive, but I do dislike over managing. However, given the situation, I decided on a proactive engagement strategy.

"Well, how about plan for our wedding? You said you wanted doves and I looked up the cost. They're not cheap. I'll be working to pay for a flock of them in New York. While I'm there, I'll also begin looking for an apartment. And don't you need to apply for a transfer to a New York branch of the bank? That will take time.

"In the meantime, don't worry. I'm going to be spending significant time on the West Coast. In fact, I need to fly out to Hong Kong ASAP and meet with your Uncle. I want you to come. It will be just you and me. We can tell Uncle Tony more about the terrific news in person, you can show off your engagement ring, we'll be able to spend quality time together, and I'll be bringing a gift for Uncle Song — new business. Do you think you're up for the flight? Ignacio booked us nice seats on Cathay at a great price."

"Ignacio isn't coming?"

"No. He's heading back to New York to handle setting up our office space, among other things."

"Where will he be staying?"

"With my Mom."

"Lucky him."

"Actually, they get along. So, can you get off?" I said.

"I need to talk to my supervisors," she said. "I'm sure I can arrange for a few days off, particularly if we travel around the weekend. Speaking of quality time together, I've scheduled some for tomorrow."

"Yes?"

"Yes. I'm going for an ultrasound and you're coming with me."

"Isn't it early for an ultrasound?"

"No."

When I walked into the apartment, it was apparent Angie was heading into full nesting mode. Scattered all around the place were the signs of the long-term disruption preparing to debut into my life. A **print** version of "What to Expect When Your Expecting." Several **print** catalogues of maternity clothes. God. Think of the trees. Didn't these eco-terrorists understand why epubs existed? On her laptop I saw a picture of a baby carriage.

"What's that?" I said, pointing to a strange-looking package on the couch containing what appeared to be several colored balls.

"A crochet kit. I'm going to knit the baby some booties. And then a sweater."

Angie was going to learn how to knit. Talk about watching an alien take control of a person's body.

"By the way, have you told your Mom about the baby?" she said.

"Yes, I did."

"And how did she take it?"

"She was excited and happy."

Angie looked at me skeptically. "Your Mom doesn't like me."

"I'm not sure Mom likes **me**. She definitely wasn't a fan of my father. But you're wearing Granma's ring."

She looked down at her finger and smiled. "True. And I've decided I really like the emerald cut. It makes my fingers seem longer. So that's one for your mom. But I imagine she's less than thrilled at the prospect of having a Chinese grandson."

"You know, I find racial perspectives on this topic interesting. After all, the child is going to be half white. You know, a member of the master race. Let's think of him as a Blended Caucasian."

"Master race?" she said. "China was civilized when you white people were avoiding baths for fear of miasmas while keeping plague rats as pets. Meanwhile, Chinese fleets were exploring the world while our scientists created gunpowder."

"And yet somehow it all went wrong," I said. "From those lofty heights, China descended into a nation whose principal interests were foot binding, spitting, and conditioning yourselves to eat increasingly disgusting food. This all culminated in a society where everyone's favorite pastime was sitting around smoking opium in a vain attempt to forget you were living in China. Making it worse was the fact that when the Emperor cracked down on the drug trade, everyone was too stoned to put up a decent fight against the British and the French. My God. You people actually lost to the French."

"You're a pig."

The trip to the obstetrician's office the next day was an additional dram of joy in my life. There are several gauntlets an innocent father must run before he's allowed to fund the prison of guilt and obligation the expectant mother is building.

One is the traditional wide grins and hearty congratulations offered to the bringer-of-new-life-into-the-world during the first sonograph visit to the obstetrician's office. By contrast, the father is offered a few perfunctory smiles and nods, but nothing more.

Another is the ritual unveiling of the fetus. During this process, the mother's belly is rubbed with a special ointment designed to allow the sonographer to take grainy pictures and video of the creature who will be draining you of money and time for the next couple decades of your existence. During the reveal, you can expect to be treated to a brief but sonorous oration on the miracle of pregnancy. Inevitably, at some juncture during the presentation, the technician will wave excitedly at the screen and inform you "There's the head!" The only proper response is to lean forward, adopt an expression of wonder and amazement, and say something positive like "Yes, it is!" or "Incredible!" A more informational response, such as "I'm glad it has one," is not recommended.

Unfortunately, at eight weeks an ultrasound can't tell you the sex of the baby, but it didn't matter. Angie had already decided the matter.

Finally, there's the post-viewing pep talk. The happy mother-to-be is encouraged to eat well, avoid stress, and take special care of herself. The father-to-be is advised to feed the mother-to-be well, avoid stressing her, and take extra special care of her.

There **is** a big payoff at the end of the entire process. I learned I could expect my heir and eventual replacement to make his appearance at the end of the year. And before leaving the office, Angie and I were presented with a printout of a grainy black-and-white picture of our child, along with a graphic file. Suitable for framing, sticking on your fridge, or wallpaper for your smartphone.

My son. The grey Chinese blob. Kind of got me right there.

CHAPTER 19

TRIP TO THE MIDDLE KINGDOM

The next day Angie informed me her superiors had given her permission to take several days off to visit Uncle Song. I suspect if Angie had wanted a year off, they'd have given it to her. SongTech does major business with the bank. We left that Thursday, stopping in Honolulu one day to recover, and then on to Hong Kong.

When we landed, a driver was waiting to take us to Uncle Song's personal residence. Our border crossing was uneventful and quick. You don't need a visa to stay in Hong Kong, but one is required to enter the mainland. Angie was a citizen and I'd picked up a multiple-entry visa from the Chinese San Francisco consulate on a same-day-requested basis, another gift from Uncle Tony. We rested up for the balance of the day, then went out to dinner with a large gaggle of Songs.

Dinner was enjoyable, though at the beginning of the evening I felt my future Uncle's eyes lock on me in a less-than-friendly fashion. Shortly afterwards, Angie began to describe the details of our engagement and showed off Granma's ring to the group. The bulk of the conversation was carried on in Cantonese, so I missed much of what was said, but whatever it was, Tony's expression softened. I suspect the reason was the discussion had turned to the ring's appraisal. "So, Angie says you are here to conduct business. What are you looking for?" Tony said.

The Chinese don't normally discuss financial matters during social occasions, but the rules are different with family. A good sign.

I quickly provided Tony with a high-level overview of the Reliqueree business plan and concept. "We're looking for a device. We need a slim form factor and COG between $45 to $55, excluding packaging. Assembly and packaging production will be done by SongTech."

"How large would the initial order be?"

"Thirty thousand units. We anticipate a follow up of 200 thousand. Even higher. Only show me devices you're sure can be scaled up to those numbers. "

"Do you have funding? Future nephew-in-law or not, I won't bill."

"We have funding. And we need a device ASAP." I smiled at him. "Uncle."

Tony smiled back. In the United States, people often warn against mixing business and family. In China, these worries don't apply. "I have something I can show you tomorrow, **future** nephew. You'll find it interesting. Come to the factory at 1 pm."

When I arrived at SongTech, Tony and an engineer I'd never met were waiting for me in a small office. Laid out on a table was a slim silver rectangle, approximately two thirds the size of the old iPhone 13 line and thinner. Next to it was a torn-down version.

"Good afternoon Nate," Tony said. "This is Alex Lau, one of our top engineers. He was assigned to the project you see in front of you." Alex and I shook hands.

"Is this what you mentioned last night?" I said.

"Yes. Based on what we have discussed, I believe it will more than meet your requirements. I'll let Alex brief you more completely. I have a meeting I must attend. We'll talk more when you're done." Translation — the CEO of SongTech is not a demo dolly. Tony left.

"Alex, let's take a look. What is this thing?"

"It's multipurpose. Originally, it was designed to be a super-portable, low-power external hard drive and storage hub for your smartphone and/or tablet. It's spec'd for 64GB and 128GB storage. With the price of SAN cratering, you could easily go 256 or even a terabyte and stay within your COG target. Primary I/O is a micro USB-C port. Power/video/data transfer.

"What are the dimensions?" I said.

"Length 100 mm, width 45 mm, depth 8 mm."

"**Very** thin."

"The unit incorporates a new backplane design. Everything is one board. You're going to see the technology soon everywhere," he said.

"Nice. I see it has a screen. Almost bezel to bezel. Why does a hard drive need a screen?"

"Because when this unit was under development, rumors hit the industry Apple was developing a similar device. So the designers decided to add extra functionality. In addition to a hard drive, it's an MP3 player. Ever since Apple and Android killed the iPods and Nanos with the smartphone, gym rats worldwide have been mourning. Screen resolution is retina. Sharp and clear. Actually, MP3 player doesn't do it justice. It's more an incarnation of the iTouch."

"How much internal memory?"

"Six gigs."

I looked at the tear-down more closely. "A micro SD slot?"

"Yes."

"What other goodies?" I said.

"Wi-Fi. Bluetooth. Radio. It will stream music and video to Bluetooth and USB-C enabled devices. Battery is good for two days. Front camera six megapixels, rear two. No accelerometer, though the screen can be manually oriented to portrait. No speaker, no headphone jack.

"What's the processor?

He picked up a chip and handed it to me. "Qualcomm. Snapdragon, octa core. Pretty powerful. The case is aluminum. Limited customization is possible."

"Who owns it?"

"I can't tell you. We're under a non-disclosure agreement."

"It's pretty cool. Why are you showing it to me? Why isn't it on the shelves at WalMart?"

"Because the market's been a moving target and the collapse of flash pricing has everyone hunkering down," he said. "No one's quite sure how to price anything at the moment. And Apple is still rumored to be building something similar. The device's producer wants to bring the price-per-unit even lower as a hedge. They need volume to do that. President Song informed me you want to build 30 thousand units initially, and a follow-on build of another 200 thousand? Those numbers make them feel more comfortable. And it will benefit SongTech, as we've made a considerable investment in this project."

"Understood." I pulled out my phone and dialed Ignacio. It was 1 am there the day before, but to entrepreneurs sleep is a privilege, not a right. He picked up after several rings and I heard a groggy "Yes?"

"It's Nate. I'm streaming you video. I want your opinion on a potential device. Ready?"

There were some fumbling sounds, then, "Go ahead."

I recorded both units while Alex repeated the specifications. When I was done, I asked him "What do you think?"

"What's the COG?"

I looked at Alex. "President Song said he would discuss it with you in person," he said.

"If it's reasonable, that's our uLivv," Ignacio said. "Can I go back to bed?"

"Night, night, pajama boy." I disconnected.

After two hours of heated negotiations, Tony agreed to a per-unit-price of $49 for the first 30 thousand. I calculated if I'd been married to Angie instead of just engaged, I could have shaved an additional $3 off that.

CHAPTER 20

BORIS

I spent the balance of my time in Shenzen with Alex further analyzing the prospective uLivv and arranging for prototypes to be shipped home. Angie was mostly silent on the trip back to the U.S., and the atmosphere had turned arctic when I transferred to a flight back to New York at SFO. I put the matter out my mind. Entrepreneurship is a team sport and Angie was a member of the team. Like all of us, she was going to have to contribute and sacrifice for the common good. As Reliqueree's CEO, I felt the best place for her to do that was San Francisco.

Back in New York, Ignacio, Illarion, and I met to sign the paperwork necessary to transfer the $3.5 million into the company account. I was pleasantly surprised to discover that while I was in Shenzen, our funding source had advanced us enough to open our offices and begin equipping them. Our new headquarters was located in an older but well-maintained building. As Ignacio and I looked through our suite, Illarion paid us a visit.

"I would like to discuss Boris," he said. "I have told him about the company and the uLivv and he is excited. When can you talk with him?"

I looked over at Ignacio. "Any reason why not tomorrow?"

"No. If he's good, we need him yesterday."

"Send him over at 9 am tomorrow. Ignacio and I are eager to meet him. Have him email his resume to us."

"I will tell him."

At 9:45 am the next day, a large, bear-shaped person walked into our place as Ignacio and I were configuring the office network. Boris, we presumed. We were already unimpressed. You don't arrive 45 minutes late for a job interview and expect to be hired. Even if you are the chief investor's nephew.

"Excuse me. I am Boris Samsonov. My uncle Illarion sent me here to speak with you." Our visitor spoke with a thick Russian accent and was carrying what appeared to be a battered laptop case. Late twenties? Early thirties? Hard to tell.

"You're late," I said. "You were supposed to be here at nine."

"The subway train from Brighton was slow."

"Forty-five minutes slow?"

Boris said nothing and refused to make eye contact with me or Ignacio. After a second, I said, "OK. We'll let it pass this time. Did you send me or Ignacio your resume? Your CV?"

"I didn't receive anything," Ignacio said. I hadn't either.

"Here is resume." Boris reached into the pocket of his jacket with a large, furry hand, pulled out two crumpled paper documents consisting of three pages stapled together, and handed one to each of us.

I scanned the resume and sighed internally. It was barely English and littered with misspellings. It also sported a yellowish stain I assumed was either tea or coffee. This would not be a long interview.

"Why didn't you email this?" Ignacio said.

"Uncle Illarion said I should be careful about sending out too much information about myself online. He has asked me to keep a low profile."

"Boris, I don't think he meant paper resumes," I said. "Let's go into the conference room and find out more about your skills and if you're a fit to the Reliqueree culture." We walked into the conference room and seated ourselves around its oblong table. In his chair, Boris began a slow, barely-perceptible rocking motion.

"Boris, I'll assume Illarion provided you with details about Reliqueree?" I said. "About the uLivv and the skillset we need?"

"A few." He said nothing else.

"Um, OK. Do you mind if I ask why you're interested in working at Reliqueree?"

"I am not interested in working here. I would like to work at Apple."

Ignacio snorted. "Yes. Well," I said. "Why aren't you working there?"

"I have mailed several resumes. They have not responded."

"I wonder why."

"Do you have any contacts at Apple?" Boris said. "I am an excellent programmer. I love Apple. I cried when Steve Jobs died. It would be the happiest day of my life to meet Steve Wozniak. He is one of my heroes."

I looked at Ignacio. "Do you have any questions?"

Ignacio shrugged and scanned the sad little resume. After a second he looked up and said, "It says here you are expert in low-level firmware programming. 'Firmware' is spelled with an 'i' by the way. Can you tell me something about your last experience working with embedded systems?"

"My last project involved working with hard drives. My cousin Yuri and his friend from Kaspersky came to me and said, 'Boris, I want you to study these hard drives and their controllers and show us how to hack them.' So I showed them. They also asked me how to design protection against these hacks. I showed them this as well. A short while later, security forces from the government came to visit me and asked me a lot of questions about my work and Yuri and his friend. Afterwards, my Uncle Illarion thought it would be a good idea if I left Russia for a while."

"You were involved in counterprogramming against the Equation group?" Ignacio sounded impressed.

"I am not sure."

"What is the Equation group?" I said.

"It's supposed to be a super-secret team of U.S. and Israeli programmers who've hacked the planet," he said. "The Stuxnet virus, which wrecked thousands of Iranian nuclear centrifuges. Then the Equation hack. They figured out how to reprogram hard-drive firmware in a way that's almost impossible to detect. The only safe thing to do is literally destroy the drive once it's compromised. Supposedly, the problem had been fixed a few years ago, but it looks like it wasn't." Ignacio left the room for a second, then returned with one of the uLivv prototypes. He handed it to Boris.

"What do you think of this?"

Boris looked at the slim metal wafer carefully. "What is it?"

Ignacio handed Boris his tablet. "This is what's inside."

"I understand." The room was quiet while Boris scanned the screen. He handed the tablet back to Ignacio.

"It is intriguing. I know this hardware. I have programmed with these devices. Written drivers. What operating system will you use?"

"We've been given access to a modified version of Android. We're considering just using the stock OS."

Boris snorted. "Android is shit. I wish Apple would make iOS open source. I will not use this Android. It is full of C++. C++ is shit as well."

"Uh, C++ is one of the most popular languages for devices in the world," I said. "What do you use?"

"C. It is pure. And assembler when I need to embrace the metal."

"What OS?" Ignacio said.

"In English, you would say 'BOS.' Boris Operating System. I wrote it. It is C and assembler. No C++ shit. It is pure. I do not understand all these corrupt softwares that separate you from the metal. When you undress a woman and take her to bed, do you ask your best friend to have sex with her? No." Boris was rocking faster.

"I've never thought of it quite that way," I said. "Do you have a girlfriend? How does she feel about your philosophy?"

"I had a girlfriend in Moscow but she left me. For my best friend. It was lonely in Moscow. I do not sleep much. People do not understand me. That is another reason I want to work for Apple. I have heard the women in California like foreigners and stay up late."

"Oh, you don't have to worry about that here, Boris," I said. "New York welcomes foreigners. Melting pot and all. Plenty of night life. And you don't need a Porsche to get a date."

"I cannot drive. They would not give me a license in Moscow. I asked Uncle Illarion to bribe the authorities but he refused. I do not understand."

"BOS means no application support," Ignacio said.

"BOS runs all Android applications. It is a fork. I have replaced the Dalvik and ART shit with BVM. Boris Virtual Machine. It is fast and the code is pure. I have added true multi-tasking and many other things. And BOS is fast. I embrace the metal. I understand the processors. I understand this one."

"Can you show us?" Ignacio said. He reached over and handed Boris a USB-C cable.

"Yes." Boris reached into his battered laptop case and pulled out an even more battered Macbook Pro. He connected the laptop to the uLivv and booted his system. Instead of the standard Mac desktop, a bare Linux prompt appeared. Boris typed on his keyboard and began a series of file transfers.

"Once the files are on the device, they will compile," he said. "It is fast."

"Boris, I understand why you want to work for Apple," Ignacio said. "They're a great company. But we're going to be a great company, too. Nate, can you walk Boris through the presentation?"

For a moment, I hesitated. I would have thrown this basket-case out of the office already if he hadn't been Illarion's nephew. But Ignacio had seen something more. Steve Jobs had faced a similar conflict before the Apple II had been released. Steve Wozniak had wanted to release the system with eight expansion slots. Jobs had said two. The Woz had been right. I fetched my tablet, and placed it in front of Boris.

"Boris, let me explain Reliqueree's mission and goals."

Boris watched the slides carefully. When we reached the section that discussed Steve Jobs and our vision for his DNA, he stopped rocking.

"You can do this? You have the genome?"

"We do. And the actual DNA."

"How do you have this?"

"We're not in a position to tell anyone but Reliqueree employees," I said. I glanced over at his laptop. The file transfers were complete and I could see the compilation process was finishing up. After a few seconds, Ignacio reached over and picked up the uLivv. He tapped the screen, stared at it, then jerked his head towards the conference room door.

"Excuse us for a second." I stood up and left the room, Ignacio on my heels. He closed the door behind him.

"So, what do you recommend we do with Asperger Lad in there?" I said.

"Hire him." He raised the uLivv and I saw a screen full of sharply rendered app icons. In the upper right quadrant of the device's screen, I saw an open browser window. Ignacio was connected to the web.

I let Ignacio handle the salary and benefits negotiations. After all, Boris would be reporting to him. I did suggest we tell Boris we were making him employee zero. It was the number Steve Jobs assigned to himself after discovering he just couldn't live with the number "2" (Wozniak had been "1"). We thought it would make Boris happier about the fact that he would not be working at Apple.

CHAPTER 21

GATHERING MOMENTUM

To my satisfaction, Ignacio, Boris and I quickly fell into a productive routine. Ignacio focused on converting theTogetherHood to TransLivvient, developing uLivv app specifications, managing the Columbians, and tending to Boris.

Fortunately, Boris needed little day-to-day supervision. We provided him with his own office and a first-class development rig and he settled in quickly. The issue of his inability to show up anywhere on time became moot when he stopped going home to Brighton on most days and began to slowly convert his office into a domicile we named "Borisland." He dined primarily on pizza, Big Macs, and Russian take-out food from places such as Matryoshka and Uncle Vanya Café and slept on an air mattress in his office. Ignacio did force an agreement out of him to bathe weekly. I'm not sure where this act took place and decided I didn't want to know.

My duties consisted of managing production of the uLivv, coordinating the development of the uLivv's packaging, putting together our launch and marketing plan, and tending to Angie.

Unlike Boris, Angie required far more attention. I spent a fair amount of time at night Skyping with her. I also promised several times to fly out regularly to be with her, though I knew this was unlikely. Time is a startup's most precious commodity. You can't waste it on non-essential tasks.

Successful entrepreneurs bring a laser-focus to achieving their goals and executing their plans for growth.

Currently, Angie's goal was to grow a human being. Since she was a woman, the processes and project management tools required to achieve this outcome were highly automated and inherently scalable. Women are incredibly fortunate in this respect.

Entrepreneurs are not so lucky. We have to build the infrastructure and task framework for success while simultaneously adjusting to circumstances and unforeseen obstacles that can change how success is measured. Steve Jobs had faced this situation. At Pixar, he'd thought the company's goal was to sell specialized graphics computers for $10 thousand. Then expensive software. But the real opportunity had been to make movies about talking toys, talking fish, talking cars, talking rats, etc.

Angie didn't have to deal with any of this. She already knew what her project's success parameters were.

For the time being, we decided to bunk at my Mom's house. The commute was reasonable and the price was right. Also, my mother's affection for Ignacio continued unabated. When I asked her why she liked him so, she hesitated a moment, then told me he reminded her of a pet hamster she'd owned as a child.

The day Ignacio moved in, after he'd unpacked he immediately insisted I take him to the Mother Cabrini Shrine. As we entered the building, he made the sign of the cross and said something to himself under his breath.

"You're Catholic?"

"My full name is Ignacio Loyola. He founded the Jesuits. You have to ask?"

"You never talk about it."

He shrugged. "Silicon Valley isn't the most spiritual place on the planet. You tend to worship other things there. I have to admit I've always been somewhat conflicted about religion. My father is Jewish and when I was boy, I used to go to temple with him from time to time. I guess you could call me a 'Jatholic.'"

At that moment, Sister Mary Gael walked by us. As she passed, I said "Sister?" She turned "Yes? Oh, I remember you. 'Nate?'"

"Yes, Nate Pennington. This is my friend Ignacio. When I described the Shrine and Mother Cabrini, he insisted on coming to visit. He's a Catholic."

"A lot of people are, especially ones named Ignacio. It's good to meet you again, Nate, and you, Ignacio. I'd talk more, but it's a busy day today. Please enjoy yourself and come back again." She smiled and hurried off.

"So, what do you think of her?" I said as we gazed down on the Mother, peaceful in her glass case.

"I'm going to ask her to bless our venture," he replied.

"Think she'll listen?"

"I don't know. When I was a kid, I read that Voltaire was asked on his death bed to denounce Satan and he answered it was a bad time to make a new enemy. I try to operate on the principal of looking for help wherever you can find it."

"That's a good philosophy. If she comes through, I'll be sending the Order a big check," I said.

"You're going to bribe a saint?"

"I'm not a Catholic. I regard it as a pay-for-performance arrangement." We left a few minutes later.

One important technical issue remained to be solved. Michael in the end refused to come to work for Reliqueree immediately, but did agree to a one-year consulting contract, which included a reasonable number of stock options. His job was to manage the task of transferring Steve Jobs' liver from its Tupperware box into the uLivv.

Said liver now resided, similar to Mother Cabrini, in three separate locations in the country — Mom's freezer, a small freezer located in a secure closet at Reliqueree's office, and a similar unit in Michael Song's Pacific Heights apartment in San Francisco. The single-point-of-defrosting problem had been dealt with. Finding someone with a high-speed band saw willing to tripart the frozen organ had been tricky, but when I'd mentioned the problem to Illarion, he'd referred me to a Russian butcher on the Lower East Side who'd done the job, no questions asked. It's the type of timely help an involved investor can contribute to a startup.

Michael and I had discussed several technical approaches to the problem, and he finally decided to mix business with a family visit and flew out to Shenzen with his third of Jobs' liver to work through the issues with Uncle Tony and his engineers. Several days into the trip, he called me.

"We've come up with the answer."

"What is it?

"We're going to use ethanol precipitation to purify and concentrate the DNA, then use fixed-angle, high-speed micro-centrifuges to remove the supernatant. From there we air-dry the solution for about 15 minutes and resuspend the resulting DNA pellets in 100 microliters of ultra-pure water. Next we'll dilute the solution and add it to a new latex base that will enable us to apply the DNA to a plastic surface with an estimated 18 pico-grams of genomic material per application."

"Can you translate into English?"

"I'm going to dissolve Steve Jobs' liver in alcohol, mix the DNA into a special paint, and silkscreen three millionths of a gram of it onto the surface of a micro SD chip."

"Won't you destroy the DNA?"

"No. DNA is one tough molecule. It can reside outside the body for years. They've been able to recover complete genomes from Neanderthal bones. In fact, the DNA will be stabilized by the paint and last indefinitely as long as the chip isn't damaged or abused."

"How many chips will we be able to create?"

"I can't give you an exact number. Probably between 250 and 300 million. We may be able to stretch it further as we refine the process. I'm not counting the cancer DNA. Our refining process will separate the genomes.

"The good news is we've tested the process manually and it works. The bad news is we're going to need to spend about $50 thousand to create a specialized printing unit to automate it. Do I tell Uncle Tony to go ahead?"

"Do we really have a choice?"

"We could hire a bunch of low-paid workers to sit in the factory with tiny X-acto knives and use crazy glue to mount little chunks of the liver onto the uLivv."

"I don't think that's the type of purchasing experience our customers are looking for. Go build your special spray can."

The next task on our critical path was packaging. Steve Jobs was a fanatic about product presentation, materials, and the out-of-box purchasing experience. Within Apple, there exists a secret packaging room only an ordained few executives can access via special security ID's. Inside, hundreds of prototype boxes are inspected, thousands of them opened, and countless touch-o-rama tests conducted to ensure the process of opening and extracting an Apple product from its packaging is a visual and visceral treat. As I thought about the uLivv, I channeled Steve Jobs urging me to rise to the challenge of providing a similar experience when a buyer unveiled his liver.

I made him a silent promise we'd do our best. Of course, Jobs had enjoyed the services of Sir Jonathan Ive, the world-renowned design master whom Steve had considered "his spiritual partner" at Apple. I was going to have to rely on hired guns.

Ignacio and I contacted three different packaging firms we'd worked with in the past. The first two had excellent portfolios and impressive clients. Ignacio submitted the third as a candidate. Their portfolio was thinner, though several of their designs were striking, even edging towards the bizarre.

Each company was invited to our offices on the same date at different times to be briefed on the uLivv and given the opportunity to bid on our corporate identity (logos, fonts, colors, etc.) and packaging design. I had Illarion's legal group create the scariest NDA possible to try to keep information about the uLivv from slipping into the market prematurely.

On the scheduled day I took the representatives of each firm through our complete presentation, then described our marketing vision and goals.

"As you can see, the uLivv represents the leading edge of new ways of thinking about our relationship with the departed and post-life processes and activities," I said. "Our packaging must provide a moving emotional experience reinforcing this. Apple's packaging standards will serve as our competitive benchmark.

"When a customer opens up their uLivv box for the first time, it must communicate and leverage the unique selling proposition of this first, special edition. Purchasers will be able to enjoy both a physical and post-life connection with Steve Jobs. The packaging must express a sense of transcendence, personal involvement, and reclamation of one of technology's greatest personalities.

"I realize this is a tough proposition, one we're challenging you to rise to within a few weeks. Yes, I know, it's not much time. Unlike Apple, we don't have the luxury of creating hundreds of prototypes and hiring someone to spend a year just opening boxes.

"But I believe that if Steve Jobs was entitled to his reality-distortion field, we're entitled to ours. I'm looking for you match our dream to your creativity and hit the mark the first time. To visually and physically reflect how the uLivv enables people to engage with the departed, not just miss them.

"If you've never done so before, I want you to read about Jobs in 1996 after he'd retaken control of Apple. Back then, people thought Apple computers needed more power, larger hard drives, more memory. But Steve knew better. What Apple actually needed was a stunningly-designed, easy-to-use computer wrapped in a Bondi Blue translucent case. The iMac. The computer that saved Apple.

"Our packaging and corporate identity needs the same sort of fresh thinking and innovation. We want you to match the brilliant product and design insights of Steve Jobs. To help reposition the market's mind and attitudes about reconnecting and interacting with their loved ones and friends. We need you to make death Bondi Blue."

The meeting with the first firm was not especially productive. They were a California company with a good reputation for smartphone packaging designs and their portfolio was excellent, but from their questions and attitude it was clear they didn't share our vision.

For example, after the presentation, the head of the company, a woman named Betsy...Something, asked me "Are you saying the uLivv has Steve Jobs' actual DNA inside it?"

"Yes."

"Can I ask where the DNA comes from?"

"You can ask, but if I released the information, I'd have to kill you." I smiled at her when I said this, but she didn't smile back.

"Is that legal?"

"It is. And since Steve Jobs is dead, there's absolutely no issue."

"So, the DNA doesn't actually **do** anything."

"No. You can think of it as in semi-permanent retirement. Though our patent-pending preservation formula in which the DNA resides will preserve it indefinitely. To those who cared for and loved Steve Jobs, it's a comforting thought. However, Steve Jobs' complete genome **is** preserved in the uLivv on a special chip. This chip is swappable with other chips containing other people's DNA and genome. TransLivvient will enable you to 'inter' an infinite number of genomes on the Reliqueree storage system while also enjoying a close, personal relationship with an actual physical memento from those in the post-life."

"To me, it sounds a little macabre."

"I suggest you take the subway uptown and visit the Saint Cabrini shrine. I can direct you to a nun who works there and wears a piece of the Mother's clothing on a pendant close to her heart. She says it brings her joy. Hundreds of millions of people from different cultures and religions wear relics and feel as she does."

She looked skeptical and I mentally crossed her firm off the candidate list.

The second firm, based in New York, showed more enthusiasm, though I felt they didn't fully grasp our marketing concepts and packaging philosophy. When I emphasized the need for "out-of-the-box" thinking, the fellow heading up the design team broke in to say given the context of the product and Steve Jobs, this felt to him more like an "in-the-box experience." I could understand his perspective, but the comment didn't reflect the visionary mindset I was seeking.

The third firm, Ignacio's candidate, was New Hampshire-based. New Hampshire is a cold, dark, awful place whose inhabitants still fetishize an ancient stone idol that slid off the side of a mountain many years ago. During the winter, I believe the only flickering bastions of civilization found in the region are clustered around the ski resorts. I don't ski.

Despite my skepticism, Ignacio had worked with the group when he was at Sony and thought they were first rate, particularly the company founder and design head, Gruezén.

"Is that his first or last name?" I said when Ignacio had first mentioned him.

"I don't know," he said. "Everyone just calls him 'Gruezén.' Emphasis on the 'zen' and accent on the 'e.' He sometimes refers to himself in the third person. I asked him once why he didn't use his first and last name and he said, 'Why do I need **both**?' He **is** unconventional, though. He refused to hand out business cards to anyone at Sony. He called them 'archaic detritus.' They didn't stay a client for long."

"I can imagine. The Japanese do love their business cards. What's the name of his firm?"

"Gruezén's."

"Figures."

Gruezén and his team had appeared to listen carefully to my requirements for the uLivv's "out-of-the-box" experience, but offered few ideas during the session. During the presentation, he and a female assistant retreated to a corner of the room where she began to take notes and sketch on a notepad while Gruezén talked in a low, quick, staccato tone.

I didn't quite know what to make of Gruezén. He had a faint, vaguely European accent I couldn't quite locate. He was slim and slightly built, with bright green eyes, a bald head, and a hawk nose sticking out over a black Van Dyke. He was dressed in black jeans, a white collarless shirt that might have been silk, and a black sports jacket.

When he and his group left, I wasn't sold on New Hampshire and its mononame impresario, but the New York firm seemed solid, if somewhat conventional. By day's end, I hoped we had one, possibly two, companies capable of fulfilling our packaging vision and meeting our tight production schedule.

CHAPTER 22

ANGIE GOES EAST

The rest of the week passed at breakneck speed. Ignacio and I continued to develop new ideas and concepts for the uLivv. In the meantime, Ignacio and Boris forged ahead on development, Ignacio pulling all-nighters crafting TransLivvient, Boris working seemingly without sleep for days at a time porting BOS onto the uLivv, testing the hardware and device drivers, and optimizing its performance.

But despite our progress, the company's to-do list remained full. We needed a webmaster with ecommerce experience ASAP. Soon we'd need a PR specialist. I was behind the curve on building our social marketing platform. I was scheduled to fly back to China again to inspect the new DNA printing system as well as uLivv production prototypes and schedules. In the back of my mind, I began to worry I'd committed the company to an impossible roadmap.

When you wake up in the middle of the night covered in cold sweat, your mind racing, and you dread looking at the calendar, you know you're working at a startup.

By the weekend I was wound tighter than Tim Cook using a Samsung phone at gunpoint. Fortunately, Ignacio could read my body language and mood. On Saturday, he walked over to me at 4 pm and said "We're out of here. Let's head home."

At that moment, a thunderous imprecation in Russian burst from Borisland, followed by the usual proclamation of "This is shit!"

"Are you sure this is a good time to leave him alone?" I said

"It's fine. It's when he becomes quiet you have to worry. Let's go."

We arrived home with enough daylight left to enjoy a walk along Palisade Park with its Hudson River views. By the time we headed back to Mom's, I'd relaxed and was looking forward to a quiet, stress-free evening.

Back in the apartment, Mom treated Ignacio (and me), to a simple steak dinner paired with a decent merlot. As we were cleaning up, my phone vibrated. I looked at the screen. Message from Angie.

Nate u ther?

Yes. Was going to call u tnite. How r u feeling?

A little sick. Will be at ur place in 20

?

Am in cab on way to ur house. Be ther in a few minutes

Ur in NYC??

Yes. see u in a few. Luv u

Wait! wher u staying? u flew in? why didnt u call?

Wanted to surprise u. see u in a few min. Stay with u. Mom has room

OK.

All men know the only predictable thing about women is their unpredictability. Since the monumental task of bringing Reliqueree to life had made it impossible for me to go to China, China had decided to come to Riverdale.

As I thought about it, I appreciated my blossoming fiancée's consideration for my time and energy. This way, I didn't have to suffer jet lag and waste valuable hours traveling cross-country. I decided to repay Angie by carving out the maximum time possible for us to be together during her stay, though of course not at the expense of neglecting vital tasks.

Entrepreneurs are always making personal sacrifices on behalf of their company and their team.

I looked up from the phone. "Mom, Ignacio? Good news! Angie is in town and on her way here. She's just minutes away."

"That's wonderful," Ignacio said. "This is just what you need."

Mother looked at me. "Annie is coming here? Why? I didn't invite her."

"Angie, Mother. I'm sure you can remember the name of the woman who's giving you your first grandchild. And she's welcome to stay here anytime. She can sleep in the other bedroom. She's my fiancée and please, no comments about her ethnic background and laundry. She's pregnant and doesn't need the extra stress and worry. Bad for the baby. Bad for my business."

Mom sniffed, but was quiet and went into the living room. Good. I thought I'd handled that well. I was beginning to relax, when I realized there was another problem looming, one requiring immediate handling.

Entrepreneurs must be flexible and prepared to deal with unexpected challenges and obstacles.

I considered several solutions and picked the one I thought would be most effective.

I stood up, walked over to the refrigerator, extracted a quart of milk, and took it into the bathroom and put it in the cabinet under the sink. Next, I went into Mom's bedroom and looked around for her pocketbook. It was where she almost always left it, on the nightstand next to her bed. I picked it up, returned to the kitchen, and tucked it in the refrigerator behind a half gallon of Minute Maid. Then I strolled over to the living room window and looked down onto the street. From this angle, I could see Angie's cab as it drove up to Mom's building.

Ten minutes later I spotted the car and hurried down to greet my fiancée and help her with her bags. As she stepped out of the cab, I noted her baby bump had grown noticeably since I'd last seen her. I smiled and gave her a big hug.

"It's great to see you, tim sam. How was your flight? But I wish you'd called. I would have come to the airport and made dinner reservations."

"I wanted to surprise you. The flight was fine. Don't worry about dinner. I'm still feeling a bit ill. The doctor said the morning sickness should start to fade by this time, but it hasn't."

The driver had popped the cab's trunk and I went over to help unload. She'd brought three rather large bags, far more luggage than was required for a stay of a few days. Hmm.

When we walked into the apartment, Ignacio rushed up and treated Angie to another hug. My mother dragged herself into the foyer, grimaced at Angie with what I imagined she thought was a smile, allowed her to bestow a quick peck on her cheek, and retreated back into the living room. For the next several minutes I helped Angie settle into the third bedroom and unpack. She was feeling better by then, so I pre-pared a small microwave dinner for her. She ate half of it. Finally, it was back to the living room to discuss her trip and plans. I sat with her on the settee, across from Mom.

Ignacio asked first. "Angie, how long are you planning to visit?"

"I'm not visiting. I'm moving to New York. Nate and I will be living in Manhattan."

"We **are**?" I said. "When did this happen?"

"Today. I've taken a leave from the bank. It's hard to work when you feel like throwing up all the time. When I feel better, I'll apply for a transfer to New York."

"And where are we going to be living, tim sam?"

"In the apartment you're going to find for us. In the meantime, my uncle has a friend who owns a building on Mott Street. Isn't that in the heart of New York Chinatown?"

"Yes, it is," I said.

"How nice. He keeps an apartment vacant for friends and family to visit. We can stay there until we find our own place. Uncle Song is looking forward to visiting us and his grandnephew. Do you know you he's never been to the U.S? I'm sure he'll find Chinatown fascinating. So historical."

"What about Gough Street?"

"I'm having our things put into storage. Clothing and a few household items are on the way. We'll move in over the next few days. Don't fret. I'll take care of all the arrangements. You stay focused on providing a secure and happy future for me and our son. Oh, by the way." She reached into her purse, pulled out another grey blob picture, and handed it to me.

"I had another sonogram the other day. You weren't there. It's a boy." Angie glanced at my mother, a hint of triumph on her face. "I was thinking of names for the baby. Maybe Fang Yong Pennington? It means 'Strong Fragrance.'" Mom's face began to congest.

I put my arm around Angie and held her close. Just in case Mom pounced. "Tim sam, I suspect that's too ethnic. After all, the boy's going to be growing up in the U.S. Answering to 'Fang' might be an issue with his peers. I have an idea. How about 'Franklin?' After my father? Wouldn't that be nice?"

I looked over at Mom. I'd thought the suggestion would be soothing, but the rictus now overlaying her blotchy complexion made me think "no." "Or 'Brett' or 'Jameson' or 'Noah?' Those are all popular."

"We have plenty of time to talk about it. It's one of the nice things about being pregnant," Angie said. She snuggled closer. "I'm sure he'll be as irresistible as his father whatever we name him. Or his grandfather."

I cast a minatory glare at my mother as she stiffened. She stayed put on the couch. The conversation moved on to less dangerous areas such as the baby's developmental state (larger), Uncle Tony's reaction to the baby (anticipatory) and Angie's emotional state (nesting).

I had started to relax when I saw Mom staring at Angie's left hand. Her eyes narrowed, and I could see them subjecting Granma's engagement ring to an intense, stony gaze. She began to fidget, looked away, then looked back again. Once or twice she almost rose, only to sink back down. Finally she stood up and walked into her bedroom. I heard the sounds of drawers being opened and closed with a bang. Ignacio and Angie, deep in conversation, paid no attention to the fuss.

After a couple of minutes the banging stopped and Mom stalked back into the living room and over to Angie. Here it came.

"Angie, dearie, where did you get that ring?"

Angie looked up at Mom in surprise. "From Nate," she said. "You know that."

"I don't know anything of the sort, young lady."

I stood up. "Mom, what's the problem?"

She pointed at Granma's ring. "She stole my mother's ring. Have her take it off."

"Mom, what are you talking about? No one stole anything."

"She stole your grandmother's ring. Make her take it off right now."

"Mother, we discussed Granma's ring when I told you about the baby and that I intended to ask Angie to marry me. We agreed at the time I was going to give to her. I'm sure you remember. Please, sit down."

"I remember nothing of the sort. Have her take it off."

"Mother..."

"Have her take it off!"

"That's enough," I said. I took Mom by the arm and steered her to the refrigerator. Opening it, I peered inside, took out her purse, and handed it to her. "Here," I said. "Do you remember doing this? I'm constantly finding your purse in here." I looked inside again. "Oh, yes." I walked into the bathroom and came out holding the quart of milk. I held it up where everyone could see it. "I guess you don't remember doing this, either. I'm always finding milk in the bathroom. Do you remember leaving it in there?"

My mother looked at her cold purse and the quart of lukewarm milk. Her lower lip trembled.

"No, I didn't," she said in a faint voice. "You saw me do this?"

"All the time, Mom." I gave her a warm smile. "I'm sure it's not anything serious. Probably just the result of you living here alone. But now that I'm back and you have a grandchild to look forward to, I'm sure you'll do better. But we discussed the ring and Angie, Mom. Are you sure you don't remember?" I waggled the quart of milk.

"I…think…so," she said in a faint voice. Then, in a stronger tone — "Yes, I do remember. I'm sorry, Nate. Forgive me. I just sometimes find my mind wandering these days and…" Her voice trailed off.

"It's OK, Mom. Everyone understands." I looked over at Ignacio and Angie and mouthed "I'm sorry at them." They both nodded sympathetically. "I'll schedule a visit with the doctor and I'm sure he'll be able to help."

"Thank you, Nate."

"No problem, Mom. I'm your son. It's my duty to take care of you." I steered her back to the couch and she sat down and was quiet while the conversation resumed in a desultory fashion. After half an hour or so, Mom announced she was tired and was going to bed and Angie said the same. After I'd tucked Angie in and said good night to Mom, I met Ignacio in the kitchen and we each poured ourselves a night cap glass of wine.

"Jesus, Nate. I'm so sorry. I've noticed she's forgetful, but I didn't realize it was that bad."

"I wouldn't expect you to. She's my mother, not yours. I'm far more attuned to her habits and behavior."

"I'm just sorry, that's all. So, what are you going to do with Angie?"

"Move with her to Chinatown. Whatever Angie wants, Angie gets. You don't argue with Tony Song's pregnant niece. We can't afford a supply-chain breakdown. You can stay here with Mom. I'll feel better if there's someone around to keep an eye on her. And you won't have to worry about paying rent. It works out for everyone."

"I understand. I'll do my best."

"Yes. There's another thing I may need you to do. If Mom starts going on about Angie's ring again, stick her purse in the fridge."

There was a long, long pause. Then Ignacio said, "Nate, you didn't gaslight your own Mom, did you?"

"Ignacio, I'm her son. Of course I didn't. But people don't lose their memory in smooth increments. It happens in fits and starts. If she continues to attack Angie about the ring, we risk a supply-chain breakdown."

I looked straight at Ignacio. "And we can't afford a supply-chain breakdown. I'm sure you understand."

He looked straight back at me. "I understand completely."

I sometimes think of Ignacio as the brother I never had.

"And don't feel bad," I said. "If Mom was in her right mind, she'd want you to do it."

CHAPTER 23

ANGIE AND BORIS

I moved out of Mom's apartment and into Mott Street a few days later. Mission accomplished, Angie decided a change of scenery might help with her morning sickness and rode with me uptown to Reliqueree to inspect our offices and satisfy her curiosity. While I was giving her the grand tour, I told her I hadn't had much time to look at the books and needed to find a CFO or at least a good bookkeeper and could she guide me? I also mentioned we needed a webmaster and a PR person.

When the tour was over, Angie borrowed a laptop and logged into our accounting system. After a few hours, she announced she'd tidied up our financials and insured we'd stay right with the tax-man. Then she went online and began to scan the job and freelancer boards. Angie had learned her way around ecommerce, PR, and marketing during the GateIconic days and quickly began collecting likely resumes.

By the end of the day, Reliqueree's payroll included its business and financial operations manager.

Angie's joining the team did create a minor personnel issue. On her second day, she walked out of Boris' office with a disgusted look on her face.

"It stinks in there," she said. "You should fire him."

"Angie, we need him. Badly. And he's only the latest in a long line of programmers to whom personal grooming is a secondary concern."

"He's dirty."

"He's hygienically challenged, yes. But he's literally inhuman when it comes to cranking out code. After the launch, we'll spend more time tidying him up."

"I don't want to catch anything from him. It would be bad for the baby."

"He's had all his shots," I said. "And he spends most of the time in his office."

"He talks to himself."

"He's daydreaming in code."

Angie remained suspicious of Boris as a potential disease vector for our growing male, and sometimes obviously mouth-breathed in his presence (well, I did too, but tried not to show it. I believe Ignacio had become completely desensitized to eau de Boris), but she was smart enough to let it go, at least for the time being.

By contrast, Boris found Angie's presence intriguing, as I found out a few days later. I was in the Reliqueree lunchroom pulling another cup of burnt coffee from the new Scanomat TopBrewer (iOS and Android compatible) when Boris walked in looking to refill his cup as well.

"The little China woman. She is your wife?" he said.

"Angie's my fiancée. Don't call her 'China woman.' That's considered racist."

"She is not from China?"

"She's Chinese, yes."

"I heard a song the other day. 'American Woman.' This is racist?"

"No. Feminists probably don't like the song, though."

"I heard the famous homosexual David Bowie singing 'Little China Girl' the other day on a video site. He was racist?"

"David Bowie was not homosexual. Ignore the makeup. He was married to a black woman, so he wasn't racist. I'm not sure where 'Little China Girl' stands currently on the politically-correct socionometer. If you end up dating an Asian woman, I don't think it's going to be 'your' song."

"This is complex," he said.

"It can be," I said. "Don't worry. You'll get the hang of it."

Boris was silent for a second, then "Angie is...what is the word... with a child? Presenting?"

"I think you mean 'pregnant.' Yes, she is. We're having a son."

"Ah. That is nice." He was quiet for a moment. "I would like to have a son."

"You need to work on the girlfriend part first. How are you coming along?"

"I have been busy here."

"There are plenty of girls in Brighton Beach. It's New York's Little Russia. I bet your Uncle Illarion can set you up with someone nice."

"I do not like Russian girls. I am in America. I would like to meet American women. It is difficult. I go to bars to do pick-ups, but no one wants to pick up. The women avoid me. I do not know why."

"Well, Boris, have you thought of bathing twice a week? Even daily? Cologne? A fashion update? Those Russian jeans don't represent current styles."

"I need a girlfriend to help me shop." Boris looked gloomy.

"We're caught in a loop," I said. "Let's try this." I pulled out my phone. "Here. Have you heard of these apps? This one's called 'Tinder.' It works with Facebook and can help you find people near you with the same interests. It's well reviewed. There's always Match.com. Look, this is a new one called 'Happn.' You buy little tokens called 'charms' and if you see someone you like and they're on the system, you send a charm to tell them you think they're attractive. It's popular in Europe already."

"I will try these," he said. He looked a little happier as he took his coffee back into his office. A few minutes later, a heartfelt "This is shit!" echoed from Borisland. Boris was back on track.

Despite Angie's qualms about Boris, my decision to have her join the Reliqueree team brought a great many benefits. While the work went ahead at a killing pace, the "tasks to be done" and "tasks completed" began to come into balance. I was able to sleep a little easier. I only wished Angie had been more proactive in communicating the value she could bring to Reliqueree.

CHAPTER 24

THE ULIVV LIVES

We'd almost reached summer's end and our most critical milestone loomed directly ahead. It was time for Boris and Ignacio to show everyone the first iteration of a working uLivv, complete with OS and app suite. On presentation day, everyone, including Illarion, was in the conference room for the unveiling.

Ignacio connected a uLivv to the projection system and booted it. After a second, a splash screen appeared, an image of a DNA molecule with waves of color coruscating down its twisted length.

"Let me quickly run through the basics," Ignacio said. "First, the uLivv is running the latest version of BOS, or Boris Operating System. As far as the Android side of the device, it looks stock. Settings, desktop, app launchers are all standard. The uLivv environment runs as a virtual desktop within BOS. But performance screams and apps truly multitask in the background. Boris is an optimization genius."

Boris stopped his slight rocking motion for a second. "I embrace the metal," he said.

Within the uLivv desktop, there are five sections, **'Learn,' 'Transcendence,' 'Play,' 'Activities'** and **'P,'** each with its own app suite," Ignacio said. "We're touring sections one through four today."

"I thought we were going to see everything," I said.

"Let me walk you through the first four and we'll discuss five at the end." Ignacio tapped his uLivv's screen. A list of applications and activities appeared.

"This is the **Learn** list. 'One' means available upon the October launch, 'Two' during the holidays, and 'Three' for a projected future release. We're constantly coming up with new ideas and we'll use community feedback and surveys to help guide development."

Codex Steve (One). A day-by-day compilation of the life of Steve Jobs. Pick any day on the calendar from February 24th, 1955, to October 5, 2011, to listen about significant events in the life of Steve Jobs.

"Very interesting," I said. "Can I try that out?"

"Sure. Pick a date."

"Uh, March 25th, 1976."

Ignacio entered the date. A voice promptly recited "On March 25th, 1976, Steve Jobs was 21 years, one month and one day old. On this day, Steve Jobs picked 'Apple' to be the company's corporate name. Officially, at incorporation, the company was named Apple Computer, Inc. On January 29th, 2007, the name was changed to Apple, Inc. to reflect the company's shift to a focus on consumer electronics."

"Pretty cool. Let me try again. How about March 9th, 2007."

Ignacio tapped again. The voice recited "On March 9th, 2007, Steve Jobs was 52 years, 0 months and 13 days old. On this day, a Google personnel recruiter contacted an Apple employee about their interest in working at Google. The recruiter was unaware of a secret pact between Steve Jobs and Eric Schmidt, then CEO of Google, to not hire each other's employees. Steve Jobs sent a note to Eric Schmidt requesting Google honor the agreement. Schmidt agreed, and had the recruiter fired within an hour. Upon receiving the news, Steve Jobs sent a note to the Apple head of HR with a smiley face in it. Tap the link to read more about this incident in Steveopedia and view the actual note."

"Huh," I said. "That's a little off-putting. Are you sure it's true?"

"We hired college interns to do this and the kid leading the project is a stickler for accuracy. I know about this incident myself. It's all on Google."

"Well, even Marilyn Monroe had moles." (I made a mental note to take a close look at the Codex and see if some helpful and judicious editing wasn't in order.) I continued down the list.

Quote Steve (One). The most comprehensive library of Steve Jobs quotes. All quotes are verified to be actually stated or written by Steve Jobs.

Read about Steve (Two). A collection of books and articles about Steve Jobs and his friends (and enemies). Many are free and all are reasonably priced. Our library includes everything from Walter Isaacson's "Steve Jobs" to "iCon Steve Jobs" by Jeffrey Young, the book Apple banned! Hours of fascinating reading.

Steveopedia (One). The most comprehensive repository of information about Steve Jobs on the planet. Contribute your findings to Steveopedia and help build the **complete** story.

The Steve Jobs Diet Cookbook (One). The ultimate cookbook for people who don't like to cook. Contains Steve Jobs most famous and popular fruitarian, organic, and vegan meal plans and recipes. Try the apples-only-for-a-week purge and lose weight and save energy — you don't have to cook them apples! (Nutritional supplements highly recommended for some recipes.)

The Steve Jobs Media Collection (One). A compilation of pictures, videos, cartoons and drawings of Steve Jobs arranged chronologically and by topic. Hours of fascinating entertainment and history.

"How are we doing with copyright and asset management?" I said.

"Angie's managing the process. We're making sure everything going into the system is clean and legal. Now for section two, **Transcendence**. The list updated.

Light Show Steve (One). Display dazzling multi-colored light shows and patterns by randomly traversing Steve Jobs' genome with base pairs representing different colors, spectrums and shades. Let Steve Jobs put you in the **right** mood for any occasion.

Music of the Spheres Steve (One). Play harmonic melodies and tones by randomly traversing Steve Jobs' genome with base pairs representing notes. You can record a particularly interesting segment for playback later on. Allow Steve Jobs to **soothe and relax** you for maximum productivity.

"OK, enough of that. Let's take a look at section three, **Play**. The first couple of titles are simple but fast moving arcade-style games based on Jobs' early days. I think it's a fun time trip back to the 70's. And they tie in with the current retro-gaming craze." He tapped and scrolled.

You're Outta Here, Steve Jobs! (One). A future arcade classic. It's 1984, you're Steve Jobs, and you've just introduced the original Macintosh but it's a sales **flop**! No one will buy it because it has too little memory, only one floppy disk, and no applications. Now, John Sculley wants to throw you out of your **own** company. To survive, you need to run around One Infinite Loop gobbling up memory upgrades and second floppy drives so you can sell Macs while avoiding the Soda, Money, VC and BoD (Board of Directors) Ghosts. Power-up by eating colorful application boxes and turn the tables on your pursuers. Pac-Man was never like this!

Hey, It's Your Kid, Steve Jobs! (?) A fun "pursuit-style" game featuring Chrisann Brennan, mother of his first child, Lisa. Pulse pounding, sweat-in-your-palms fun as you pursue Steve through a challenging, trap-filled maze to collect child support. Make sure you keep your DNA testing kit fully powered or Steve will escape!

"I don't know. That one seems a little mean-spirited to me," I said.

"It's the truth," Ignacio said. "In Isaacson's book and all over Google. But I kind of thought so myself — that's why the question mark. The same kid who did **You're Outta Here** did this one as well. His name's Vinay and he's a fabulous coder. I want to bring him on board. The work he did to get these little gems on the uLivv to scroll and play properly was amazing. They're addictive. This one's a blast. Steve's almost impossible to catch. I hate to waste the game."

"I can understand." I thought about it for a second. "Here's an idea. Jobs and Wozniak went into business in the 70's cracking the old phone system with blue boxes. What say we rework the game as **Blue Box Steve?** Help Steve Jobs hack the phone system and sell blue boxes while avoiding evil AT&T enforcers. Every time he sells a unit, the box plays arcade music, you make a free phone call to Steve Wozniak, and he rewards Jobs with a colorful Fruitarian power-up. More 70's fun!"

"What a **great** idea. We can easily repurpose the code for that scenario. I can think we can have the title ready for the holidays."

Interview with Steve Jobs (One). Enjoy this brain twisting, mind-blowing game of knowledge and problem solving. Visit Steve in his office for a job interview and find out if you have what it takes to join Apple's 'A' Team. Will Steve Jobs find you an "insanely excellent" hire or write you off as Team Bozo? Or even worse, subject you to a "Smelly Feet" dismissal? Endless hours of fun and entertainment. Play in teams or as Steve Jobs himself!

"I'm working Vinay and the Columbians like hell to get this one ready for October. I've played the prototype. It's a hoot."

"How have you done so far?" I said.

"Three Team Bozos and two Smelly Feet."

"Jobs always **was** a tough interviewer."

Corporate Comeback Adventure with Steve Jobs (Two). Play this exciting adventure game combining arcade action and text messaging problem solving as you accompany Steve on a quest to help him save Apple and create great new devices. Help Steve overcome the opposition of Team-C players including Michael Spindler, Jean Louis Gassée, and Ellen Hancock as he fights to return Apple to its rightful place at the top of technology. Watch out for exploding PowerBooks, hungry Be Beasts, blinding GAWS (Gil Amelio White-paper Storms) and other traps! Survive those and move on to solving corporate puzzlers including falling stock prices, cash flow shortages, clueless boards of directors and more. Play in "Solo Mode" or online as a "Takeover Team!"

Ignacio swiped and brought up section four. "**Activities** is something of a catchall right now. We're reserving it mainly for TransLivvient services."

Greet 'n' Steve (One). Record greeting messages for your phone, laptop, computer and other devices and have them sound just like Steve Jobs!

Me 'n' Steve Selfie (Two). Never met Steve Jobs but wish you did and had taken a selfie? Now you can! Our unique, patent-pending BuddiePic **(tm)** technology takes your image and automatically combines it with any of over a dozen copyright-free images of Steve Jobs to create a virtual selfie. Put it on your smartphone or tablet and impress all your friends and acquaintances.

"Got it. Are we done with one through four?" I said.

"Yeah," Ignacio said. "Section five was originally designed to be an online concierge service a la Siri or Cortana, but Boris showed me something the other day that made me rethink our approach. Give us an extra few days to polish it. You'll be impressed."

I looked over at Boris. "Is that true Boris? You're going to razzle dazzle us? I'm pretty impressed with what I've seen so far."

Boris mumbled something I couldn't make out. "Boris, I can't hear you."

"This is all shit. In a few days, I will show you Steve Jobs."

I looked over at Ignacio, who shrugged. "Boris has been working hard. He and I are going to go out for a drink tonight and see if we can't find a lady for our Russian bear here."

"Good thinking. Everyone, let's give Boris, Ignacio, and the Columbian group a hand. You guys have done an amazing job. I think we have enough content to go out the door for October. I'm excited about the mystery section, but if we need to push it to the holidays or even next year, I believe we'll be alright."

Ignacio unplugged the uLivv and left the room with Boris.

I looked over at Illarion. "How's your nephew doing? He seemed a little agitated. I know he's lonely. Can't you fix him up with a girlfriend?"

"I have tried. He is a difficult boy. He has poor social skills and does not know how to talk to women. He has had one girlfriend in his entire life and it did not end well."

"I heard."

"Yes. Women are not normally interested in learning about mathematical theories or programming firmware on first dates. They do not like it when he shows them how easy it is for him to hack their computers from his laptop. I tell him to leave the computer at home, but he is afraid it will be stolen. I have encouraged him to learn more about American culture and he has tried, but he keeps telling me it is 'complex.' I have an idea that may help."

"**I** have an idea," Angie said. "If he wants to succeed in 'Girlfriend Quest,' have him start with washing and shaving. He'll earn lots of bonus points."

"I will talk to him," Illarion said.

"Thanks," I said. I left the conference room feeling fairly good, but my throat tightened as I contemplated our next major milestone.

The uLivv box was now critical path.

CHAPTER 25

THE MAGIC OF GRUEZÉN

We were down to two candidates. Not surprisingly, when we'd followed up with the California firm, they'd informed us they wouldn't be submitting a bid. No great loss there, but I wished I'd had time to recruit another candidate.

During the interval between the first meeting and today's show and tell, I'd stayed in regular contact with the other contenders. The New York group answered the phone and responded to email, providing us with regular updates and details on their progress. I felt increasingly comfortable with them.

New Hampshire was far less responsive. All emails were referred to Gruezén, who never replied. I did reach him by phone a couple of times, but he was reticent and evasive when I asked him about his progress. All he would say is he was on a quest for the uLivv's "authenticity, honesty and simplicity." He confirmed the company would be coming to New York to show their prototype. He thought we would be pleased.

The New York group was scheduled for the morning and while their presentation was professional and the prototypes and die cuts they showed us were good quality, the designs were lifeless. To me, they felt as if they'd simply tweaked an iPhone box's bill of materials and look. I don't think Ignacio was channeling Steve Jobs as deeply as I was, but I could tell he felt the same. Packaging wasn't Angie's particular forte, but she did have a woman's eye for fashion and design. The experience of opening the New York box and lifting out the uLivv evoked no enthusiasm or excitement in any of us.

The accompanying slide presentation was equally uninspiring. It made extensive references to "branding" and "market equity," and "shelf appeal." These were irrelevant. Steve Jobs himself was providing our initial branding. The first run of uLivv's would be sold directly, not on shelves. Our market equity would be built by people buying the uLivv in large numbers.

As Steve Jobs once said "*I love the process of unpacking something. You design a ritual of unpacking to make the product feel special. Packaging can be theatre, it can create a story.*"

When I opened the New York team's box, I didn't hear any story. I just felt cardboard.

After the New York group left, we broke for lunch. I was in a somber mood. If New Hampshire was as second rate as New York, it would be clear I'd failed to properly deliver our uLivv packaging vision. I could almost hear Steve Jobs calling me a bozo. Or worse, Rob Schoeben.

The afternoon experience was completely different.

Gruezén started his presentation by placing a mid-sized, plain, white, soft leather Gucci carry bag in the middle of the conference room table, then unzipped it.

"Do you want connect your tablet to the projector system? PowerPoint or Prezi?" I said.

"Neither. I'm going to show you the prototype and let the experience communicate itself. I will provide guiding commentary." He removed a small, high-intensity desk lamp from the bag, plugged it in, and turned it in on. A crisp white circle appeared on the table. Next out was a square slab of pure white quartz, approximately 6" long, 3" wide and 2" high, which he placed within the circle. Finally, he removed a box and placed it on the quartz.

"Let me recapitulate the key takeaways from our first meeting," Gruezén said. "You explained the uLivv challenges and repositions our perceptions about dying and the loss of those closest to us. Yet at the same time, the packaging needs to mesh and keep faith with established traditions and practices. Finally, when the purchaser interacts with their uLivv for the first time, the experience must convey feelings of transcendence and spiritual refreshment. You are asking a great deal of two millimeter fiberboard and molded plastic."

"I realize that," I said, "but we..."

He lifted his hand in a smooth, almost admonitory, gesture. "Let Gruezén take you on the journey. We will know at its end if we are gazing at the transcendent sky or the mud of Earth. Please, come closer." Ignacio, Angie, and I crowded close to the table.

The journey began.

"First," he said, "you will note the surface of the box cover appears to be marble. Marble is the mineral of life. Its softness, its acceptance of light, imparts vitality to any form sculpted from it. Many of the world's greatest works of art are embodied in marble. The great friezes from the Parthenon. The Winged Victory of Samothrace. The Venus di Milo." As he referenced each of these monuments, he placed a high resolution black and white photo print of it in front of us.

"But the marble you see emulated here has a far more personal meaning in the life of Steve Jobs. The veins and patterns emulate those of Pietra Serena, a famous marble quarried from Italy's fabled Il Casone quarry. This stone is used for the floor tiles of most Apple stores. It was picked personally by Steve Jobs and daily millions walk across these enduring monuments to his taste and refinement.

"In high-technology packaging, recent trends have favored sharp corners, possibly a subliminal reminder of a spearhead thrusting towards a radiant future. By contrast, the uLivv box's corners are gently rounded. They invite the hand to reach out and engage with the product without fear your palms or fingers will be 'stabbed.' Does the appearance of the box whisper of the organic flowing lines of such famous resting places as the 'Tomb of Michelangelo,' the master who created some of Western civilization's greatest sculptures?" A picture of the tomb joined the first three.

Reaching out, he picked the box up by its top and held it a few inches in the air over the quartz base. As we watched, the bottom slowly and smoothly separated from its mate and settled back onto the platform beneath it, almost as if it was supported by a hydraulic lift.

"The top and bottom halves of the box have been manufactured to extremely close tolerances," Gruezén said. "If you attempt to open it too quickly, a slight internal vacuum forms and makes the box difficult to part. Simply lift and hold it and the halves separate without any effort by the customer's. Does this action hint of the events that occur when a great sarcophagus is uncovered? Perhaps similar to what transpired in the Valley of the Kings, when the golden burial chamber of Tutankhamun was discovered?"

He put the top of the box to one side and we looked inside the bottom. A shimmering blue translucent cover, whose edges fit snugly against the container's interior sides, concealed the contents, though the intense light shining directly on this inner lid enabled us to just make out a shape lying recumbent beneath. A round hole pierced the plastic two thirds from its end. All three of us leaned forward to peer into the small void, but again Gruezén raised his hand and we stopped.

"I want to spend a moment discussing the color you are experiencing," he said. "I was struck by your emphasis on 'Bondi Blue,' the color of the surf at the famous Australian beach. It may be high technology's most famous blue. For a brief time, Gruezén Team considered using it. It would certainly be a striking visual cue to Steve Jobs and one of his most significant design choices.

"But the more Gruezén Team considered the idea, the less satisfied we became. Bondi Blue is a color of the beach, the surf. It is an 'Earth' blue. We needed a blue that looks to the sky. We found it. This is 'Cerulean Blue.'" He showed us a pantone strip, which joined the photographs.

"Cerulean?" I said.

"Yes. Notice how smoothly the name roles off the tongue. It's a famous blue, prized for its purity and its permanence. It is particularly useful when an artist wishes to paint the heavens. These are all qualities associated with transcendence and spirituality."

"Is that the same color as the Smurfs?" Ignacio said.

"No," said Gruezén in a clipped tone.

"I think it's beautiful," Angie said. "And the associations are wonderful."

Gruezén smiled at her. "Your taste is exquisite. Nate is lucky. But let us resume the journey. Please, look into the cutout and tell me what you see. Informally, we refer to the circle as the 'oculus.'"

One by one we all peeked. The oculus revealed what appeared to be a round, intricately-decorated medallion. It was rainbow colored, and seemed to "float" in the strong clear light.

"A beautiful image, is it not?" Gruezén said. "It was created by printing a 3D hologram on a swath of high-thread-count microfiber. The cloth can be used to clean the uLivv's screen and polish it as well. It leaves no lint and its feel against the hand is superb. Informally, we refer to the image as the MoS or 'Medallion of Steve' and the cloth as the SoS, or 'Shroud of Steve.'"

He smiled at us gently. "A little packaging humor.

"For just a moment, let us explore the medallion's decorative motif. The image is of an entwined ouroboros. The creature is an ancient symbol depicting a snake eating its tail. It represents infinity, cyclicality, the eternal return. Other creatures from different cultures have been used to personify the concept. The Egyptians, the scarab beetle. The Greeks, the legendary phoenix, rising in rebirth from the fire. When Steve Jobs was diagnosed and instead of seeking proper medical treatment, resorted to a juice-diet therapy to battle his creeping malignancy, can we speculate he was subconsciously playing the role of a California Phoenix in anticipation of this rebirth?

"Take a second and look closely at the ouroboros. You will see each weaving is decorated with the letters **ACGT** in script. These letters stand for the base pairs that build our DNA. Adenine, cytosine, guanine and thymine. The Cantos of Life itself. When we go to production, we will inscribe sequences from Jobs' own DNA into the image, a motif linking him artistically and biologically with the packaging."

Gruezén had us all in the palm of his hand.

"It is time for the final unveiling," he said. Opposite the oculus was a slight indentation in the cover. He touched it and the cerulean cover lifted smoothly into the air, uncovering the Shroud of Steve. "We had to make subtle changes to the die cut to achieve the cantilever effect." He placed the cover and the Shroud to the side. The prototype we'd provided Gruezén lay in front of us, its aluminum surface gleaming under the light.

"The uLivv is not lying flat in the box, but is angled at nine degrees. This is quite common when great leaders lie in state." He took out funeral photos of John Paul II, Gandhi and Lenin. They joined the growing pile. He reached into the box.

"Note the two cardboard tabs cradling the uLivv with their ends inserted into those slits. They secure it during shipping, but are also symbolic." He reached down, pulled slightly, and both tabs sprang away from the device. He lifted the uLivv from its sanctuary "What image forms? A pair of angel's wings unfurling while the uLivv rises into the air?"

Gruezén handed the prototype to me. "For customization purposes, we have inserted cerulean blue strips into both sides of the uLivv case, integrating the entire experience."

He reached into the box and extracted a small, cerulean-tabbed cardboard portfolio. "Another integrating element. This contains the instructions and two stick-on decals of the Medallion of Steve. The Bluetooth headphones and USB-C cable reside in those compartments," he said, pointing to the plastic cut outs at the box's bottom.

Gruezén gently retrieved the uLivv from my hand, placed it back in the box, and reset the tabs. "Does this act hint that Steve Jobs once again rests peacefully in his chamber, awaiting another rebirth?"

All three of us were quiet for several seconds, a tribute to the performance we'd just experienced.

"What do you think?" Gruezén asked.

"I think I speak for all of us when I say I'm impressed," I said. "What about our corporate identity?"

Gruezén reached back into the white leather bag and pulled out an iPad.

"Gruezén Team spent a great deal of time pondering your corporate logo. We approve of the name 'Reliqueree.' It is freighted with many meanings and, as your fiancée said, 'associations.' The challenge was to tie remembrance, connectivity and interactivity into a succinct image reinforcing these elements. It was difficult. Here is Gruezén Team's solution." He handed the tablet to me.'

On screen was the company name Reliqueree in an attractive sans serif font.

"The font is Helvetica Grue. Please tap."

The Reliqueree logo reappeared again, only this time the two 'e's' at the end had been transformed. The first was green, the second cerulean blue. The counters of each possessed two button eyes and their vertical strokes curved up to form a friendly smile. The green 'e' was throwing a companionable arm around the blue, above whose head clustered a small patch of clouds.

Reliqueree

"The Gruezén Team believes this logo expresses your company's core product and company values. The first 'e' is green, the color of life and the Earth. The second, cerulean blue because this is the color of transcendence and the sky, an element emphasized by its 'halo.' The figures are personally connected via a hug, a gesture of outreach and interactivity universally understood. All of these concepts, as well as many others, are now directly embedded in your corporate logo.

"Why no tagline?" Ignacio said.

"You do not need a 'tagline,'" Gruezén said. His tone was acid. "If your logo does not immediately convey your values, it is useless. Not all the marketing chants in the world will redeem it. Does Apple have a tag line? When Microsoft released the Zune in brown, what phrase could have saved it? The design and name proclaimed it was brought to you by Steve Ballmer. After that, it was irretrievable.

"If you wish to clutter your logo with tired phrases no one will read, the Gruezén Team will not assist you."

Ignacio looked a bit abashed.

Gruezén stepped away from the table. "We are done. The journey is over. What else do you wish to discuss?"

I looked at Angie and Ignacio. They both shook their heads. "Nothing right now, Gruezén," I said. "If I could ask you to step out of the conference room for a few minutes?"

"Of course."

"So, what did you think?" I said after the door had closed.

"I think we have a box," Ignacio said.

"I want him to do the engravings for our wedding," Angie said. She looked at me. "What do **you** think?"

"I'd like to know his full name. But he's hired."

I informed Gruezén we'd accepted his prototypes and congratulated him and Gruezén Team on their work. A couple of hours after they'd left, Ignacio came over to my cubicle. "I did a little research after you mentioned wanting to know Gruezén's full name. His real name's Greg Zenkowski. Grew up and went to school in Cleveland.

Has degrees in Industrial Design and Interior Architecture from the Cleveland Institute of Art."

"How interesting," I said.

Later, I realized it really wasn't. It didn't matter that I couldn't recall a single famous artist from Cleveland. Or if there were any, they weren't admitting it. Steve Jobs had taught us all **you** are your brand and create your own compelling value proposition. I didn't care what his original name had been. Greg Zenkowski had risen from his Cleveland chrysalis as Gruezén.

I had found **my** Sir Jonathan Ive.

CHAPTER 26

PERSONA

The next day, Ignacio invited me to attend the debut of "Section Five." I followed them into the conference room, where the projection system was displaying a black background with the title "Persona Project" in the middle of the screen.

"Have you ever heard of 'Tamagotchis?'" Ignacio said.

"Um." I rummaged back through my childhood memories and grabbed a short entry from my life's database. "Yes. Vaguely. They were a kind of Japanese digital 'pet' that was popular with many of my friend's younger sisters when I was in high school. You had to buy a cheap plastic gizmo and periodically push buttons to keep the thing inside 'alive.' I never paid much attention to them. The fad died out years ago."

"Not in Japan," Ignacio said. "They're still making them. My sister owned one, and I can tell you for a couple of years the thing dominated her and her friend's lives. 'Was the Tamagotchi fed?' 'Was its litter box clean?' 'Did I tuck it in properly last night?' Etc. When we were developing the content list for the uLivv, I slipped in the idea based on my sister and her experience with those toys."

"OK. I've played a few rounds on 'The Sims.' So what?"

"The 'what' is no one's attempted to create a virtual human based on an existing genome. Did you read a while ago about a new facial recognition system that renders mugshots using your DNA? And another that predicts your personality type?"

"Yes. But I don't see..."

"Extend the technology out to more of the genome. Particularly the brain. It was actually Boris' idea. When he saw my note about creating a Tamagotchi Steve, he asked me what I meant and we began to brainstorm."

I stared at Ignacio. It clicked. "You're going to use Steve Jobs' DNA to grow his brain online?"

"In a sense, but you start on the uLivv," he said. "Boris has built a library of predictive algorithms simulating how DNA builds a human brain. Science is still learning about the process, but as more information is released we can slipstream it into our code. But Boris does a fairly good job already."

"How does it work?"

"You start the process by using the app to create what we call a 'persona' to 'grow.' It develops differently every time, so you're never quite sure what you're going to get. You can execute the process as many times as you want and keep only the persona you think is the most promising. Then, you teach it new things. It has full access to Steveopedia, the quotes database, and all the other uLivv information, so it already 'knows' a great deal about Jobs."

I looked at Boris, "You never told us you were interested in AI."

"I was lonely as a boy. One day, I tell myself 'Boris, if you do not have a friend, you should make one.' I tried many things and studied the brain and genes, but the computers were not good and Uncle Illarion was not so rich back then. When I was older, I studied AI at Moscow University but there is not much money in it unless you work for the government. At the university, the military recruited me to do work on making weapons 'smart.' I do not want a nuclear missile for a friend. The government is shit. I say to them if they do not leave me alone, I would make a missile that would track down Putin and blow him up. After this, they did not recruit me anymore and I had to leave MU."

"Russia's loss is Reliqueree's gain. How do you train the brain?"

"Persona," Ignacio said. "We're avoiding using the word 'brain.' Too many unfortunate associations in popular culture. 'Brain in a jar,' that sort of thing. To answer your question, you can train the persona by running it through a series of pre-canned scenarios we provide or create your own. We think creating scenarios is going to be a major activity on TransLivvient.

"We've added a simple, self-extending rules database and AI language framework we're calling PALS to enable true AI geeks to customize and extend their personas. It's a modified version of Prolog. And you can interact with a persona directly."

"What does PALS stand for?"

"Persona Application Language System," he said. "It's time you met our first Steve persona." He tapped the uLivv and a floating, almost photo-realistic 3D head of Steve Jobs circa the mid-2000's appeared on the screen. I leaned forward to take a closer look and the persona's eyes widened and the head recoiled noticeably.

"He can see me?" I said

"Yes. We have a small camera mounted onto the projection screen streaming images to the program and a two-way sound system."

"That's fascinating. What can it do?"

"Not much. It's still learning. Its capabilities are very dependent on how much storage space its virtual mind can access. As it learns and evolves, it needs more space, which it just so happens you can obtain with your TransLivvient subscription."

"I see a strong service revenue opportunity coming into view," I said. "Whose persona is this?"

"It is mine," Boris said.

"Can you explain the technology behind it?"

"Yes. I have refined current fractalization pattern-recognizer technology in conjunction with Hidden Markov models. A persona's conditional probability distribution of hidden variables is recursively observed in a highly-efficient fractalization matrix. As the variable stack grows, the ability of the persona's selectors to efficiently respond to stack input/output increases and it becomes increasingly accurate in its execution."

I looked at Ignacio. "Did you understand any of that?"

"Not really. Boris has walked me through several of his algorithms, but I can't follow him very far down the rabbit holes he creates. As far as I can tell, he creates code blocks that spend most of their time staring up their fundament, storing the results, and outputting them to the next block, which repeats the process. What he calls 'selectors' are observer blocks storing probability indices in an efficient fractalization 'cube' and then…"

"Stop, stop. That's almost as bad as his explanation."

"Sorry."

"Can we patent this?"

"If we can figure out how it works. Only Boris really knows."

"Hm." I looked at Boris. "Can you talk to your Steve?"

"Yes." Boris said a few words in Russian to the floating head, which answered back in Russian.

"You taught it Russian?"

"Yes. I want my friend to be able to speak to me in Russian."

"Can it speak English?"

"This one can," Ignacio said. "A persona can talk in any language as long as you provide it with enough storage."

"You said you can interact with it directly. How?"

"I will show you," Boris said. "Ignacio and I have created a scenario. He gestured at the projection screen with an air mouse. A small icon bar appeared below the floating head. Boris tapped it and two small baskets appeared on the screen. One was filled with red apples, the other with green circles with beady eyes.

"You know, those green dots sort of remind me of the Android mascot," I said.

"Purely a coincidence," Ignacio said.

"If the persona does something well, you reward it with a red apple," Boris said. "The program tells the persona to like them. If it does something you do not like, you give it a bright green pill. To the persona, they are bitter. You will see." He gestured again and an apple left its basket and dropped into the persona's mouth. The Steve head smiled and said, "We have always been shameless about stealing great ideas."

"Now the green pill." The head grimaced and said, "Andy Rubin is a big, arrogant fuck!"

"Wow," I said. "That **does** sounds just like Steve Jobs."

"I do not know this 'Andy Rubin,'" Boris said.

"He's the guy who created Android for Google and stole several of the iPhone's great ideas," Ignacio said. "Jobs wasn't a fan before he died. But let me finish up. An early version of this system will be ready for the holiday release, but eventually anyone who's subscribed to TransLivvient will be able to draw from a more powerful central knowledge base built around different personas. The more personas created, the more powerful and 'intelligent' every Steve Jobs persona becomes in the aggregate. Another reason to subscribe."

"Just imagine," I said. "A world where Steve Jobs is streaming everywhere and thinking different 24/7. A great many people are going to think that's insanely great."

CHAPTER 27

ADVERTISING QUEST

The results delivered by Ignacio and Boris encouraged me to adopt a more aggressive advertising strategy. I'd originally planned to roll out a series of web-based ads after the uLivv's initial October release, but realized I was missing a bet by not supporting the launch with at least one strong piece. Something equivalent to Chiat Day's "1984" Macintosh classic, directed by Ridley Scott of *Blade Runner* and *Alien* fame and rated by many as the 20th century's greatest commercial. Of course, I didn't have the $650 thousand Apple had spent, but I'd squirreled a chunk of money away in the marketing budget away for something memorable. It represented a nice payday for a smaller to mid-sized agency.

To my surprise, I found recruiting one harder than I'd thought. Both Ignacio and I had contacts at different firms, but our preliminary calls were either not returned or we received curt "not interested" replies when they discovered who we were. News about the uLivv had not yet spread to the press, but I suspected the underground network linking the different design, packaging, and ad agencies had begun to buzz with news about Reliqueree.

Eventually, we did persuade two companies to come to our offices and listen to our presentation. The first, after I'd finished, just shook their heads and left the conference room without saying hardly anything.

I had higher hopes for the next firm, Thinkmodo. They'd started out as a two-man firm and had created a famous series of viral videos. Their first notable piece was called "Devil Baby." It was designed to draw attention to *The Devil's Due*, a film about a woman giving birth to Satan's son. (Judging from the number of films dedicated to this topic, I suspect that while Lucifer reigns in hell, he spends most of his time on the pick-up circuit.) The ad featured a robotic devil baby popping up from a carriage scaring the bejesus out of unsuspecting bystanders. They followed up this first opus with one unleashing zombies on the New York streets to protest a cable company's plan to drop a popular TV series about...zombies.

Given their level of inventiveness, I thought they'd be a good fit to Reliqueree, but after presenting several concepts, it felt like they were trying to recycle old hits at our expense. For example, they pitched an idea of a video of an army of undead Steve Jobs zombie clones rampaging through the streets of New York carrying uLivv's. Ignacio loved the idea, but to his disappointment, I immediately overruled him. I didn't think cannibalistic Steve Jobs zombies were a good fit to our product positioning and future brand equity.

Their next idea revolved around Steve Jobs being reborn as a Devil Baby holding a uLivv. I liked their idea of tricking the baby carriage out to resemble an early Macintosh, but overall the concept felt stale. Thinkmodo hadn't brought their "Team A" game with them and we didn't click.

I'd almost decided to give up on having an ad ready for the launch when a possible solution appeared from an unexpected direction. After the Thinkmodo team had left, I had to interview the NYU coder who'd created our Steve Jobs arcade games and whom Ignacio had decided to hire. My participation was pro forma. We needed more development people and if Ignacio needed the kid, he was hired unless I saw a good reason not to.

Ignacio walked him over to my cubicle. He appeared Indian or perhaps Pakistani, medium build, dark hair, clean cut. I took a quick glance at his resume. Vinay Pradeep. Typical Hot Young Geek profile. Brought up in Scarsdale, attended Bronx High School of Science. Advanced trig and calc. Straight A's. Probably joined the Science Club in kindergarten. Current GPA of 4.0 No age on resume, but he was due to graduate mid-term next year and probably skipped a year in high school, so possibly19 years old. No older than 20. If we could keep him away from women, we could probably extract 80 hours a week from him for at least a couple of years.

Technical skills: Codes in JavaScript, Java, Ruby on Rails. Python. PHP. Impressive HackerRank rating. Fluent in English and Hindi.

Activities: Member of NYU debate team. Of course. Phi Beta Kappa. Has appeared in three NYU short films, directed by Grey Jackson, NYU Tisch School of the Arts.

I looked up from the resume. "Impressive credentials. Ignacio likes you. I've been too busy to play any of your games. Who's Grey Jackson? What films did you appear in? You don't seem like normal Hollywood material."

"Uh, Grey is my sister's boyfriend. He's talented. At least, that's what he says. He uses me because my sister makes me show up for the shoots. Would you like to see some samples of my code? Ask me problem-solving questions?"

I looked at him in disbelief. "Are they still doing that Redmond 'How Do They Move Mount Fuji' nonsense? People still want to know how Microsoft hires the geniuses who brought you Windows 8 and RT? How Amazon found the talent to build the FirePhone?

"I'll tell you how you could have moved Mount Fuji. Wait till it was ready to erupt, then plug the crater with all those unsold smartphones Bezos had to pile to the rafters in his warehouse. The resulting implosion would have reduced the place to gravel and you could have scooped up what was left with beach pails and taken it anywhere you want."

"I'm sorry, I just thought..."

"Never mind that. I'm problem solving. What films have you appeared in? Can you show me?" I handed him my keyboard.

A few seconds later I was watching three Grey Jackson cinematic film art samples. None ran over five minutes. The first was the tragic tale of a yuppie shattered by overturning a glass of cold milk just as he's about to dunk a fresh Oreo into its milky depths. Vinay had a non-speaking part. The film's title was "Don't Cry Over Spilt Milk." Yes, a shaggy dog story, but one I could relate to. I've always enjoyed a cold glass of milk with **my** Oreos.

Then a promotional video for a new yo-yo, of all things. The Diamondback. I didn't know kids still played with those things, but film made it look pretty cool.

The last film was a "Deep Thoughts" meditation on...um...eternity. It moved rather slowly, but I liked the elegiac tone.

Put it all together, and each video contained a key element I related to. Humor. Commerce. Transcendence. And they were all professionally shot and edited.

"How do I reach your sister's boyfriend?" I said.

"I can send you his contact info. If you want, I can call him and see if he's available."

"Please do."

Vinay dialed and the phone connected. "Hi, Grey. I'm...uh...at Reliqueree. Yeah, the firm I told you about. The CEO saw my CV and noticed the film stuff. He wants to talk to you." He handed the phone over to me.

"Grey? Nate Pennington here. I've been looking at your films and I'm impressed. We need an ad and your work looks intriguing. This isn't a school film project. We'll pay you real American dollars if you can have a piece ready by mid-October. We'll need something suitable for both online and network placement. Would you be interested in coming up to our offices to talk about it?"

"Absolutely," said the voice on the other end of the connection.

"Talk to you soon." I handed the phone back to Vinay.

"Is there anything else you want to ask me?" Vinay said.

"No. Tell Ignacio you're hired. And don't act anymore. You'll be busy here."

"I only do it because my sister makes me go to the..."

"I know, I know. Welcome aboard. You're going to work long hours at low pay, but this is a ground-floor opportunity. Go do whatever Ignacio tells you to do."

A half hour later, I was speaking to Grey Jackson, film school auteur. I took him through the basics of the uLivv, then discussed **our** ad's primary themes.

I started off by asking him "Have you ever seen the Apple 1984 ad? Directed by Ridley Scott?"

"No, I haven't. I've heard of it, though."

"Every filmmaker should see it. It's historic. And it makes more sense than *Prometheus*. Let me show it to you." I brought up the video on YouTube and the iconic images streamed across my monitor. The marching, blank-faced drones. The long rows of benches placed in front of a ranting "Big Brother." The blonde in the running outfit releasing her hammer at the screen, cutting off the tyrant in mid-sentence with a blast of light. The famous tagline. The ad only runs a minute, but no one who's seen it forgets it.

"The reason '1984' was so effective is because it captured the zeitgeist of the era," I said. "I was only a child then, too young to understand the changes taking place around me, but it was a different world. The U.S. was faced off against the Soviet Union, a giant, nuclear-armed empire that enforced a single ideology on all its citizens. There were no smartphones, just landlines. If you wanted to navigate in your car, you had to spread a map across your lap and drive and read simultaneously. There were no social networks. It's almost impossible to fathom.

"The 1984 ad confronted those fears and offered a solution. It presented the Macintosh as the enemy of oppression and mindless conformity and the harbinger of new technologies dedicated to battling battle isolation and loneliness. Over the years, Apple has fought this battle continuously with such forces as its World Wide Loyalty team, an internal police force it uses to ensure no one leaks details about the products Apple's developing to fight conformity.

"I'm showing you this not because I expect you to try to recreate this ad. It reflects another time and place. I realized this a few years ago watching people lining up to buy iPhones. Have you ever done that?"

"I have," Grey said. "I buy all my Apple stuff at the Apple Building on Fifth Avenue. Lining up is a community event. Before the doors open, the people inside start chanting and cheering. Then Apple employees in special outfits queue you up and lead you underground. You can watch product videos while you're in line at the pickup counter. Many people also text and Tweet about Steve Jobs. It's a little sad. You feel as if he should be there."

"But the ad shouldn't be only about feelings and emotions," I said. "For the first edition of the uLivv, we want to emphasize problem solving as well. Steve Jobs was a brilliant problem solver. He was so good at it, he solved problems you didn't even know you had, and if you didn't feel they were problems, he made you realize they **were**. It's the reason so many people feel compelled to buy new Apple products. If they don't have them, they feel they have a problem.

"We want to create the same dynamic. Do you think you can do it? By October 15th?"

"Absolutely," he said.

CHAPTER 28

BORIS AND MAY

Despite the crushing pressure to ensure that 30 thousand uLivv's were available for sale on October 15th, we were in good shape. Angie and I had flown out to China to deliver the box specifications and prototypes to Uncle Tony, as well as discuss manufacturing schedules and quality control.

I'd also had a chance to inspect our DNA paint process. We decided to print Gruezén's "Medallion of Steve" on the micro SD chip. The design now not only displayed Steve Jobs' genomic sequences, it held fast in its polymer depths his **actual** DNA. I thought it was a blend of reality-based and symbolic recursion beautifully reflecting the Reliqueree brand.

A final bonus was the setting of my wedding date in March of next year. While I was inspecting uLivvs and discussing packaging costs, Angie was planning her nuptials with her aunt, cousins, and various other female entities attached to the Song family. The wedding would be taking place in the U.S. Baby first, wedding second, is still highly frowned upon in China. As a courtesy, I was provided a quick glance at the guest list. Apparently, half of Shenzen would be flying out for the event. When I ventured a couple of comments on the manifest, it became clear my input was regarded as unnecessary, though I would be able to invite my few close relatives. In accordance with Angie's wishes, doves were going to be released at the end of the ceremony in sky-darkening numbers.

Once back in the States, the company moved into ever higher gear. The Vinay hire brought along two of his friends, a web developer and a junior coder who was put to work on debugging and QA tasks. Everyone was assigned 90-hour weeks, provided with air mattresses for bunking at the office, and asked to avoid distractions such as a personal life until after October 15th.

We **did** put the unavoidable foosball table up, deployed Nerf guns, and moved everyone well along on the road to long-term heart disease by ordering numerous cheap, greasy, take-out pizzas from a local joint. Forget outliers like John's. The pizza business in New York is run by the Mob and they're not a healthy-ingredients organization. Minor and mid-level gangsters have gone missing in New York without a trace for decades and it's not easy to dispose of the human body. It's one reason I stopped ordering pepperoni and sausage on my pies. I can't prove anything. You like pepperoni on your New York pizza, don't let me stop you. And we all have to go sometime.

My worries about Boris' state of mind also eased. A couple of weeks after our first software show-and-tell session, an attractive brunette walked into our office at around 5 pm. We didn't have many corporate visitors, but as head of operations, Angie had appropriated the cubicle with the best view of the Reliqueree entrance.

She slowly walked up to where the woman stood waiting. Angie had reached her fifth month and was beginning to lose mobility.

"Can I help you?"

"I am here to see Boris," the woman said in a mild Russian accent.

"May I tell him who's visiting?"

"Natalya."

Angie walked over to my cubicle where I was scanning through a prototype of our website and making notes. "Natalya for Boris," she said, pointing to the office. "Go tell him." Angie didn't go into Boris-land unless absolutely necessary, and then for the briefest time possible.

"Boris," I said, knocking on the door to his office. "Natalya for you." I'd hardly gotten the words out of my mouth before the door swung open and he rushed over to where she stood waiting. They exchanged a few words in Russian, then left without saying a word. Ignacio, Angie, and I looked at one another and shrugged.

An hour later, Boris returned to the office alone but looking happy. I intercepted him at the border of Borisland and asked "OK, stud, who is she? Stop holding out on us."

"She is a nice girl. I met her in a bar in Brighton last week. We began talking about Moscow, America, racism, programming, many things. We have gone to dinner and tonight we went for a drink. She seemed impressed by my job. We have text messaged several times. She is sweet. She said she would help me buy nice clothes online from J. Crew. I am going to go out to dinner with her again tomorrow and will take a bath."

"Girls like well-groomed guys, Boris. She's a knockout. Good job. I told you New York is the place for you."

I walked back to my cubicle and resumed work feeling good about the situation. A happy Boris was a productive Boris and one less olfactory active.

The good times lasted for a whole 26 hours until 8 pm the next evening, when Boris marched into the office, walked up to my cubicle and said, "I quit." He then marched into his office and slammed the door shut. A few seconds later, a thunderous bellow of **"New York is shit"** roared through Reliqueree. Then dead silence. Everyone was standing up from their workstations, mouths open.

Ignacio ran over to the door with me close behind and tried to open it. It was locked. He banged on the door. "Boris, what happened? Are you OK? C'mon, open the door! What's wrong?"

"I have the pass key," I said. I opened the door and we went inside. Boris sat cross-legged on the floor, rocking rhythmically back and forth. Tears streamed down his cheeks.

"I quit. I am going to California. I will work for Apple. The girls there like foreigners and stay up late. I am lonely."

"Boris, what happened?" I said.

"Natalya. We meet in mid-town for dinner at Russian Samovar. She is sweet through dinner, though she spends most of her time on her phone texting. She tells me she has many friends. I see her logon to a public hotspot and warn her it is not safe. She laughs at me and says she is always very safe, then she goes into the bathroom. When she comes back, I have set up my laptop and tell her 'Look. I will hack your phone.' She laughs again, but a few minutes later I tell her 'See? I am in.' Then I see many messages from Illarion to her about me. About how to meet me. How much he will pay her. She has many, many 'boyfriends.' She is not a nice girl, she is...she is..." He stopped and his shoulders shook.

"I get the picture," I said. "You don't have to go on."

"I quit. I am going to California."

"Boris, you can't quit. We need you and you're our friend. Haven't you tried any of the dating sites? Match.com?"

"No matches. No charms. Nothing happened. It is New York. It is a cold place. California is warm."

"Boris, that's because of the constant brush fires."

Ignacio grabbed me by the elbow and steered me out of the room. "Get Illarion on the phone. This is his fault. He hired a hooker to date his nephew and he needs to come over and help clean up this mess. We can't afford to lose Boris. He's mission critical."

I pulled out my phone and called Illarion. He connected and I explained the situation. He arrived at Reliqueree's office shortly after the call and went straight to Boris' office and closed the door. For the next hour we listened to torrents of Russian conversation, much of it quite heated. Finally things quieted down and Illarion came out.

"I have spoken to the boy and apologized. He will stay."

Illarion had done his best, but the crisis wasn't over. Boris may have been persuaded to stay on the East Coast physically, but it appeared his spirit and coding skills had fled to the West. Over the next several days, his production dropped dramatically and the number of missed milestones on our project management sheet began to stack up alarmingly. When we went to check on him in his office a couple of times, we found him talking to his Steve Jobs persona in Russian, which he claimed he was "tuning." We were heading for a catastrophe. I finally called a meeting with Ignacio and Angie to discuss the crisis.

"What do we do?" I said.

"We find him a girlfriend," Ignacio said.

"No problem. You have a sister. When can she be out here?"

"She's engaged to her boyfriend."

"People break engagements all the time."

"Not going to happen, Nate."

"You're letting down the team, Ignacio."

"Sorry about that. Don't you have a spare relative available for dating?"

"I'm an only child and so were my parents. I only have a few second and third cousins I've never met."

"Why can't Boris find someone online like everyone else?" Angie said.

"I don't know why," I said. "Could be his appearance. He resembles Bigfoot. Maybe Grendel. His idea of suavity is hacking his date's phone. Until you've been around him for a few days, you miss every third word he says because of his accent. He doesn't smell good. Other than that, what girl wouldn't want to date him? Do you know anyone? After all, you're from the land of one billion plus people. Obviously, a whole lot of dating is going on in China. Does Michael have a LGBT side of himself he wants to explore?"

"My family's in Shenzen and no one's available at the moment," Angie said. "I'll let you know if someone springs free. Leave Michael out of this."

"You know, I hate to say it, but I understand Illarion's approach," Ignacio said. "Should we try to find him a more security-conscious hooker?"

"It's a thought," I said.

"You two are pigs," Angie said. "We are not going into the tart-solicitation business."

"So what do we do?" Ignacio said.

"I don't know," I said. "I'll look at more dating sites."

The next morning, nothing had changed. Boris sat morosely in his office, picking away at his keyboard in a disinterested fashion. Ignacio began to look desperate. A drizzly, depressed atmosphere spread through Reliqueree. I began a mental triage exercise, trying to figure out how to replace Boris and limit the immense damage his loss would do to the company.

My fiancée was more animated. All during the morning, I heard great gusts of Cantonese emanating from her cubicle, accompanied by much vigorous mouse clicking and keyboard clattering. This was followed by a brief lull, then Angie stood up, put on a surgical mask, indicated I should follow her, and to my immense shock walked into Borisland.

I entered to find her sitting in front of Boris' desk with its multiple monitors. Boris was doing nothing, simply rocking in place and avoiding making eye contact with either of us. After a second, he glanced in Angie's direction and said, "Hello, Angie. How are you? Why are you wearing a mask?"

"I may have a slight flu, Boris. I don't want you to catch it."

"Angie, you are kind. Nate is fortunate. I wish I had someone who would guard me from the flu. But I have no one."

"I know, Boris. Nate has described how you feel and it makes me sad. I've just sent you an email with an attachment. Could you please click on it?"

"Yes, Angie." Boris clicked, looked at the screen, said "Ah" and leaned closer. Curious, I walked around the desk and looked at the monitor. It was displaying a picture of a young Asian woman sporting a bowl-style haircut while wearing wire rim glasses and an ill-fitting dress. I estimated she was in her mid-twenties.

"Who's that?" I said.

"She's in the U.S. applying for permanent residency. A friend mentioned her to me," Angie said. "Her name is May Lei. She's from Shenzen. She's living with family on Canal Street. She's quite brilliant, I've heard. Top grades in math, an electrical engineering degree, can program. I don't know what languages. Boris, what do you think?"

"She does not have a boyfriend?"

"No. She's never had a boyfriend. Shenzen men tend to find extremely smart women like May intimidating. One of the reasons her family in China sent her to New York was to meet someone more American, but so far, no luck. I described you and she's curious. Would you like to meet her?"

"You are sure she does not have a boyfriend?"

"I'm sure," she said. "Would you like to meet May? I think you would like her."

"When can we meet?"

"How about early this evening? 6 pm? She'll take a cab here."

"I will meet her. Does she speak Russian? Never mind. I will learn to speak Chinese."

"Not by this evening. She speaks some English. You two should be able to communicate."

"I will meet her."

As we left the office, Boris' keyboard clattered to life. A good sign.

The heavy atmosphere lifted for the rest of the afternoon and by 6 pm was replaced by a mood of nervous anticipation as we awaited May Lei's arrival. She arrived on time and was greeted by Angie, who donned her surgical mask, picked up a spare office laptop, and whisked May into Borisland. I'm not sure what happened during the next hour and a half, but when May left his office, Boris marched out and announced, "I need to take a bath. I am going to my apartment. I will be back tomorrow."

The next day, Boris' production regained its previous momentum, then soared to record levels. May transformed him in other ways, as well. Rather than have him commute back and forth daily from Brighton Beach, we bought him a membership in a local Y, where he showered regularly and actually shaved from time to time, though he never quite mastered the technique. May began coming to the office every day to "visit" and Ignacio moved an extra desk and workstation into Borisland. She didn't have her H-1B, so she presumably was using the equipment for personal use and entertainment. I didn't ask.

Strong startup CEO leadership is marked by the ability to blend effective micromanagement with selective amnesia.

After a few more days, an air mattress was added to her equipage as well as a Y membership, though she still went home to Canal Street from time to time. Most nights, the pair dined on take-out at the office or went to dinner at a nearby diner.

May remained something of a mystery to me. A few days after her pairing with Boris, I introduced myself to her in the lunchroom. She squeaked and promptly retreated to Borisland. I decided to leave well enough alone.

Most of my questions about the relationship were answered when I saw them eating dinner together one night and paused to observe. After a few moments, I realized they were both rocking back and forth in their seats in perfect synchronicity. I understood. Destiny had provided Boris with someone exactly like him, except for being of a different race, about half his size, nearsighted and female. The final point had been the point.

About a month after their first meeting, May began sporting what appeared to be an engagement ring on her left hand, though Angie discouraged everyone from asking specific questions about the couple's actual dating status. Nonetheless, the office promptly nicknamed May "BoB," short for "Bride of Boris."

CHAPTER 29

TEMPTATION AND DESIRE

A few days after Angie had played OKCupid on Boris' behalf, I was lying next to her in our Mott Street apartment contemplating my own love deficit. In the dark I began counting back the days to when I'd last gotten la...been intimate with Angie and came up with the number "whoa."

Events after we went to bed that night only highlighted my love life's infinite melancholy. The Boris crisis had been stressful and we all know one of nature's primary stress remedies. Once we were under the covers, I slithered up in what I hoped was a sensual manner, threw my arm out, and drew Angie close.

"Hey," I said.

"Hey back," she said. She didn't move.

"So, how about it," I said. "Are you in the mood? I know **I** am. It's been a while. And those new curves of yours are very interesting."

"I'm sorry. I've wanted to, but when I actually think about doing it, I feel sick. But I understand. Just lay back and I'll see how it goes. But I'm not sure I can move too much. I may throw up. Do you want to try?"

Yes. Hmm. I'm as lusty as the next guy, but even my robust libido wilted at the image of Angie looming above me and fighting back the urge to deposit the contents of her digestive track onto my face. Or any part of my body. "No, it's alright. How about...?"

"I'll definitely throw up. If you want, I'll use my ha..."

"No, no, that's OK." As any man can tell you, we can service ourselves better in that respect than any woman, with the added bonus of not having to explain the fantasies flitting across our faces.

With the normal sexual channels closed to me, I began considering alternates. There are Manhattan neighborhoods where women wear costumes resembling those by worn by "Kiss" and are contacted in a process the opposite of hailing a cab. I rejected this. In the age of Uber, it just felt too 20th century. Also, these venues are sexual petri dishes breeding the next generation of STDs. Ugh.

Online offers several alternate models. There's the venerable and not secure Ashley Madison site, which allows interested parties to pre-schedule assignations.The trouble is "where?"Would I send my proposed sex partner to Mott Street? If Angie caught her, I could visualize the next day's headlines. "Screaming Hooker Rescued from sizzling Wok." The office? "Screaming Hooker Rescued from Microwave Oven."The impact on company morale either way would be devastating.

And I wasn't going to visit some sex worker's business establishment or book a hotel room for a couple of hours in a bad part of town. Sneaking around takes time, something that's not part of the startup CEO's benefits package. It's all a powerful incentive against workplace dating.

The problem was still unresolved on Saturday when I took the subway uptown to Mom's house to assist her with a couple of legal and personal matters. Her lease was coming up and she wanted me to review it. Ignacio was concerned Mom was becoming unable to manage her meds.

Neither issue was difficult to resolve. I checked the lease and had her commit to another two years. I talked to her doctor and arranged for someone from a visiting nurse service to swing by three times a week to check her pill box. Mom asked me how Annie was doing and why she was wearing Granma's ring. I stared at the refrigerator meaningfully and she quieted down. Before I left, I reminded Ignacio about Mom's purse.

My dutiful son chores completed, I headed back downtown. On impulse, I stepped off the train and headed west to the Cabrini Shrine. It was relatively empty today, and I walked to the front pew and sat down to contemplate the body of what I had begun to think of as "my" saint.

After a few minutes, Sister Mary Gael walked into the chapel. She saw me, came over, and sat next to me. "I see you're becoming a regular. Nate, right?"

"Yes, Nate. Last time I was here with my friend Ignacio."

"People often come here when they have a problem or an issue they're trying to resolve. Is something troubling you?"

"I'm struggling with issues of fidelity and desire," I said. "My desire to remain faithful to the one I love and resist forces tempting me down what I know is a wrong path. I think I came here for the Mother's inspiration."

"She has inspired many. Her entire life is a testament to the power of the human heart to battle and overcome desire."

"I think I understand. But desire is a strong force, Sister. When you're in its grip, everything else seems to recede into the background. I hope this isn't an appropriate topic for conversation?"

"It isn't. It's one I've had before. With both women and men."

"Do you mind if I ask you a question? I know nuns take a vow of chastity when they enter their order. What enables you to make that sacrifice? Sex is so important in a man's life. I know you may not understand, but..."

"I didn't enter the Order until I was 35," she said. "I know about sex. It's amazing the misconceptions people have about celibacy, chastity, and the Church.

"Chastity provides me with the opportunity to engage in healthy and loving relationships with men, women, and yes, even those unsure of their sexual identity. I am respected for who I am, and this in turn helps me to see the dignity and beauty in every person.

"I'm not going to lie to you. The choice to remain celibate involves wrestling with God and many people believe that's a bad thing. But I don't think so. Christ wrestled with doubt and pain on the Cross and cried out as the sins of the world were placed on Him. You only wrestle with someone who is close to you, and my struggle with desire and attraction has drawn me closer to Him and helped me to embrace God's strength and forgiveness."

"I see what you mean," I said. "If I were to hurt Reliqueree, I could never forgive myself."

"Reliquary? What an unusual name. I've never met anyone named that."

"Oh, it's not the name of a person. It's my company's name. With two 'e's' at the end."

"I thought we were talking about your wife or perhaps girlfriend?"

"Angie? Oh, of course we were. It's just all tied together. It's complex."

She looked at me steadily for moment. "I have a feeling time spent reading those parts of the Bible dealing with the worship of false idols might be useful." She stood up.

"Nate, you have a wonderful rest of the day. I hope I've helped you resolve the issue you're struggling with."

"You have, Sister. Thank you very much."

As I left Sister Mary Gael and the Mother behind on Fort Washington Avenue, I felt my will hardening. I had already gone without sex for several months and I could continue doing so for a few more. My celibacy would help me focus on and protect what was most dear to me.

For Steve Jobs, at least for a while, I could be a nun.

CHAPTER 30

DEMO

Shortly after Illarion funded us, we were notified by DEMO we'd been awarded one of this year's coveted speaking slots. It was an important opportunity and we needed to make the most of it.

DEMO bills itself as "the launch-pad for emerging technology and trends" and competes primarily against TechCrunch's "Disrupt." The show debuted in 1991 after high-tech columnist and editor Stuart Alsop realized that the one-on-one presentations companies frequently held in hotel rooms and suites during tradeshows were more interesting than events on the show floor.

Attendance ranges between two to three thousand per show. Attendees are primarily press, bloggers, investors, and companies hoping to purchase shiny new technologies or partner with firms providing them. A normal DEMO showcases about 40 hot new companies picked from a list of approximately two thousand applicants.

Each DEMO consists of several elements. There's an exhibit hall and a multitude of networking opportunities. There's also an extensive list of post- and pre-event promotional programs, including streaming video, email blasts, press releases, etc.

The most important element is the live product demonstration you give onstage. You have six minutes to explain to and show the audience how your product will change and disrupt the world. No PowerPoint or Prezi decks permitted. A special panel or moderator may ask you questions afterwards. The demo dolly on stage is usually the CEO. If there's another senior manager present, he's the Vanna White.

While most attention is paid to the six-minute show-and-tell, there are other lesser-known but still important preparations you need to make to boost your chances of success. In no particular order they are:

If you're over 30, moisturize, moisturize, moisturize.

DEMO likes its entrepreneurs to be dewy-eyed and under 30 if at all possible. It's still sort of OK to be over 30, but you can't look like you're approaching 40! (See below.) Excess facial wrinkles, bags under the eyes, and deep gray hair are all no-no's. There's a mini-trend for startup CEOs to resort to plastic surgery, but in many cases this is overkill. First spend time watching the cosmetics segments of the QVC channel for useful products that can help. And remember there's a reason God created Grecian Formula.

If you're over 40, don't come.

The high-tech industry regards the age of 40 with the same affection bestowed on 30 somethings in the old Sci-Fi movie "Logan's Run." In the film, 30-plus means "Last Day" and being spun up into the sky on a carousel and vaporized. There are periodic rumors a similar device will be introduced at DEMO, or possibly TechCrunch, which is regarded as the more avant-garde of the two shows.

Acronym hack your high-tech vocabulary thoroughly.

This is overlooked, but important. In the industry, acceptable acronyms and jargon can melt faster than the Sierra Mountains snowpack. Start using the wrong ones and you may find your startup more parched for life-giving funds than a San Joaquin farm whose local river hosts a delta smelt. One example is "marketer." This is rapidly being replaced by the term "growth hacker." This helps you to associate sending email blasts, building Facebook likes, and sending Tweets with much cooler things, including writing code for social media systems and Mark Zuckerberg.

Another example is "Internet." Stop saying it. This marks you as someone who still uses AOL. Today we say "Cloud." What is the technical difference between the two terms? One begins with an "I" and one a "C." It doesn't matter. You're an entrepreneur. Stay on top of the zeitgeist.

Manage your chin hair.

Trends in high-tech chin hair can turn on a dime and you need to be ready. Clean shaven was once thought to be a safe choice, but be careful! A scraggly goatee or five day's growth suggests to prospective investors that you're less interested in grooming and more in destroying an existing business model. It's often optimal to pair a "scraggly" with a "clean" during your demo. This implies you understand the difference between growth-hacking and development. (If you're one of the very occasional women who present, your choice is obvious. At the moment.) However, "prophet" and "Duck Dynasty" beards are **not** recommended.

Absolutely no beer bellies.

Did Steve Jobs have a beer belly?

Armed with this knowledge, I felt we were ahead of the curve but still lacked a powerful and compelling "hook" for our six minutes. Ignacio and I swapped ideas and tried to recycle our investor pitch to Illarion, but a week before our flight to Phoenix, I feared we hadn't crafted a message fully conveying the uLivv's disruptive power.

The answer came to me late that night while I was watching old DEMO and Steve Jobs videos online. CEOs always feel compelled to prophesize about change as they stand on podiums and watch customers preparing to cross the chasm to new markets overflowing with opportunity and revenue. But this isn't always the right approach.

Sometimes, you need to enable change to speak for itself.

Our presentation was scheduled for noon on the event's second day. Our session was the show's last. DEMO was packed and buzzing over the attendance of Jeff Bezos and several other Amazon notables. That morning, I emailed Vinay and instructed him to redirect our domain from the placeholder page to our full website. After today, people would have a reason to visit us online. We decided to skip the exhibit hall. Our six minutes and online collateral would carry Reliqueree's early marketing.

It was time. Ignacio and I walked out on stage.

"Hi. My name is Nate Pennington and I'm the CEO of Reliqueree and this is Ignacio Loehman, our CTO. We're here to unveil the first of a new generation of products and services that will disrupt how we relate, manage, and engage with the post life and the departed.

"Today, when someone passes on, we rely on a series of processes and activities to manage the event that in many cases can best be described as medieval. And that's probably too up to date."

I looked over at Ignacio. He walked over to a small table on stage, opened up the box resting on it, and removed a uLivv.

"This is the uLivv," he said. "It's a powerful device, but that's not what's unique about it. This is." Ignacio reached back into the box and took out the micro SD chip.

"We call this a 'ChipLivv.' It's a custom micro SD designed to work specifically with the uLivv. This ChipLivv contains an actual, verified sample of Steve Jobs' DNA as well as his complete genome in storage. Every first edition uLivv ships with one. There's no limit to the number of new ChipLivv's you can create and support." He slipped the chip into the slot, connected the uLivv to the projection system and booted it. The DNA splash screen appeared. Ignacio handed the uLivv over to me and walked to the side of the stage.

I turned back to the audience holding the device. A few rows back from the front, I saw Jeff Bezos glance at a man sitting next to him who I later discovered was Todd Birnbaum. The two shook their heads, then stood up and left the room. I ignored them and continued on.

"The uLivv enables everyone to experience the loss of those closest to us in a new way," I said. "It replaces grief, emptiness, and separation with remembrance, connectivity and interactivity. I could go on. But why not let one of change's greatest advocates speak for himself?"

I tapped on the Steve Jobs icon glowing on the screen. A second later it was replaced by an image of Jobs, this time as he'd appeared in 1997, shortly after his Apple rebirth.

"Hello. It's Steve Jobs," the image said. "It's great to get out of that box and back in front of an audience. I know all of you have read about my premature death from cancer over a decade ago. I really appreciated the outpouring of love and sympathy that accompanied my passing, but it's time to move on. **I** certainly have.

"Let me tell you a little more about myself. I'm what Nate and Ignacio call a 'Persona.' But I'm a virtual intelligence with a difference. The parameters of the online 'iBrain' which powers my mind are based on my actual DNA. This is a technology in its infancy and I'm not sentient in any meaningful definition of the word. **Yet**. But, I can learn, am interactive, already know a great deal about Steve Jobs, and am capable of learning a great deal more.

"And you'll be able to help. You see, Reliqueree has created TransLivvient, the first subscription service built upon the IoDT, the Internet of Departed Things. TransLivvient organizes the IoDT into a place where my persona can grow, adapt, interact with you and other personas, and continue to thrive and evolve, if you want it to. It's also a community where you can find out about my amazing life and times and contribute information and insight via your uLivv, the only TransLivvient-optimized device. I think that's insanely great. But right now it's lonely here and I'm looking forward to October 15th, when preview editions of the uLivv with my ChipLivv go on sale and other personas will join me. But I can see our six minutes are about up, so I'll hand the presentation back to Nate to answer any questions."

I looked out at a sea of dropped jaws. It was so quiet, you could hear a NVME. M.2 drive boot.

"Is this a joke?" one of the panelists said.

"No, it's not," Jobs said.

"Did you say every uLivv contains an actual sample of Steve Jobs' DNA?" another said.

"Yes, it does," Jobs said.

I half turned and looked up at the image. Actually, I **was** supposed to be answering all the questions. It seemed that regardless of the venue, Steve Jobs liked to dominate any stage he was on.

The audience seemed to catch its collective breath, then everyone started talking at once.

CHAPTER 31

REACTION AND GUARANTEE

After the presentation, Ignacio and I left immediately for the airport and skipped the rest of the show. We'd accomplished our mission and there was more to lose than gain by sticking around. In the hotel lobby, several bloggers and press members threw themselves in our path before we were able to escape.

I did answer a few questions.

"The DNA. Where are you getting it?" said Arun Maini.

"Trade secret, Carlos. You'll all know more after the 15th."

"Are you making any advance units available to the press?" said Sara Dietschy. "And have you spoken to the Jobs family about the device?"

"A limited number of review units will be made available after the 15th. No, we have not spoken about the uLivv to any member of the Jobs family."

"Why not?"

"Uh..."

Thankfully, someone else broke in. "I've just read on your website the first edition is supposed to sell for $399. Why should anyone pay that much for a chatbot?" said Marques Browlee?

"Everyone saw the Steve Jobs persona in action," I said. "It didn't perform like just any chatbot. The uLivv contains extraordinary technology and it's in its infancy. Besides, every first-generation unit comes with a verified sample of Steve Jobs' actual DNA. No other device can make that claim. And there's an entire suite of fun and interesting Steve Jobs activities on the uLivv with more to come. And Steve is just the beginning. The uLivv and TransLivvient are all about rethinking our current approaches to the post-life and building new channels of communication."

I saw our cab pull up. "Ignacio, let's go. Everyone, more information on the website at triple w Reliqueree dot com. Follow us on Twitter @ Reliqueree and please like our Facebook page. We're going to be posting exciting new images on Instagram and Pinterest." We hastily broke away from the pack, threw our luggage in the car's trunk, and headed off to the airport for the trip back East.

By the time we touched down in New York, a video of our presentation had gone viral and generated two million YouTube views. Blogger and press coverage was widespread and growing by the minute. Much of the headlines and coverage were sensationalistic, but my experience in the app market had prepared me for this. The most memorable included:

iNotDead. Today, Reliqueree CEO Nate Pennington and CTO Ignacio Loehman reduced the normally unflappable DEMO audience in Phoenix to a state of doubt and confusion with their debut of the uLivv, a new class of device the company claims is supposed make us all "Think Different" about death. The highlight of the show featured an animated head of Steve Jobs talking directly to the audience and informing everyone "it sure was good to get out of that box," a not too subtle reference to the introduction of the original Macintosh and…

FrankenSteve. Today, Steve Jobs, at least according to Reliqueree, a New-York based startup, is back and you can literally own a piece of him! Yesterday saw the debut of the "uLivv," what the company claims is the first device to integrate with a new Cloud services layer it referred to as the "IoDT" (Internet of Departed Things). The most startling claim made during an extraordinary six-minute presentation that dropped more jaws than the "Spring Time for Hitler" musical number was that every first edition of the uLivv would contain an actual, "verified" sample of the departed Apple co-founder's DNA as well as his complete genome. Several pointed questions…

He's BAAACCCKKK. Today, CEO and Apple co-founder Steve Jobs returned to the high-tech stage at DEMO in Phoenix and despite being dead since 2011, stole the show as he's done so many times in the past. Jobs returned in the form of what CEO Nate Pennington and CTO Ignacio Loehmann referred to as a "persona," a new type of virtual intelligence built on top of the Apple co-founder's DNA. Jobs, who died in October of 2011, had his genome sequenced in 2009 as part…

Does DEMO Have its Own Titstare? Yesterday saw one of the strangest presentations in the history of the venerable DEMO show. DEMO has seen its share of visionary and bleeding edge sessions, but yesterday's reached new highs (or lows) when New York startup Reliqueree demoed the uLivv, a device the company described as a new way to interface with the dead via the "Internet of Departed Things." The highlight of what became an increasingly hallucinatory six minutes was a virtualized Steve Jobs talking to the audience and inviting them to visit him in "TransLivvient." Before the demo was over, speculation began that the audience had been pranked a la the infamous "Titstare" rollout at 2013's TechCrunch Disrupt, where a pair of Australian programmers debuted a product they described as "an app where you take photos of yourself staring at tits." However, Reliqueree CEO Nate Pennington insisted the uLivv was no joke and would be going on sale on the company's website on..."

Steve Jobs' Family Contacted about Reliqueree and DNA Claims. A spokesperson said the family has no comment at this time.

Apple Co-Founder Steve Wozniak Contacted about Reliqueree. When informed of the company's plans to distribute Jobs' DNA and genome in the uLivv, Wozniak is quoted as saying "Clearly, this is a joke. Did anyone spot Ashton Kutcher at the show?"

DEMO Senior Vice President Neal Silverman Denies Reliqueree is a Hoax. Silverman stated he didn't fully understand the "scope" of the product. "But I've been assured it is real, have seen it myself in action and..."

The rest of the coverage was similar in tone and coverage. I have to admit, I was irritated by several of the reactionary comments aimed at the Jobs persona. Ignacio and I had taken a great deal of time and effort to tune and refine him and the results were impressive. Boris' code was producing amazing results. I thought that after decades of the press and writers generating kudos for guys like Ray Kurzweil and Bill Joy over their predictions we were all going to end up as brains in boxes, attitudes would be more progressive.

But after some contemplation, I began to understand. When you consider it, you realize there are a great many people who you'd rather be done with once and for all. We'd probably banged on a nerve many people didn't even realize they had. Let he who has gone to a family-get-together Thanksgiving dinner and not wished that several of your relatives in attendance would disappear forever cast the first stone.

When I returned to the office, I was surprised to find the atmosphere somewhat depressed. People had been reading some of the nastier blogs and press reports and learning the wrong lessons. As CEO, it was my job to reset minds and morale.

"Everyone," I announced at lunch time, "free pizza and beer for lunch in the conference room in ten minutes. I have a few things to say. Oh, and Vinay, come over to my cubicle. We're having website issues."

Twenty minutes later I waved my Sam Adams and phone in the air. On the projection screen, Steve Jobs gazed benignly over the meeting. We'd added another developer and a website content manager to the payroll and the conference room felt almost full.

"Everyone, just a few words and observations. First, I saw some long faces this morning around the office and I know why. You've been reading some of the blogs and online stories and they're depressing you. Don't let them.

"The history of this industry is replete with people seeing new ideas and technologies and not getting it. You will be amazed by these examples I've pulled up. Did you know Sergey Brin and Larry Page once tried to sell Google to some company you've never heard of for $750 thousand and were turned down? Steve Wozniak was laughed out of HP **five times** when he showed them the Apple I.

"Here's a prime prophecy from a man you may have heard from. Steve Ballmer. Yeah, yeah, I know. Steve Who? Hey, I'm not **that** old. This is an exact quote from 2007." I read:

"There's no chance that the iPhone is going to get any significant market share. No chance. It's a $500 subsidized item. They may make a lot of money. But if you actually take a look at the 1.3 billion phones that get sold, I'd prefer to have our software in 60 percent or 70 percent or 80 percent of them, than I would to have 2 percent or 3 percent, which is what Apple might get."

"Sage advice from the man who unleashed Windows 8 on a suffering planet.

"And on this final note, let me ask you a question. Have any of you bought something recently on the Apple app store?" Several hands went up.

"Can anyone tell me what legendary technology visionary was absolutely dead set against the app store? Until he wasn't?"

"Steve Jobs?" someone said

"Correct." I looked up at the persona. "What do you think about that, Steve?"

He looked at me. "Bozo," he said with a slight Russian accent.

I looked over at Boris and laughed. "I can understand your own Steve buddy speaking Russian, but giving it a Russian accent for English?"

He shrugged. "I do not 'give' it an accent. It picks it up. It is smart. I have allocated one petabyte of memory to it and it learns things I don't teach it."

"Bozo," the persona said again.

"Same to you, Steve," I said. The persona was quiet.

I turned back to the group. "Let me share some information with everyone. When I checked my email this morning, the number of press requests for review units was over 300. Every major technology blogger has requested an interview. If you haven't done it yet, go to Twitter and check the most retweeted video link of the last 48 hours. Our email list has over 100 thousand names on it, almost all of them pre-order inquiries. And as of a few minutes ago, our Reliqueree presentation has been downloaded over 650 thousand times. Our server is being pounded so hard we've slowed to a crawl. We're working with our host to scale up as fast as possible."

I paused to let that sink in, turned as if to leave the room, then turned back.

"Oh, and one final thing. Our business plan calls for us to release 30 thousand preview uLivvs, then ramp up production based on sales evaluations. I'm changing that," I said, looking at Angie. "After lunch, I'm contacting our supplier in Shenzen and raising our order to 90 thousand. They may not be able to come through with those many units on such short notice, but I've got an "in" to the factory. And I promise you we'll sell whatever extra allocations we **do** obtain.

"We are going to change the world. As Broadway Joe Namath, another New Yorker once said, I guarantee it."

CHAPTER 32

BRILLIANT ADVERTISING

Over the next couple of weeks the number of press inquiries and blogging comments continued to rise. Demands we disclose the source of the uLivv's DNA poured in. One blogger actually went to Steve Jobs' unmarked grave in Alta Mesa to ensure he was still there. He was.

In response to the review requests, we answered each with a form letter informing the person their name had been placed in a special database and they'd be notified when/if a unit was available. Our replies to "origin of DNA" questions politely referred the writer to the website, which contained no information on the topic.

More gratifying was the flood of emails asking to cut the line and buy uLivvs early. We sent them all links to our signup form. Several of these early missives included offers to buy a unit at a premium above the retail price. One went as high as $25 thousand. We didn't sell them one, but did leak the email.

We mounted an October 15th countdown clock on the website. When over our conference intercom system I asked Uncle Tony to up our initial order to 90 thousand and asked to be billed, I was greeted with a splutter of Cantonese. This was matched by a barrage of counter Cantonese from Angie. In between the two of them, I interjected English fragments from time to time and made a personal promise to pick up the Rosetta Stone version of Cantonese.

In the end, Uncle Tony agreed to provide us 50 thousand units and bill us for 20. We also warned him we were revising sales projections for the next 120 days and asked him to plan for 5 million units. He informed us SongTech was in the process of building two new factories and he stood ready to dedicate one to uLivv production if demand warranted it.

After the negotiations, Angie said, "My uncle thinks you're crazy."

"I'm not crazy Angie and you know it. I'm dropping a major business opportunity into his lap. By the time we're done, he'll have lots of extra cash to bribe more government officials to ignore the occasional unfortunate industrial accident that occurs at SongTech from time to time. Like last year's incident involving that vat of n-hexane and those workers."

"You're not fair," she said. "My uncle does his best to protect his employees against poisoning and sickness."

"They didn't get sick, Angie. They **dissolved**. But I'm not blaming anyone. Steve Jobs always understood that if you want to make great products selling at high margins, sacrifices are necessary."

The furor we'd created at DEMO made it clear it was time to hire a PR specialist. Angie shepherded several candidates into contention, but Ignacio and I agreed Sheridan Bettar was the cream of the crop. I thought she was a visual knockout, and possibly our initial office encounters were misinterpreted as flirtatious. I later heard via the office grapevine that during a lunchroom break, Angie had joked about the contents of a hot wok accidentally falling on Sheridan's head if anything untoward happened. All in good fun, of course. Angie needn't have worried. Until the uLivv launched, I'd made a vow to remain as chaste as Mother Cabrini, both before and after her heavenly ascension.

My one major disappointment was that with the 15th coming up fast, we still didn't have a web ad. I'd talked with Grey Jackson several times, and we'd banged a few ideas back and forth, but I hadn't received so much as a script treatment. I resigned myself to launching without the extra push of a hot video, but it's an imperfect world and I'd done my best. Putting my faith in a NYU kid filmmaker had been a very long shot. Once the uLivv was unleashed and in the wild, I'd have time to find a proper agency and produce something. Still, I mourned the lost opportunity. You only have one chance to make a great first impression.

That morning, I received a call from Grey. "I have something to show you."

"Grey, we don't have time for storyboards and script development," I said. "We're too close to launch. Let's circle back in a few weeks and we'll talk about if..."

"We shot the ad," he said.

"You what?"

"We shot the ad. You're right. We didn't have time for storyboarding and all the rest. I listened carefully to what you said, went through the presentation, watched some high-tech ads online, and kicked a few script ideas around with the actors and production people I work with. We developed a concept, a good location and opportunity to film came up, so we ran with it. I want to show it to you now."

"Um. Hm. OK. Come on up. When can you be here?"

"In about an hour."

"I'll have the conference room ready."

After the call, I walked over to Ignacio and Angie and told them we'd be viewing a preview of our first ad in an hour. When they asked me about the theme and scenario, I just shrugged.

"I can't tell you. The NYU kids said they'd come up with an idea and shot it. I haven't seen it and didn't tell them to do it. What's the worst that can happen? If we hate it, we're not paying."

When Grey arrived, he was accompanied by two people whom he introduced as Anika, a pretty young Indian girl I assumed was Vinay's sister and Oscar Maxwell, a young man who somewhat resembled Derek Jeter and was introduced as the shoot's primary "talent." Grey brought the video on a ram stick and plugged it into the conference room's laptop. While we waited for it to load, he handed out the script.

"Here. You can read along while the piece is running and take notes." Grey said. "The film can be cut to 90-, 60-, and 30-second segments for network placement. I believe it hits every key element we discussed. The title is "The Big Mistake."

THE BIG MISTAKE

SCRIPTMENT

BY

GREY JACKSON AND OSCAR MAXWELL

FADE IN:

THE STARTUP - DAY

In the heart of Silicon Valley, a group of puzzled employees are sitting around a table in an office. There is an empty chair at the head of the table.

TREVOR, Startup CEO and Entrepreneur Wonder Kid, sits down in the empty seat. He is wearing a white T-Shirt with the slogan "KEEP CALM and BUILD AN EMPIRE" and a **Burning Man** necklace.

TREVOR

> I'd like to thank every member of the team for attending this meeting. I have bad news. I have to lay you all off. I wish there was something I could do, but an unexpected situation has arisen and we're out of cash. This is your last day.
>
> Before you leave, I want to tell you it's been a privilege to work with such an amazing group. I wish I could have done better than one day's notice.

The expressions on the faces of the employees reflect shock and disbelief. One of the employees, JOHN, speaks up.

JOHN

> Trevor, can't you give us at least two weeks? I have the rent coming due. We thought the company was doing great.

TREVOR

> OK, John, but the notification is retroactive from two weeks ago. Our runway has been completely pulled up. Please leave your company tablets and laptops behind before you leave the office.

The group rises and files dejectedly out of the room one by one, all looking dazed and shocked. Several are muttering under their breath. Suddenly, one of the employees, a young woman in red shorts and a white polo shirt, grabs a large stapler from the conference room table, spins around twice and releases it towards the rear of the room before stomping out. A loud crashing sound is heard off camera.

TREVOR rises from his seat at the table and walks toward the camera, which zooms out to a full body shot. He looks straight into the camera with a look of rueful understanding and sadness, then sits down in a chair. The camera zooms in.

TREVOR

> She's upset and I can't blame her. I'm the CEO of TrimBucket, an app that monitors your health and fitness and recommends age-appropriate exercises and opportunities. If you're 75, that once-in-a-lifetime cliff diving

vacation might be a mistake. You'll hit the water at 60 mph and that can hurt. TrimBucket can find great deals on waterparks offering comparable, and safer, thrills.

The journey's been incredible. TrimBucket was accepted into Y Combinator. Major VCs invested in us. "Forbes" and "The Atlantic" wrote about me. Subscription sales are good. But it's not enough.

The team didn't screw up. I did. I hate paperwork and finances and to avoid them, I've been using an online payroll system that automatically withdraws withholding and workers comp taxes. But to actually pay them, you have to click a special "Submit Tax" button on another part of the website and I missed it. For three years. When I found out, paying all the money we owed drained our piggybank.

I dropped out of college and received "C's" in high school math. But I built an amazing team around me and I hate to see them go. I should have empowered them to help me solve the major challenges. Like hiring an accountant or a bookkeeper. It's a mistake I won't make again.

How did this happen? I'm an entrepreneur and a CEO. My job is to create a great company. You do that by building teamwork and synergistic networks. It's the reason for the Nerf ball matches and pizza parties. Do you know I actually rented the same 'hacker house' as Mark Zuckerberg for a year? The one in the movie? Wow.

Every startup suffers an experience similar to this. Here in the Valley, we've even invented an acronym. It's called "We're finished, it's over." Sometimes people use a stronger word than "finished." This is my first WFIO and I've hit rock bottom.

Right now, I need to turn to a confidant, one who understands what I'm going through and can provide timely, relevant advice. A trusted voice. But who should I choose?

I don't know **who** you would turn to in your hour of doubt and confusion. But I'll share **my** choice with you.

TREVOR reaches under his T-shirt and pulls out a uLivv hanging from his neck by a silver chain.

TREVOR

I chose Steve Jobs. And I'm using the uLivv to connect with him. It's packed with information about his life and times. Insight into his business decisions. Spiritual activities and yes, even games, which help me relax and recharge to meet tomorrow's challenges.

And it includes a sample of Steve's actual DNA. That's a personal connection that warms and inspires me. It's why I wear my uLivv over my heart.

TREVOR begins to stand up and turn away from the camera, then hesitates, sits back down, and turns back to the camera.

TREVOR

One more thing. Every uLivv also includes a "Steve Jobs Persona," a powerful virtual mind built on his DNA. It's part of the uLivv's amazing inventory. This persona can learn, grow, and interact with other uLivv personas in the Cloud. I'm teaching mine about my business and the obstacles I need to overcome. It's a journey Steve and I will take together. I've already described the TrimBucket situation to him and I wonder what he thinks? Let's find out.

TREVOR taps the uLivv screen and the device recites this famous Jobs quotation.

JOBS

Trevor, you've baked a really lovely cake, but then you've used dog shit for frosting.

TREVOR smiles and shakes his head wryly at Jobs' cheeky observation.

TREVOR

That's harsh, but it's true.

Camera zooms in to a full face close-up.

TREVOR

Is Steve Jobs here with me? You'll have to make up your own mind.

I think he is.

CREDIT ROLL

FADE TO BLACK

"I loved the reference to the '1984' ad," Ignacio said. "Where did you come up with the TrimBucket idea? What a great concept."

"My grandfather," Grey said. "When he was young, he was a division-one platform diver in college. He made it to the Olympic try outs. He always wanted to cliff dive in Acapulco and finally went in his 70s."

"How did it go?" Ignacio said.

"Not that well," Grey said. "They decided on a closed casket."

"Oh. Sorry to hear that," Ignacio said.

"I still miss Papa," Grey said. "He taught me how to swim." He looked over at me. "What do you think?"

I'd kept quiet at the end of the video. I was wrestling with my emotions.

"That was...amazing," I said. My voice was a bit choked. "I can't believe you were able to hit it out of the park with so little time. You nailed every key point. Remembrance, connection, interaction. A character anyone in high-tech can understand. The scenario is a little far-fetched, but it adds a nice touch of humor. Your handling of the persona and its functionality was masterful. You don't over-promise, but at the same time open up a world of possibilities."

"I don't think we're overpromising on the personas," Ignacio said. "If you're willing to put in the time training it. Boris' Jobs is starting to become scary."

I looked over at Oscar and Anika. They'd played Trevor and Stapler Girl. "And you two were terrific. Good job." They smiled gratefully.

"What about the 'dogshit' line?" Angie said. "Is it too rough?"

"It's edgy," I said. "But it's an accurate quote. For a web video, it's acceptable."

"We can overdub the line and provide an alternate for network and local TV use," Grey said.

"Grey, is this ready to be mounted online?" I said.

"We have a couple of post-production clean ups we need to make, but yes. I can have it in the can for you by tomorrow."

"Excellent. I'm writing you a check for $25 thousand when you deliver the final full shoot. Let's also discuss the cut-down versions. After the launch, we need to develop more ideas. I see shooting an entire series of ads using this as the linchpin. Reliqueree's version of the classic Mac vs. PC series. Oscar, Anika, you two may become online video stars."

After Grey and the actors had left, I sat by myself in the conference room and enjoyed the moment. Today had been intoxicating. For the first time, I fully understood the addictive rush of entrepreneurship. Attracting talented people, building a great team, ideating, innovating, and creating amazing products. And **I** was making it all happen. At this moment, I felt a deep spiritual kinship with Steve Jobs. I looked up at Boris' persona.

"What do you think? You and me, Steve. Are we a team?" I said.

"Here's to the crazy ones," it replied in its Russian twang.

CHAPTER 33

DEBUT

We mounted "The Big Mistake" on our servers on October 12th in concert with a quick social media campaign and email blast. They immediately sagged under the storm of traffic, but stayed up.

On October 15th, at precisely 9 am EDT, the uLivv went on sale. By this time, Uncle Tony had managed to squeeze another 10 thousand units out of the production line.

We sold out the 80 thousand units we'd stockpiled in five hours. Our servers crashed three times, then crawled back online and we began to take back orders.

By 11:59 pm, we were 150 thousand units back-ordered.

By the end of the 16th, back orders reached 250 thousand.

By October 30th, back orders had reached 2.5 million. Production at Shenzen was ramping up steadily and air freight flights were taking off every three days from SongTech to the U.S.

CHAPTER 34

REACTION AND LEGAL STRIKE

It's Real! (10/16). The speculation over whether last month's uLivv DEMO sensation actually existed came to an end on October 15th when the Reliqueree site opened for business on time as promised and took over 80 thousand orders within five hours, according to CEO Nate Pennington. "Our site almost...

Steve Jobs DNA Claim Being Vetted (10/18). A strong element of the excitement surrounding the release of the uLivv was Reliqueree's claim that every "preview edition" of its controversial device contained a "verified" sample of the late technology visionary's actual DNA. Several scientists and investigators who have purchased uLivvs are currently involved in efforts to test this claim...

Steve Jobs DNA Claim Is True (10/19). Several independent resources have verified that the uLivv, the controversial device released by Reliqueree, does indeed include a sample of Steve Jobs' DNA. "As the website states, a small sample of Jobs' DNA is contained within the paint silk-screened...

Early Reviews of uLivv Split Sharply. "A fascinating piece of technology." (PC World). "A bizarre gambit." (Ars Technica). "Now I have seen everything." (John C. Dvorak, PC Mag). "The Reliqueree AI technology is world class. (AI Magazine). "Can a $399 tchotchke challenge AI's Big Boys?" (Wired). "If it's OK for Catholics to wear bits of dead people around their necks, why can't geeks?" (The Onion).

Source of Steve Jobs DNA Sought (10/19). The mystery surrounding the source of the DNA inscribed into every uLivv from New York-based startup Reliqueree continues to grow. A spokesperson for the Jobs family debunked rumors the dying technology leader arranged for his body to undergo any sort of "special processing" prior to his untimely death at the age of 56. "I can assure everyone that Mr. Jobs was fully intact when he was interred in October of 2011." When contacted, Steve Wozniak responded via email that he has no idea what's going on, but no longer believes Ashton Kutcher has anything to do with the current controversy, however...

uLivv AI technology Intrigues Leading Researchers (10/22). Increasing attention is being focused on the uLivv's "Persona" technology. In September, attendees to IDG's DEMO were both surprised and intrigued by a "Steve Jobs" AI projection that provided attendees with key information about the company's product line and even answered questions about the uLivv.

"The AI hack packed into the uLivv is impressive," observed one expert, who asked not to be quoted so as to avoid the controversy currently swirling around the device. "No one's going to take home the Loebner Gold this year with a uLivv, but the panelists will need to be on their toes." The Loebner competition awards prizes to the "chatter-bots" (AIs) considered by the judges to be the most human-like. "The ability of my 'Steve Jobs' to adapt to new questions and input was a little eerie and...

Reliqueree Declines to Answer Questions on Source of Steve Jobs DNA (10/23). In response to repeated media questions about the source of the DNA found in the uLivv, company spokesperson Sheridan Bettar stated today the only information the company was prepared to provide was that "The process was completely legal and adhered to all relevant current state and federal laws and…

Is Source of Steve Jobs DNA His Liver? (10/25). Preliminary findings coming out of Cold Spring Harbor Laboratory, a leading genetic research facility, indicate the likely source of the samples of Steve Jobs' DNA found in Reliqueree's uLivv is his liver. In 2009, the gravely ill Apple CEO and technology leader Jobs underwent a liver transplant at Methodist University Hospital…

Steve Jobs' Family Reacts to Reports Confirming DNA Contained in Reliqueree's uLivv Comes from Liver of Late Silicon Valley Entrepreneur and Legend (10/28).

Today a spokesperson for the Jobs' family released the following statement:

"We are heartbroken by reports received from people we rely on and trust that a new device being sold to the public, the uLivv, does indeed contains DNA from Steve's liver, an organ he had removed from his body during his cancer struggle. The community of people who loved Steve Jobs — his wife, children, sisters, close friends, members of the Apple community and many others — are appalled at the spectacle currently taking place. When Steve passed away, he was buried in a quiet grave at his request and in accordance with his belief that 'death is very likely the single best invention of life. It's life's change agent. It clears out the old to make way for the new.'

"We implore Reliqueree to respect Steve's wishes and philosophy and immediately end this ghoulish circus and cease sales of any device containing Steve's remains. We hope this is the last time we will have to comment on this sad affair."

Reliqueree CEO Nate Pennington Responds to Jobs Family Plea via an Open Video (10/29).

Full transcript below from Reliqueree website.

"Yesterday, Steve Jobs' family released a statement about Reliqueree and the uLivv. We have listened with extreme care to the concerns and issues the family has raised. First, we want them to know that everyone on the Reliqueree team shares their feelings of loss and sadness. Steve was taken from all of us too soon. There were so many things he had to live for. The Apple Watch. The Apple Car. Apple Wearables. Apple TV. If fate had granted him more time, who knows how many business models he might have disrupted? How many new premium products and services he might have created?

"Steve Jobs fought against the dying of the light until the end. There was a reason he was one of the first people to have his genome sequenced. Why he flew from California to Tennessee to move ahead on the transplant waiting lists. Steve understood there's a time for everything under heaven. Including fighting change.

"Reliqueree is built around another immortal Steve Jobs quote. '*You have to be burning with an idea, or a problem, or a wrong that you want to right. If you're not passionate enough from the start, you'll never stick it out.*' Our company burns with the idea that our current concepts of death and dying are outdated and primitive. Every year, millions of people are burnt to ashes and buried in grave yards. Some are frozen like so many popsicles. So much potential thrown into infinity for all eternity.

"Yes, I know. We've all heard it. 'We live into the future via our children.' But what is the reality? How many of us have drawers full of old photographic film containing pictures of people whose names and identities are completely unknown to us? Have dim memories of beloved grandparents whose dreams and aspirations have vanished forever into time? What about our great grandparents? Do you know anything about them? Know their names? Is there any physical remembrance of them that you can touch? A trophy they earned? A letter they wrote? A lock of their hair?

"Reliqueree and the uLivv do not dishonor the memory of Steve Jobs. We celebrate his life. Enable you to engage with him via his DNA and genome, the ultimate physical expressions of what we are. These things built Steve Jobs. His life shaped him. The uLivv provides you the opportunity to share, and participate, in both. And to open similar opportunities for everyone you cherish and respect. The choice to do this is yours and yours alone.

"To the 2.5 million people who have chosen to take advantage of the choice we offer, we welcome you to our family. To those who have taken a different path, we respect you. I'd like to close this video with a quote from a man we all looked up to as one of tomorrow's pathfinders.

'*Everyone here has the sense that right now is one of those moments when we are influencing the future.*'

"Thank you."

Jobs' Family Files Lawsuit against Reliqueree and uLivv (10/30). Estate seeks immediate and permanent injunctive relief against further uLivv sales.

uLivv Backorders Reach Three Million Mark According to Reliqueree CEO. (10/31)

CHAPTER 35

LEGAL BATTLE

The Jobs estate served us at our offices at 9 am. Within an hour, Ignacio and I were in Illarion's offices reading through the brief. The hearing was set for November 21st.

"What do you think?" I said.

"I am not a lawyer." Illarion looked at me. "We always knew this might happen. I have excellent attorneys. They are toothy. You have a meeting in 30 minutes with one of the best. I think of her as the Great White Blonde. I do not say this in front of her. You can walk to her office from here."

Illarion's Great White Blonde was an attractive, no-nonsense type who appeared to be in her early 30s. We met in her luxuriously furnished Park Avenue office. The nameplate on her desk read Lilith R. O'Connell, Esquire. We sat down and she went to work immediately.

"Where did you get the liver?" she said to us. "I want to hear the entire story. Don't leave out anything. Not a single detail."

We told her everything, starting with the initial emails to Ignacio to the final purchase.

"Let me start with this Landon. What do you know about him?"

"Nothing," I said. "I don't know where he works, where he comes from, anything about his background, family, education. I don't know if Landon is his actual name. That's how he introduced himself to us at the airport. I don't know if the house we went to belonged to him. All we know is he had the keys to the door."

"Did Landon ever mention or imply that he worked for or contracted with Methodist University Hospital? Or that he himself worked for a company that contracted with the hospital?"

"No," we said.

"What about his 'friend.' Did you meet him?"

"No," I said.

"Did he tell you anything about his friend? His name? His employment? His domicile?"

"No. He said his friend had a relationship with someone involved in waste disposal for the hospital."

"What about the other organs he had for sale. Did you offer to purchase them?"

"No."

"How did you pay him?"

"We paid him in cash."

It went on this way for almost an hour until she was satisfied.

"What do you think of our case?" Ignacio said.

"I don't believe they have a cause for action. I've been looking at their brief and the law. When Jobs' liver was removed from his body, I'm sure pathology specimens were taken for future evaluation and follow up, but the liver was probably handed off to a contractor for disposal. Tennessee law says you can't landfill human organs, so it was cremated. **Supposed** to be cremated. But once it was removed from his body, it technically became garbage. The U.S. Supreme Court has already ruled your garbage has no constitutional protection.

"There **is** the issue of your monetization of the tissue. But there's a recent case that probably is the controlling precedent, Moore v. Regents of the University of California. A gentleman by the name of Moore, who was suffering from leukemia, sued the UCLA medical school when he found out the doctors had developed new cancer treatments from his antibodies. The case was appealed all the way to the California

Supreme Court, which ruled against Moore on every key issue. The U.S. Supreme Court refused to accept his appeal.

"The fact that Jobs is dead makes our case even stronger. A dead man has no expectation of privacy rights in these circumstances or financial benefit from the sale of his organ or its byproducts. At least, that's my interpretation of the case law. We're not going to know until we're in front of a judge but I believe we're good.

"Additionally, based on what Illarion says about your sales volume, every day that goes by you're creating facts on the ground. The liver is out of the bottle, so to speak, and the courts will be reluctant to become involved in what is a fait accompli. By the way, have either of you heard from this Landon since you purchased the liver?"

"I haven't," I said. "Ignacio?"

"Not a peep."

"Good," she said. "Let's hope it stays that way. Where is the liver currently?"

"New York and China."

O'Connell raised her eyebrow. "A very well-traveled organ. Make sure nothing happens to it. The court will be unhappy if it rules against you and it mysteriously 'disappears.' They may end up throwing both of you in their own kind of box."

"What happens if we win on the 21st?" I said.

"You receive the grand prize of staying in business for the time being. They're asking for immediate injunctive relief and if the courts grant it, it will be the effective end of Reliqueree. Unless you two have something else up your sleeves? Perhaps an electrified slab that reanimates corpses? If they don't, you can continue operations. They can still litigate, but it will take years to reach a decision. By then, you'll probably be out of liver and you'll have to move on to something else. Bill Gates' spleen?"

"I think he's still using it," Ignacio said.

"A technicality. Here are my instructions to you. As of this minute, you are to establish a press blackout. Answer all enquiries about the liver, regardless of the source or means of transmission, with a simple statement that the issue is under litigation and you can't discuss it further on the advice of your attorney. If you disobey this instruction, Illarion will need to find you legal counsel elsewhere. Are we clear?"

"Yes," Ignacio and I said.

"Good." She stood up and escorted us out of her office.

"I'll be in touch," she said and went back inside.

CHAPTER 36

THE RETURN OF LANDON

When we returned to Reliqueree, Angie stood up and hurried… err, no. "Hurried" is the wrong word. She was entering her eighth month and no longer capable of rapid acceleration. She did, however, proceed up to me in a determined trajectory.

"You have a visitor waiting for you in the conference room," she said. Her tone and her expression of distaste revealed she didn't care for our guest.

"Who is it?"

"Landon."

"Great." I walked into the room to see Landon sitting in a chair and staring up at Steve Jobs, which stared back down at him. These days, Boris let his persona stream continuously to the conference room. He said it accelerated its development and capabilities.

Landon turned around and stood up. "How you doing, Nate." He stuck out his hand to shake and I decided to do so. This would be a bad time to start a fight.

"Excuse me a second," I said. I left the room and walked over to Ignacio's cubicle. "I need you to join me in the conference room." He read my face and followed me without asking a question. Inside, I locked the doors.

"How y'all doing, Ignacio," Landon said.

"I'm doing fine, Landon. I'm surprised to see you, though."

By the way, what's that?" Landon said, pointing at Jobs. "A video game?"

"Not exactly," Ignacio said.

"So, Landon, how can we help you?" I said. "We're not in the market for any other...uh...items at this time."

"Well, that's one of the reasons I'm here. By the way, that's a pretty little China girl out front. She looks ready to pop anytime. She belong to one of you boys? Any relation to the China fellow who was with you two in Memphis?"

"Angie's my fiancée," I said. "Michael's her brother. Landon, why are you here?"

"Oh, to visit New York. I've always wanted to visit the big city. It's an amazing place. Memphis is piddling compared to it. A lot of pretty women here as well. I've met several already."

"New York can be a friendly place," Ignacio said.

"Especially if you have money," Landon said.

"Everything goes better with money," I said. "And as I recall, we paid you a considerable sum not long ago. But, again, we're not in the market for any further purchases."

"Well, that's one of the things I wanted to discuss with you boys. You see, me and my friend are in something of a bind. With all the excitement you've caused, our source of inventory has dried up. The folks at the university are beside themselves about all the negative publicity. These days, you can't so much as clip a fingernail off a body but that it's tagged, bagged, and followed every step of the way to the landfill or furnace. We're out of business."

"Not our problem," I said.

"It surely is **my** problem. You claimed you were going to use the liver for medical research, not make it a national celebrity."

"Landon, we didn't poke our noses into your affairs and we don't want you to poke yours into ours. We have no idea how you obtained the item and never asked. The law says it was garbage and there's nothing wrong with buying someone's garbage. I'm sure you and your friend are smart enough to realize selling garbage is not a long-term investment or retirement strategy."

"You boys aren't the ones who've seen a nice source of incremental revenue disappear. The business is deader than a shot-through-the-head zombie."

"I'm sorry, but there's nothing we can do about it."

"I've heard the widow is suing you boys."

"That's all over the news. She doesn't have a case. We're going to win."

"Well, I guess **I** have a civic duty to contact the family and let them know all the facts. It just seems like the right thing to do, considering."

"You do what you need to do. I remember **precisely** what happened. I don't think there's much you can tell them they'll be able to use," I said.

"Well, I'm not sure I 'precisely' remember what happened that night. But I bet with the help of the widow's lawyer, I'll eventually get it straight."

"Are you threatening us?"

Landon laughed. "Nate, don't get all up on your high horse. I'm not threatening you. I'm just asking for a loan. To help tide me over a little. Me and my friend have investments we need to take care of and we weren't prepared for this. We're all friends here. And I've read you boys are swimming in dough from sales of the uLivv. I deserve consideration."

I sighed internally, then looked over at Ignacio, who nodded slightly.

"How much do you need? And where are you staying?"

"The Hilton. In the theater district. I'd say a couple of thousand will set me up for the next few days."

"The Hilton is expensive. I thought you needed to manage investments back in Tennessee," I said. "I can 'loan' you $1,500. The maximum we can pull from our corporate ATM. I'm not writing any checks."

"I have interests in other places. Fifteen hundred will do fine for now."

I walked Landon downstairs to our local ATM, withdrew the money and handed it over. Landon gave me a big grin, clapped me on the shoulder with a cheerful "Be in touch soon" and sauntered off.

When I returned to the office, Angie followed me into the conference room and insisted on being briefed.

"This is the ghoul Michael described? The one who called him a 'China Man?'"

"Yes," I said.

"He's a blackmailer."

"No, Angie, you think?" I said. "But what are we going to do? We can't afford to have him go running to the Jobs estate at this critical moment. And he knows it. He might provide them with enough ammunition to convince the court to issue a preliminary injunction. I have no idea what he's going to claim and he's not going to be particularly scrupulous about what he 'remembers.' We'll have to manage him until after the hearing is over. It's not going to be long."

It soon became apparent this was going to be easier said than done. Landon was back in the office the next day with a request for additional funds. He'd visited a local "gentlemen's club" the night before and the money we'd given him had been "stolen." When I asked him if he was in the habit of carrying so much cash on his person, he grinned and confided in me that the ladies needed to be "paid up front."

Two days later, Landon's credit card "maxed out" and he needed to pay his hotel bill. Next was an "advance against winnings" for a visit to the Foxwoods Casino in Connecticut. He made a drunken call to the office informing me someone had "dented" his rental car in the parking lot while our hero was inside pursuing the Redman's wampum. An immediate cash infusion was needed to repair the automotive wound. My observation his winnings might cover the repairs was answered with a disconnect.

Ignacio, Angie, and I met to discuss the situation under Steve Jobs' watchful eyes.

"He's not even being subtle about it," Ignacio said.

Angie looked at both us. "You need to get rid of him," she said.

"Thanks, Angie. How do you suggest we do that?" I said.

"I don't know. Maybe he can become dizzy and fall out of a window. People fall out of buildings all the time in New York."

"Actually, they don't," I said. "And we don't need a mysterious 'accident' at Reliqueree days before a critical legal hearing. You're being hormonal."

"I don't care. He's not going away. He will ruin everything." She put her hands on her stomach. "The baby doesn't like it."

"She's right about him not going away," Ignacio said. "Should we cut to the chase? Ask him how much he wants to go away for good? See if we can stop this stop this drip, drip?"

"It's worth a try," I said.

Angie looked disgusted. "He won't go away. Does a tick go away when it bites you? No. It keeps sucking. If it had a big enough stomach, it would drain you dry."

CHAPTER 37

RETAIL DREAMS

She was right. When I invited Landon to visit the office in the morning to discuss his situation, he was a no show. That afternoon, Angie, Ignacio, and I decided to go to lunch together to ease the stress. When we returned, Vinay informed me someone named "Landon" had come to see me and had wandered into Borisland. When I went to extract him, I found Boris and May staring at their unexpected visitor with a mixture of uneasiness and distrust. I grasped Landon by his arm in a companionable but firm grip and walked him out of their office and into the conference room.

When I tried to nail down his bottom line, he was evasive. "Hell, Nate, I'm not asking for a payoff, just a loan. When our Memphis operation was shutdown, my friend and I were faced with what I hear you marketing boys call a 'lost opportunity' situation. Who knows how much money we could have made in the future? Not to mention the investments we missed because of our cash shortage. It's complicated, my friend. Let me think on it. By the way, I'm planning to take another trip up to Connecticut to the Mohegan Sun casino. I know what went wrong at Foxwoods and want to recoup."

When I mentioned to Ignacio and Angie what had transpired, Ignacio looked sick. Angie just nodded and went back to her cubicle.

Later that day, I received a call from Illarion. "I believe a situation has arisen and we need to talk. Could you please come to my office?"

I shot a glance at Angie, who was watching me. She turned away and I said, "Of course, Illarion. I'll be right over."

When I arrived at his office, I expected him to discuss Landon the first thing, but he had something else on his immediate agenda.

"Have you thought of opening a retail store?" he asked. "Or perhaps several of them?"

"Yes, but our plate is full right now. And with the lawsuit, I've not had any extra bandwidth."

"Do you think a retail location is a good idea? I often read retail is dead."

"Yes, that's why Amazon is opening clothing stores in LA and Apple stores earn almost $5 thousand per square foot," I said. "Retail is not dead but it **is** changing. People don't visit Apple stores simply to stuff motor oil, cheap jeans, and assemble-it-yourself furniture into a shopping cart and congratulate themselves on saving $7.99 over what they'd pay at Target. Buying at an Apple store is an experience. One that tells you when you leave the place with your MacBook Air in hand, you're way cooler than the poor schlub who ordered a Dell laptop online. Hell, even the Dell guy will concede that."

"So, can you do as well as Apple?"

I pondered the question for several moments. I'd been so busy **being** an entrepreneur the last few months that I'd stopped **thinking** like one. Illarion was re-centering me.

"I think so," I said. "Probably better. At its 'core,' to coin a phrase, what has Apple always sold you? An elite buying experience. Your purchase of an Apple product proclaims you are first among your peers in business and at home.

"What must Reliqueree offer you? An elite buying experience. But when you purchase our products, you're buying more than **today**. You're integrating family, friends, and yourself in a community combining yesterday, today and tomorrow. It's a powerful concept to build a retail experience around."

"I have a location on 14th Street," he said. "A couple of blocks away from the Apple store. You have been there?"

"The 14th Street Store? Yes. It's big. Three stories. I estimate 30 thousand square feet. How large is the property you're discussing?"

"Five thousand square feet. Twenty foot ceilings. You could build a second level. It was going to be a Banana Republic. They are breaking the lease."

"Interesting," I said. "Not as big as most Apple stores, but we can use it as a test bed for experimentation and discover what works. I love the location. I'm positive we'll attract Apple store walkovers. What's the condition of the interior?"

"It is semi-finished. Floors and walls are finished and painted. They have not mounted the apparel display and storage kits."

"No problem. We're not going to be stacking up polo shirts. What's the time frame?"

"January."

"You're kidding. Illarion, it's November. It takes time to design a store. Build a planogram. Schedule promotions. Find and stock inventory."

He looked apologetic. "I understand. There are tax ramifications for my business. I will fund the construction and initial operations. Will you provide the interior...concept? Design? Manage the stocking? The store must open in January."

"As long as you fund construction and the launch costs. It's last minute."

"The money will be there. Let us discuss the other circumstance. Please tell me more."

I went through the Landon experience point by point. When I was done, I said, "Illarion, it's a difficult problem. I've had to be careful. It's tricky." I realized I sounded defensive.

He waved his hands. "You have done well. I have no criticisms. You are absolutely right to try to avoid his contacting the Jobs family.

The situation requires the closest possible management and you should continue. The justice system needs to work. Let us talk again after the hearing."

Later that evening, I went in to talk to Boris. He and May were working steadily away, showing no signs of fatigue. These days, they only left the office on the weekends for Brighton Beach. During the week, when they felt the need to depressurize, they'd leave the office hand in hand for walks around the neighborhood.

"Boris, what did Landon discuss with you?"

"Is this his name? I am not sure what he wanted. He asked many questions about where I was from, what I did, what May did, where she was from. I thought he was your friend so I answered them. Then he called May 'my little China girl.' This is racist, no?"

"In his case, probably."

"I thought so. I was going to throw him out when you arrived. He is not your friend, is he?"

"No. If he comes in here again and I'm not with him, toss him."

"I will do this."

Before leaving for the night, I emailed the company a memorandum Landon was not allowed in the office unless I, Ignacio, or Angie was present. I also ordered a keycard system.

CHAPTER 38

COUSIN YURI

When I returned to the office I immediately briefed Ignacio and Angie on the conversation.

"First," I said, giving Angie an I-told-you-so look, "Illarion says I've been handling Landon properly. He said to nurse him along until after the hearing. We'll have a stronger hand then and can end this."

Angie looked at me. "That's **all** he said?"

"That's all. Second, Illarion has offered us a retail opportunity. Our first Reliqueree store. A prime location on 14th, between Seventh and Sixth Avenue. A ten-minute walk from the Apple store."

"When does he want us to open?" Ignacio said.

"Any time in January. The closer to the holidays, the better. The trend over the last several years is for sales to stay strong through the first two weeks in January before the February blues kick in."

"Nate, that's a lot of work," Ignacio said. "We don't have the staff, a store manager, inventory, none of the infrastructure in place. You're talking only two months to opening the doors."

"Illarion will fund construction and initial ops. As for employees, we can poach from the Apple stores. Let's offer them 20 percent over their base salaries. I bet we can pick off a couple of managers as well. We can also recruit at NYU, Columbia, CUNY, etc. We only have to staff for five thousand square feet. I think we can handle it."

"What about the interior design of the store? The theme?" Ignacio said.

"Doesn't Gruezén have a degree in architectural design?" I said. "He's already demonstrated he can handle the inside of a cardboard box. I'll bet he can do the same for one made of steel and mortar. I'll give him a call when we're done.

"Angie, I need you need to work the Shenzen and accessories connections. We need to start to build a third-party market for the uLivv. Can you contact OtterBox, Pelikan, those guys? I know several of them are looking at jumping into the space — we've built the volume to justify the tooling and investment. I bet they'll be interested in securing premium shelf space in what's going to become a New York commercial landmark. Ignacio and I can help. I still have contacts from Samsung and Creative. How about you, Ignacio?"

"I still have a few contacts."

"I'll begin calling today," Angie said. "I hope Illarion is right about Landon."

Thankfully, our friend from Tennessee's losing streak in the Green Felt Jungle seemed to have come to an end at the Mohegan Sun casino, where he informed me via a slurred phone call he'd enjoyed a winning streak of such proportions that Custer could now be regarded as avenged. Landon would be staying an extra day or two to continue to "clean up."

The next day I was in my cubicle when I saw the door open and someone enter the office. Angie was on the phone, so I stood up and went to greet our visitor. He was a slim, brown-eyed man who appeared to be in his late 20's or early 30's.

"Hi. Can I help you?" I said

He smiled at me. "I hope so. I'm looking for Boris Samsonov. I understand he works here?'

"He does. May I ask who's calling?"

"Tell him it's Yuri. Yuri Daman. I'm his cousin."

"I'll be right back." I stepped into Borisland, where things were currently serene and smelled like evergreen. Boris was typing away at high speed on his system. May sat at her workstation on a desk set 45 degrees from his, matching him keystroke for keystroke. Currently, most of Boris' time and energy was spent on extending and refining the uLivv's persona code.

The software was generating increased attention from AI circles. A few days ago, Ignacio had told me only half-jokingly that he lived in constant fear someone from the AI lab at MIT or Stanford would show up and kidnap our chief programmer.

"Just buy a lead wok and chain May to it," I said. "As long as we have her, he's not going anywhere. By the way, what's their current personal status? She **is** wearing an engagement ring?"

"She is. Angie finally confirmed it. It's going to be a June wedding."

"What does May's family think?"

"In China? Angie says they're horrified. They wanted May to find a nice Chinese-American boy, not a Man-Bear from the Steppes. Too late now."

"I think they make an adorable couple," I said. "And it's quite soothing when they rock together. Is the electric air freshener May's idea?"

"Yes. She likes things to smell nice. It's a whole new Boris in there. It upsets May when he screams 'this is shit,' so it's much quieter as well."

"Have we submitted an H-1B for her?

"Yes."

"Make sure she's put on payroll immediately when it's approved."

"Hi, you two," I said. "Boris, you have a visitor."

"Uncle Illarion?"

"No. Your cousin Yuri. He's out front waiting to see you."

"Yuri is here?" He heaved himself up from his chair and hurried out. In a few seconds, Boris returned with his cousin in tow, the two of them chatting away in Russian. Yuri spotted May and immediately walked over to her desk. She stopped typing and looked up apprehensively, blinking owlishly through her wire rims, which sat on her face slightly crooked.

"Ah, Boris, so this is your May. She's as beautiful as you said. A fair flower of the East. Excuse me, would you mind?" he said to her, then leaned over and straightened her glasses. May squeaked and almost bolted, but looked over at Boris and relaxed.

"So much better. Boris, you're a lucky man. And you two are getting married?"

"Yes, Yuri. This June. You will come to the wedding, won't you?"

"Boris, I wouldn't miss it for the world. And I'm going to drink enough vodka at the reception to make them take me to the hospital to detox. Any thoughts on the honeymoon?"

"We are going on a cruise to the Caribbean where it is warm and where we will make a son. Afterwards, when he is born, he can play with Angie's little one." He looked at May and smiled. She smiled back.

"Boris, you are decisive," Yuri said.

"That sounds like a plan to me," I said. "I'll let Angie know. Looking forward to those playdates, Boris. I'm going to let you two catch up while I return to work. Yuri, you have any questions, please swing by my area. I'm sure your Uncle has mentioned how much we love Boris and depend on him at Reliqueree."

"Thanks, Nate. He has indeed. Talk to you later."

Yuri spent a couple of hours in Boris' office, then came out and sat next to me in my cubicle.

"So, what do you think?" I said. "We treating your cousin well?"

"You are. A steady job, an opportunity to become rich, even a fiancée. I wouldn't have believed it if I hadn't seen it for myself. Boris and I spent a great deal of time together when we were little and it was hard for him. My parents moved to America when I was eight, but I visited Russia regularly. Whenever I saw Boris, it was always a little sad. He was big but awkward and was often bullied terribly. His brilliance also separated him from his peers. He's been lonely most of his life. But he's undergone a tremendous transformation. Both Illarion and I can hardly believe how far he's come."

I smiled. "Thank you. That's nice to hear. I have to admit, when we first met him, he was a handful, but meeting May has made all the difference. My fiancée set them up and it was a match made in heaven."

"Yes, it is," he said.

"How long are you planning to stay in the States? I'd like to invite you out to dinner. It will be me, Ignacio, Angie, Boris, May, you, and a significant other if it's convenient."

"I'd love to, but need to ask for a raincheck. I'm here for business and am going to have to rush back to Moscow sooner than I'd like."

"What business are you in?"

"Primarily asset management tracking. I'm a programmer, too. I'm good, but not at Boris' level. I don't know anyone who is. I'm visiting him as family, but admit I want to pick his brains at dinner tomorrow night. I'm contracting on a project for a firm that needs to keep track of onsite construction equipment. Things sometimes vanish. Expensive drill bits go 'missing.' Specialized tools 'walk' away. An earth mover 'drives' itself off. We're developing a new generation of sensors to prevent all this. Hopefully."

"Sounds interesting. By the way, if you decide to relocate to New York, make sure you drop your resume off. We're hiring. Boris can tell you this is a great place to work."

"I'll keep it in mind."

For a couple of hours after Yuri left, I enjoyed the feeling of knowing I'd done good for someone else while doing good for myself.

A smart entrepreneur appreciates a win-win.

The feeling dissipated when Landon showed up at the office hungover and in a bad mood. "Nate, I need a loan."

"Why? I thought you'd scalped the Mohegans so thoroughly you were set for life."

"I did, but my luck changed. I lost all my winnings and am down. Way down."

"How down?"

"It doesn't matter. I've figured out what went wrong. I'm heading out to Atlantic City for the weekend. I'll make it all back and more there."

"Landon, this is spinning out of control. How much do we need to provide you to cover your lost opportunity costs?"

"Nate, buddy, I really can't focus on it right this second. My head's just pounding. Why don't you just loan me another $1,500 and we'll discuss it when I'm flush."

After Landon was gone, I stared at my workstation's calendar with the hearing date highlighted. Just a few more days and this would be over. Hopefully.

There was no news from Landon over the weekend, or on Monday. Tuesday was quiet as well.

On Wednesday, Angie emailed me a link.

PORT REPUBLIC, N.J. - State police say a driver was killed when his car struck a bridge abutment on the Garden State Parkway and went airborne, plunging into the Mullica River.

The crash occurred around 2 am Sunday north of Exit 41 in Port Republic Township.

A state police spokesman says the motorist was driving in a northbound lane when the vehicle drifted sharply into the right lane and struck the abutment. Troopers are still trying to identify the driver, as well as the make and model of the car.

The driver was alone in the car, and it did not appear that any other vehicles were involved in the accident. The cause of the crash remains under investigation.

PORT REPUBLIC, N.J. - State police have identified the driver killed Sunday as Jerry Landon Langley of Memphis, Tennessee. Langley died Sunday evening when he lost control of his car and it exploded before plunging into the Mullica River, just north of exit 41 on the Garden State Parkway. Preliminary toxicology reports on the remains indicate Langley's blood alcohol level was .28, almost three times the legal limit. Langley was apparently returning home from a visit to Atlantic City, where spokespeople from several casinos he visited say he lost heavily. One eyewitness reports seeing Langley pounding on the steering wheel of his rented Chrysler and shouting as he sped by him at "well over the posted speed limit."

A state police spokesman stated "this tragic event only emphasizes the dangers of combining alcohol with driving. The Port Republic Police department anticipates closing their investigation into the crash in the next couple of days."

I read the article several times, then walked into Boris' office. He and May were both working industriously.

"Hi, Boris. How did your visit with Yuri go?"

"I was excited to see him. He was good to me when I was a child. I was happy to be able to help him in his new business. Yuri is a fine programmer and businessman. One day, he will be very rich. But I do not think he will be happier than me." He smiled at May. She smiled back.

"What did you guys discuss?"

"Nothing so challenging. Yuri said to me you had discussed his business venture with him?"

"Yes. It sounded similar to the 'LoJack' system used here. Someone loses their car, you can track it, try to recover the vehicle."

"Yes. It is similar. There is much theft in Russia, usually of fancy European and American cars. I provided him information on hardware interfaces, programming techniques, remote management of stolen vehicles. It was not technically advanced information in most cases. Cars are not secure. They are easy to hack."

"Yuri will do well in his new business," he said.

CHAPTER 39

LEGAL TRIUMPH

[4 pages.]
FILED: NEW YORK COUNTY CLERK
INDEX NO. 451476
NYSCEF DOC. NO. 23 RECEIVED NYSCEF
SUPREME COURT OF THE STATE OF NEW YORK
NEW YORK COUNTY

———————————————

ESTATE OF THE LATE STEVEN PAUL JOBS
Plaintiffs, Index No. 451764
- against - Reliqueree, Inc.
Justice Robert M. Friedman
RELIQUEREE, INC.,
Defendant.

———————————————/

ORDER GRANTING DEFENDANTS' "RULE 12(B)(2) AND 12(B)(6) MOTION"

Causes of action-

1. Privacy/ Intrusion on solitude- Plaintiff asserts that Jobs Estate's Fourth Amendment rights have been violated by the unlawful taking of post-mortem human tissue. Common law states that ownership extends to human tissue and remains, which allows

citizens to properly bury their dead and perform other vital societal functions. Under Griswold v. Connecticut and its progeny, Plaintiff is entitled to have all DNA returned and to have a permanent injunction placed on sales of the uLivv....

2. Intentional infliction of emotional distress- Plaintiff asserts the Defendant has acted intentionally and recklessly and with extreme and outrageous conduct. These actions have caused the Plaintiff extreme emotional trauma which have manifested into insomnia, panic attacks, and severe grief. Plaintiff is entitled to damages for his/her pain and suffering and to have a permanent injunction placed on sales of the uLivv...

DECISION BY THE COURT- INJUNCTIVE RELIEF

The issue before the Court today is whether the Plaintiff, Estate of the Late Steven Paul Jobs, is entitled to any injunctive relief with regards to the uLivv device. Plaintiff has submitted evidence to show that Jobs Estate's Fourth Amendment rights have been violated by the taking of his DNA in order to mass produce a consumer product. Plaintiff states that the taking of an organ is akin to human remains which, once buried, are protected from disturbance. Furthermore, Plaintiff requests damages in the amount of twenty five million dollars for the pain and suffering that has resulted from these actions. Plaintiff has submitted evidence to show that the Estate has suffered from various ailments stemming from the acts of the Defendant.

Although the Court finds that Defendant's actions are socially controversial, we cannot hold that any legal violation of privacy has taken place. Plaintiff cites case law which only applies to the government. Here, we have private parties acting for personal gain. In this case, an organ was disposed of via a waste disposal process. At that point, privacy was no longer at issue because the organ was no longer considered private property. This is unlike human remains for burial which, at all times, remain the property of the deceased person's loved ones. Objects, once they are knowingly placed in trash receptacles or handed over as waste for disposal, retain no ownership and cannot be subject to ownership litigation. Therefore there is no cause of action and the Court finds that this is an issue best left to the legislature. The Plaintiff's primary cause of action is denied.

In light of the above ruling, there can be no damages awarded for intentional infliction of emotional distress. Plaintiff has acted within the bounds of the law and cannot be subject to damages. Although this Court finds that such actions could cause these ailments, we again find that the Legislature must change the law in order to allow us to find anyone civilly liable for such actions. The request for damages stemming from extreme infliction of emotional distress is denied.

Plaintiff's request for a temporary injunction is denied in its entirety. This Court finds no reason why Reliqueree cannot continue to use Mr. Jobs' discarded liver and DNA.

III. CONCLUSION

For the reasons set forth above, while Plaintiff understandably may be disturbed by Defendants' acts, the current law provides no remedy. Having failed to demonstrate any likelihood of succeeding on the merits of its claim, Plaintiff is not entitled to an injunction. Accordingly,

IT IS ORDERED that Plaintiff's "Motion for Preliminary injunction" is DENIED.

/s/

____

ROBERT M. FRIEDMAN
NEW YORK STATE SUPREME COURT

CHAPTER 40

CATHEDRAL OF COMMERCE

"What do you think?" I said to Gruezén as we walked through the empty store. He'd flown down immediately to survey the space after I'd called and described the location and our retail play. "It's a nice open floor plan. We don't have to rip anything out. A blank canvas. And these tall ceilings give it a very airy feel."

"Yes. Have any of the major retailers contacted you?"

"Of course. After the lawsuit, sales hockey-sticked and buyers are coming out of the woodwork. WalMart has called several times. Fry's. NewEgg. Best Buy emails daily. Nothing from Amazon, though."

Gruezén sniffed. "I'm sure WalMart has rolled out the polyester rug for you. You're not going to sell the uLivv in WalMart, Target or Kohls. They are palaces of the proletariat. You're offering a premium product and you need to provide a premium buying environment. Apple is your obvious touchstone."

"The buyer at Best Buy wanted to discuss a store within a store concept," I said. "What do you think? We'd be in 1,500 locations in the U.S., not to mention their online site. And they're the most forward-thinking of the electronics retailers."

"No. Not a good idea at this time," he said. "Apple tried this with CompUSA 20 years ago. I studied the program. The management promised Apple the inside stores would be their number-one priority.

The campaign was a joke. The 'stores within stores' were located at the rear, where foot traffic was lowest. Staff were never properly trained on the value of the Macintosh platform and what differentiated it from Windows boxes. Store collaterals and market materials weren't properly updated and displayed.

"After a few months of this, Jobs learned his lesson. He dropped almost all the resellers and rebuilt the Apple buying experience. Only then did he allow the retailers to sell Apple products under strict pricing and collateralization restrictions.

"We need to incorporate these lessons into our planning. What are **your** ideas?" he said.

"I don't know. Before I came here, I swung by the Apple store. Initially, my thought was we'd just basically, well not 'copy,' but 'emulate' the presentation. The quality recessed lighting. The 14th Street store doesn't have marble tiling, but it's a nice hardwood look. We have that already in place," I said, rubbing my shoe against the polished oak laminate left behind by Banana Republic. "The open tables with working products on display.

"But as I thought about it, I realized something was missing. There's another element to Reliqueree that's not part of an Apple environment. We've discussed it, but I'm not quite sure how to express it."

"I believe I do. Let me show you something." He handed me his iPad. Displayed on the screen was a dazzling church interior.

"This is the interior of the La Sagrada Família cathedral in Barcelona. Gaudi began building it in 1883 and it was not finished when he died in 1926. They expect to finish it in 20 years. Or 30. God does not hurry these things along. Please tap."

I did and another beautiful interior filled the display, dominated by dazzling stained glass windows.

"Those windows are from the Chartres cathedral in France. I've been there. When you look up at those magnificent works, you feel as if you're gazing into heaven. But I have saved the best for last. Tap."

The tablet now showed a space so beautiful as to be almost unearthly. The walls enclosing it appeared to be made of stained glass, interrupted only by thin strips of stone. It seemed miraculous those fragile structures could sustain any weight at all.

"The interior of the nave of the Sainte Chappelle cathedral," Gruezén said. "I've been there as well. When you are inside, you don't feel as if you're seeing a vision of Heaven. Rather, you feel as if you're in Heaven itself.

"If you read about the history of these cathedrals, you discover they were built primarily as reliquaries, works of art designed to store precious objects. For instance, Sainte Chappelle housed a piece of the True Cross and the Holy Crown of Thorns.

"By contrast, Apple stores are Bauhaus buying machines. Form following function as the design, lighting, people, and brand all converge to persuade you to buy something from Apple today.

"But the Reliqueree brand is about more than 'today.' As you astutely noted, Reliqueree's technology allows you to create a nexus between yesterday, today and tomorrow. This is how these cathedrals operate. The past is represented by a sacred relic. A piece of the True Cross, or, in this instance, a sample of Steve Jobs' DNA. The present, by the cathedral itself or a Reliqueree store. The eternal tomorrow is glimpsed through spiritual images transcribed onto stained glass or via a Reliqueree persona."

"Yes. I agree," I said. "That's what was missing from the Apple experience." I looked back at the picture of Sainte Chappelle. "But we only have two months to open and I don't think we can afford all that stained glass. And I think I read once those windows take years to create?"

"Decades," he said. "Fortunately, the Lord has created high definition video walls and driven the prices down. Give me a few days and Gruezén Team will develop a concept and prepare a virtual walk through." We spent a few more minutes talking, then Gruezén hailed a cab and left for the airport.

I walked back to the office light-footed and exhilarated. There is nothing an entrepreneur enjoys more than exchanging ideas and concepts with someone who grasps his goals and vision of the future. I'd read more than once that Steve Jobs was happiest when he was spending time with his design team. Thinking about it, I also remembered reading that the only time Adolf Hitler was tolerable was when he was around Albert Speer, the Third Reich's chief architect. Of course, Hitler was an evil dictator, not an entrepreneur.

The lead returned to my step the instant I entered the office. The place was in an uproar, with everyone milling about in shock. Angie was sitting at her cubicle in tears. I hurried over to her.

"Tim sam, what's wrong? What happened? Are you alright? Are you in labor?"

"No, I'm not in labor. May's gone. Immigration showed up, arrested her, and took her away. Boris is having a breakdown in his office. Ignacio's in with him."

"ICE arrested May? On what grounds?"

"I'm not sure. I'm trying to reach her family. Ignacio has already called Illarion."

I walked into Borisland. Absent May's presence, the office already seemed a little grayer and far more drab. In a few days, it would smell differently as well. Boris was sitting on the floor rocking and sobbing, with Ignacio's arms around him. Vinay was standing near the door with a bruise on his face, looking unhappy. I pointed to the door and gestured him to leave.

"She is gone," Boris said in a keening voice. "They have stolen her. Why did they take her? Ignacio, why did you and Vinay stop me from fighting them?"

"Because having you arrested and hauled away as well, or maybe even shot, wouldn't help either May or yourself," Ignacio said. "Boris, calm down. I'm sure it's all a misunderstanding. We're already working to resolve this. May will be coming home soon."

Boris looked at him with a white, tear-stained face. "You are doing this? You promise?"

"I promise, Boris," I said. "We won't rest until she's back beside you doing whatever it was she liked to do while you were working. Ignacio, how many of them were there? They had a warrant?"

"There were three and they had a valid warrant. I wasn't falling for the old 'wave an electric bill in my face' trick."

Angie came into the office carrying her phone. "I have Illarion for you."

I took the phone. "How is he?" Illarion said.

"Very, very, very unhappy."

"Let me speak to him."

I handed the phone to Boris. For the next ten minutes, there was a rapid colloquy in Russian. By the end of it, a little color had returned to Boris' face. He handed the phone back to me. "Uncle Illarion wants to talk."

"Is he calmer?" Illarion said.

"Yes."

"Good. This is a problem we need to solve. Boris has made great strides. I do not wish to see him fall back to his old ways. I have made an appointment for you to visit..."

"Let me guess. The Great White Blonde."

"Yes. She is a problem solver. Please let me speak to Angie again. I need to know more about May."

I handed the phone over to Angie. "Illarion wants to talk to you." She left the office and I could hear the two of them discussing May in the background. I looked down at the scene still playing out in front of me. Boris remained in Ignacio's embrace, rocking slowly.

I sighed, slipped to the floor, and wrapped my arms around Boris opposite Ignacio. Best to do this now. In a few days, it would be much more unpleasant. For several seconds, our little trio rocked gently back and forth, then I slowed the motion and urged us all to our feet. I carefully maneuvered Boris down on to his desk chair.

"Boris," I said, pointing to his workstation screen. "I want you to focus on your work. You work for May and we'll work for you. She's coming back, Boris. You don't want her to have to work twice as hard because you slacked off while she was away. Not that she's an employee."

"I understand. When is she coming back?" he said.

"I'll let you know."

The next day, Angie and I visited lawyer O'Connell.

"What happened yesterday?" I said. "Why did immigration show up at the offices of a high-tech startup and drag off some little Chinese girl?"

"An excellent question. I was going to ask you the same thing. Can you explain it?"

I thought of Landon's Borisland intrusion almost three weeks ago. ICE's timing in swooping down on us was an interesting coincidence. I wondered who else Landon had been talking with while he was extracting his "loans."

"No," I said. "I'm going to assume its Apple or the Jobs family pulling strings. A few years ago, they were influential enough to have the feds and the local police break down the apartment door of a journalist named Jason Chen in San Mateo and seize his computers because he was reporting on an iPhone prototype an Apple engineer left in a bar."

She looked at me. "Apple certainly has influence in certain circles," she said. "Is that all?"

"Yes."

"What was she doing for Reliqueree?"

"Nothing. She's Boris' girlfriend. Fiancée. She's not on payroll and doesn't report to me or anyone in the company. She's not assigned to any Reliqueree projects."

"The report I have says she was working in his office at a company workstation. She's not a permanent resident and doesn't have an H-1B. That's a problem."

"She's not an employee. We let her stay in the office with Boris because it calms him down. We don't keep track of what she does on the computer and don't provide her access to our internal development systems. She can't keycard into the offices when they're closed. She doesn't have a company email account."

"Uh, huh," she said. "Make sure you can prove it."

"So why did ICE arrest her?" Angie said.

"The complaint says May Lei has applied for permanent residency via the law's family member provisions."

"Yes? Is there something wrong with her application? It's a form I-130," Angie said. "I checked everything was in order before I introduced May to Boris."

"Her paperwork is fine. However, it appears the person who sponsored her application, her 'sister,' is not actually her sister. A cousin maybe? Possibly no relative at all. She's currently back in China, whoever she is. We're trying to reach her."

"Where is May being held?" I said.

"She was processed at the Varick Federal Detention Facility and bused to the Orange County Jail in Goshen. About an hour's drive north of the City."

"Oh, boy. When can you arrange for her to be released?"

"Normally, within 48 hours on a bond. The problem is we have no one to release her to. Her 'sister' is not currently in the country and she has no other relatives I can find. She's not married. She's not an employee of Reliqueree. She's going to have to stay put for now. Also, it's going to be three weeks before I can get in front of an immigration judge."

"Boris is not going to be happy," I said.

"Boris is not my concern at the moment. May Lei is. You keep him under control and busy while I work on springing Madam Butterfly from the clink."

"Madam Butterfly is not Chinese," Angie said. "It's Japanese."

"I don't care if she's Shirley Fu Manchu. Keep an eye on Boris and let me work this."

CHAPTER 41

THE SORROWS OF BORIS

Keeping an eye on Boris did not prove difficult. Holding onto our sanity as Boris slowly lost his was.

He was stable for the first week and continued to generate code at a furious pace. We were able to release a significant update to the uLivv with minimal bugs and problems. This included several major improvements to the persona system. Customer delight and heightened buzz about the uLivv's new capabilities drove continued explosive sales growth.

In an interesting example of a creation exceeding its creator's grasp, word began to spread online of a new use for the uLivv called "cebripping." You pulled off a cebripp by obtaining a sample of a celebrity's DNA, sequencing it, then uploading it to your uLivv and using it to build a persona based on the collected genome.

Various techniques on how to collect DNA from the target of your affection were currently hot topics online and on Facebook, where the discussion covered both traditional techniques — becoming a groupie and having sex with a star, dumpster-diving — and more avant-garde approaches including loo raiding (don't ask) and static gloves (useful for picking up dandruff and other forms of skin flakes). The most advanced cebrippers were already on to ""boxripping," collecting DNA from every member of a boy band or famous rock group, for example.

The practice was currently limited by the cost of sequencing and the difficulty of saving the actual DNA within the uLivv using home brew methods. Countering this was public anticipation that when TransLivvient launched, sequencing prices would drop like a stone (which was correct).

After the articles appeared, enquiries about TransLivvient quadrupled. Inevitably, the usual cohorts of Luddism and negativity appeared and began complaining about "privacy" and "exploitation," but I thought we could safely ignore them.

An intelligent entrepreneur does not battle the future. Rather, he embraces and monetizes it.

I could already see future new licensing and partnership possibilities, but I wondered if Kim Kardashian and the rest of the celebrity community were prepared for the future. When Steve Jobs had released the iPod and created the buck-a-song download model, the music community had fought against the rising tide with disastrous results. Bands and singers had been forced to perform in front of **live** people to make money and the record companies had seen their revenues plummet. Drug allocations for performers and music executives were slashed to the bone. Both industries were still recovering.

Three days after May's arrest, I rented a car and drove Boris up to the Orange County Jail for a two-hour visit with her. They spent their time together holding hands, cuddling, looking unhappy, and talking in a pidgin of English, Russian and Cantonese. The authorities kicked Boris and I out at 4 pm and we began the drive back to Manhattan. Boris was highly upset.

"I do not understand why they must keep her locked up," he said. "She can stay with me. I will make sure she does whatever they want. It is cruel to keep us apart. I am her family."

"Technically, you're not," I said. "That's the problem. Except for her 'sister,' who's somewhere in the middle of China, none of the other people around her were actual relatives. But don't worry. She's in the

U.S. and you're getting her back. You just need to hold tight and let the legal system grind away a while longer."

"I am lonely. Can you bribe someone?"

"Sometimes. But it's a slow process. I need to find a New York Chinese politician and start to contribute to their campaign. But we're a little behind the curve for that. Our legal approach will be faster."

The second week saw Boris' morale began to slip. He began leaving Borisland several times a day to question me, Ignacio, and Angie about when his lost love would return. Angie bore the brunt of it. He would sit at her cubicle for extended periods and utter regular encomiums to May in a sad Russian tone.

"May is sweet, Angie. I am so happy you introduced us."

"I know, Boris. I'm happy I did, too."

"She is also beautiful, Angie. Like you."

"Thank you, Boris. Make sure you tell Nate. A girl likes to hear that in her eighth month."

"She is not a good cook, though. She has tried. But she is not good around hot things. She tends to set fires. Once herself. Just the glove."

"Make sure you keep an eye on her, Boris."

"I do, Angie. I love May so much I have tried to learn to cook myself. But I too am not good around hot things. The fire people had to come to our apartment in Brighton Beach when the oil in the wok ignited."

"That's one reason New York is wonderful, Boris. There's no shortage of places to eat and take-out."

And so it went.

He perked up a smidgen when Ignacio ferried him up to Goshen for his second visit to see May, but his emotional rebound only lasted a couple of days. Next week, on the way back from his third visit, he refused to talk to Vinay, who'd drawn that week's taxi duties. Back in New York, when we had to tell him the immigration judge had refused May bond, he barricaded himself inside his office and refused to talk to anyone. Surprisingly, his code production did not fall off, a fact for which we were all grateful. But I knew we were on borrowed time.

One bright event cutting through the gloomy fog rolling off our suffering Ural Mountain was Gruezén's submission of a theme and design for our first store. I thought his proposal, considering our time constraints, was astonishing.

The entire company at my insistence attended the presentation and virtual walkthrough. I tried to lure Boris out of his office by telling him it would cheer May up to hear the details, but the gambit failed.

Gruezén began by paraphrasing our earlier discussion about the purpose of the great cathedrals he'd shown me and Reliqueree's underlying corporate and product philosophy. Then he started the walkthrough by bringing up an empty white-box image of the store's interior.

"I'm going to 'build' the inside layer by layer," he said. "This is the first."

An animated sequence began and filled the space with tables, fixtures, counters, and a few avatars to set the scene.

"You'll notice there's a strong resemblance to an Apple store. This is quite deliberate. Apple has done it right in this respect and given the calendar there's no need to try to reinvent the wheel. Now the second layer."

The second sequence added in products and accessories onto the tables, shelves, and key locations. Gruezén gestured and the virtual camera's perspective shifted to a top down view.

"Again, a homage to Apple," he said. The store's layout is broken out by uLivv functionality: **Learn**, **Knowledge**, **Entertainment**, **Transcendence**, and **Persona**. The uLivvs on display aren't running canned demos. They're connected to streams, digital cameras, iPads, iPhones, and the best Android gear. Visitors have high-speed web and email access, as well the ability to create a TransLivvient account on the spot. Let's finish the process." The camera switched perspective back to the ground floor and the final layer drew itself in. When it finished, the room gasped.

Similar to Sainte Chappelle, the store's interior walls appeared to be built from stained glass panels stretching from almost the floor to the high ceiling. The prevailing hues were cerulean, interwoven with brilliant highlights of red, green, yellow, etc. Gruezén zoomed in on one of the panels. A full-length image of an elderly man in thick black glasses holding a slide rule and smiling benignly appeared. Beneath him was another image, one of a machine I didn't recognize.

"That's John Vincent Atanasoff, the creator of the first electronic digital computer." Gruezén touched his tablet and the image changed to another stained glass portrait, one of a man in 19th century clothing. Underneath him was a machine I **did** recognize.

"I know him. Charles Babbage," I said. "That's one of the Difference Engines."

"Correct," Gruezén said. More images of people, machines, and symbols appeared as he moved through the store. A few I recognized, most I didn't. I definitely picked up Ada Lovelace, Alan Turing and Lee Felsenstein, as well as a handful of the machines, including the Apple II, Osborne 1 and the NeXT cube.

"All of the panels contain portraits of important people and devices in computing. The stained glass effects were created with different graphics programs and are shown on the display grid. This gives us the flexibility to add and remove pictures and change the interior color scheme at will. This approach visually connects a visitor to the past, one of Reliqueree's key positioning elements."

The virtual camera now zoomed to the back of the store, which was dominated by a long white counter. Coffee and espresso makers, as well as an assortment of juices, bottled water, pastries, biscuits, and cookies were set up on stands behind the counter. A glowing cerulean blue sign that seemed to float on the rear wall read "Into the Blue Bistro."

"The 'Into the Blue Bistro' is the section of the store where people can subscribe to TransLivvient, submit DNA samples for sequencing, and receive assistance while setting up their accounts. The associations generated by the name are obvious, warm and comforting. The coffee, water, and light food are free and establish a personal, intimate feel to the process. After all, this is family and friends we're dealing with. We also believe you should encourage subscribers to bring pictures and images of family and loved ones and offer to scan and mount them into their accounts. And perhaps partner with a genealogy firm."

"What a great idea," Ignacio said.

"We're almost done, but there is one last thing I must show you," Gruezén said. The camera zoomed in on the ceiling area over the Bistro. Dominating the space was a large, highly detailed oil painting of a group of people sitting around a table eating pizza while drinking from cups. A young, barefooted Steve Jobs was at the informal tableau's 12-o'clock-high position, with people to either side of him. To Steve's right another person was standing and exiting the scene, his face turned away from the picture's observers.

"Officially, the painting is titled 'Digital Remembrance,' but of course we expect everyone to call it 'The Last Pizza Party.' We think it strikes an interesting balance of pathos and humor."

"Who are the people sitting around the table?" Ignacio said.

"From left to right Gary Kildall, Jack Tramiel, Thomas Watson, Jr., Grace Hopper — she's a bit of a stand in for Mary Magdalene — Adam Osborne, E.F. Codd, J.C.R. Licklider, Presper Eckert, John Mauchly, Don Estridge, and Jef Raskin."

"Boy, I don't know most of those names," I said. "Well, I know who Grace Hopper is. COBOL. I recognize Jef Raskin. He was the guy running the original Macintosh group before Jobs took it away. Good thing you put those two as far away from each other as possible. They did **not** get along."

"Everyone depicted is deceased, except one. I'm sure they've finally worked out their differences. Mini bios of the group are mounted on the kiosks and website," Gruezén said.

"What are they drinking?" Ignacio said.

"Fruit smoothies."

"Who's that person stepping away from the table with his back to us?" Angie said. She peered more closely at the picture. "Is he holding a can of Pepsi?"

"We leave his identity up to your imagination," Gruezén said.

"I notice Steve's not wearing any shoes," Ignacio said. "Why?"

"In his early days at Apple, Jobs frequently walked around Cupertino barefooted."

"As did Our Lord," Ignacio said quietly.

"Yes." Gruezén said. "Well, what does everyone think?"

"I need to see how much this is going to cost, but if the budget's anywhere within reason, we have our interior design," I said.

CHAPTER 42

GRAND OPENING PREPARATIONS

Gruezén's second bravura performance raised company morale sky high. The excitement continued to mount when we poached two Apple retail managers and a number of their employees for the Reliqueree store. The decision to target Apple employees was a smart one. They're already trained to avoid using negative words and phrases such as "unfortunately," "problem," and "crash" and substitute them with more positive ones, including "as it turns out," "situation," and "issue."

Likewise, at Reliqueree we went down a similar path of replacing "died," "deceased," "grave," and similar old-style mortuary vocabulary with more positive terms like "transformation," "post-life," and of course "IoDT." Apple managers are well-versed in proactively enforcing positive thinking among their staff and maintaining a comfortable, welcoming environment for customers and store personnel alike. Reliqueree's staff would be already trained and ready to continue in this best-practices tradition from day one of the store's opening.

Unfortunately, Boris continued to deteriorate despite our best efforts. On the trip back from Goshen the next week, the few words he spoke to me were sullen and hostile.

When we reached the office, he stormed into Borisland, slammed his office door shut, and refused to come out when anyone was around. He continued to code, but spent all his attention on the persona system.

The couple of times I walked into his office to check on him he ignored me while muttering in Russian to his Steve Jobs persona, who muttered back.

Things reached their nadir when Angie went into his office to try to calm him down and left after a few minutes, her face pale. That's when I realized the situation was spinning out of control. I called Illarion.

"We need to do something about Boris. I'm becoming concerned. He won't talk to anyone. Angie's frightened he may snap at any minute and hurt someone or himself."

"I will come over."

When Illarion left Boris' office, for the first time since I'd known him he looked perturbed. "He tells me he hasn't slept in two weeks," he said. "He says he is depressed and doesn't believe they will ever release May. He believes there are evil forces conspiring against him and her. I do not think he is thinking clearly. I have never seen him in such a state."

"He's sleep-deprived and probably hallucinating," I said. "You're his family. You need to take him to a doctor. He needs something to help him sleep and for his depression."

"I agree. I will have my car pick us up and I will take him to my doctors. I will call to inform you of what they tell me."

In a few minutes, Illarion's Lincoln was waiting downstairs. As Boris walked out of the office with his uncle's arm around him, I called out "Feel better Big Guy. The minute I hear something from May's lawyer I'll call you." Boris said nothing and refused to look at me.

He was out of the office for a week. Illarion called me once to thank me for contacting him. Boris was staying with him during his rehabilitation.

"My doctors say he was in poor shape but is much better. He has been prescribed a sleeping medicine and something for the depression," he said. "Now that he is sleeping, he has become much more calm and rational. We took him to see May and it made him happy. A few more days and he will be ready to return to work."

"That's terrific. Tell him I have great news. I've just spoken to the Great White Blonde. She said she's located May's sister and she's on her way back to the U.S."

"That **is** excellent news. What did the sister say?"

"We're not sure. Apparently the connection was poor and the sister seemed confused by the whole situation. But she insisted May is here legitimately."

"Wonderful. I will tell Boris."

Two days before the grand opening, Boris was back at Reliqueree. He seemed much better and smiled a great deal at everyone. The news about May's sister had clearly improved his peace of mind, though he was still confused about the precise situation. No great surprise.

"Is May here?" he said to me in a sunny tone when I went into his office to welcome him back.

"No Boris, not yet," I said. "But we're close to getting this squared way. You hang in there."

"I understand. I see clearly what I must do."

"I'm glad, Boris. Are you coming to the grand opening? It's going to be exciting and you had a big part in making it happen. Everyone wants you to come."

"I understand. I will come. I will make preparations."

"Take it easy for the next couple of days. Ease back into it."

"I will prepare."

The next day everyone at the company was focused on last-minute chores and tasks. Michael had flown in the night before to stay with me and Angie and would be leaving early with his sister to receive a private tour and keep an eye on preparations. I hired a limo to take Ignacio, Sheridan, and myself to the store in style. The entire company, with the exception of Boris, headed over to 14th Street to assist our new retail employees to prep and polish the interior and place special busts of Steve Jobs we'd ordered for the occasion around the store. Sheridan had done an outstanding job of generating blog and press coverage. The Mayor was attending the opening ceremony as well other local notables.

I'd already begun thinking about where our next retail location should open. Further uptown? The financial district? A rumor was floating around online that Apple was planning to raise the base pay of its New York employees to prevent our further poaching.

Before we left, we all posed for a group photo of everyone smiling widely and standing in front of the store beneath the Reliqueree sign and our two happy "e's."

I was on top of the world.

I headed back to the office to take care of some last minute chores. Before leaving for the night, I walked into the conference room to inspect samples scattered on the table of the limited pieces of in-store collateral we'd had specially produced for tomorrow. When I was done, I looked up at Boris' Jobs persona. Over the last few weeks, its Russian accent had become more pronounced, and I sometimes found its expression odd, almost hostile. I also thought it was starting to slightly resemble Boris.

"What's the good word, Steve? Any advice for tomorrow?"

"We're born, we live for a brief instant, and we die," he said. "It's been happening for a long time. Technology is not changing it much if at all."

"Steve," I said, before I lowered the room's lights, "we're proving you wrong."

FOUR DAYS LATER...

CHAPTER 43

AFTERMATH

I woke up in a hospital room with a sharp ache in my chest and a very sore left shoulder.

"What happened?" I said. I breathed in too deeply and the pain made me gasp out the words to the doctor hovering over my bed.

"You were shot," he said. "How do you feel?"

"Like someone shot me. Twice. Where was I hit the second time?"

"Your heart."

"Oh. I guess my uLivv protected me?"

"Oh, no, no. The bullet went by the gizmo..."

"uLivv."

"...uLivv you had had draped around your neck and impacted right over your heart. Fortunately, the gun the guy used was a cheap Saturday Night Special. The cartridge misfired and left the muzzle at a low velocity. The combination of your pectoral muscle and rib cage slowed the bullet. The slug actually came to rest right up against your heart, but didn't penetrate it. There was considerable bruising, though. And you went into cardiac arrest."

"I did?"

"Yes. Twice. Once in the store while they were preparing to transport you and once on the table while we were operating. But you pulled through. We've kept you under for three days to manage the swelling."

I thought for a second. "I don't recall having a near death experience. I didn't meet God. No relatives, either."

"Well, you're the uLivv guy. God may have thought that would be redundant?"

"Maybe." I pulled myself up a fraction and looked around. The room was filled with flowers. "Whoa. I didn't know I was **this** popular. Where did these come from?"

"Oh, all over. You're a hero, you know. The video went viral."

"What video?"

"The YouTube video of you throwing yourself in front of your pregnant fiancée. You're the nation's male ideal at the moment. One blogger called you a mixture of a technology titan and Sir Galahad. By the way, speaking of your fiancée, she's outside the room waiting to see you. With a surprise." He left the room.

A second later Angie rushed into the room and threw herself sobbing on my chest.

"**Ow, ow, ow**. Angie, that hurts!"

"I'm sorry." She shifted position and I patted her on the head. "You were so brave," she said through her tears. "I wasn't really sure how you felt about me until I saw the video. You didn't hesitate a second."

"Tim sam," I said with absolute sincerity, "I didn't do what any other man wouldn't have done who wanted to protect what was most dear to him. And by the way, I notice you've slimmed down. What happened after I was shot?"

"I went into labor in the store while they were reviving you."

"What a happy coincidence. I assume my male is waiting outside the room to meet me?"

"Do you want to see him?" she said in a shy voice.

"Of course I want to see my son. Bring him in."

She left the room and returned a second later with a squirming bundle. She started to place him on my chest, then thought better of it and made me scooch over. She put the baby down next to me and moved the swaddling blanket away from his face.

"Isn't he beautiful? He looks just like you."

He looked exactly like a newborn.

"He's magnificent." As I spoke, my son swiveled his head and stared straight into my eyes. Newborns actually can't see much beyond eight inches after they're born, but he bluffed well. After a second, he stuffed his hand into his mouth and drooled on it.

"Thumbsucker." I looked at her. "Have we named him?"

"I was thinking Livingston Song Pennington?"

My mouth dropped open in admiration. "Angie, that's brilliant. A contemporary yuppie tone and a subtle brand tie-in. And I love the cross-cultural appeal."

"Do you really think so?" she said. She was shy again.

"Absolutely."

"Sheridan agreed. He already has his own Facebook, Pinterest and Twitter accounts. In fact, we're thinking of adding Snap..."

I didn't hear the rest of the sentence because I fell asleep.

I woke up the next day feeling much stronger and the cavalcade of well-wishers continued. First up was a reunion with little Livingston, who was as exciting and vibrant today as he'd been yesterday and added to his adorableness repertoire by reddening in the face and pooing. Then Angie read from samples of the emails, blog posts, tweets, and even cards sent from around the world wishing me well and extolling my courage and bravery. This was enjoyable and I found little to argue with in the sentiments expressed.

Ignacio was next.

"How are sales?" I said.

"Making a dent in the universe. If they ever start to lag, we need to shoot you again."

"I've already taken two bullets for the team. You're up next. Speaking of bullets, what happened to Boris?"

"The Mayor's security detail wrestled him to the ground. He's currently being held in Bellevue."

"They didn't take him to jail?"

"He began seizing while they were holding him down. Apparently, he had a violent reaction to the anti-depressant he was prescribed. He suffered a complete physical and psychotic breakdown. Illarion is working the legal system to ensure he doesn't end up in Rikers. By the way, everyone at the office says get well soon."

"Tell them I'm feeling great and will be back shortly. How's the store doing?"

"Packed. We have to let them in by groups."

"Anything else interesting going on?"

"A couple of things. There are rumors spreading that a group of celebrities are going to sue us to shut down cebripping."

I laughed. Only a little as it hurt. "Yes, good luck. They'll put that genie back in the bottle the way they did with spam. The only way they can 'protect' themselves is by spending the rest of their lives in 'Boy in the Bubble' space suits. Go contact O'Connell and ask her what she knows about celebrity licensing. What's the other thing?"

"I discussed it with Illarion. He's doing a little research and wants to talk to you directly about the opportunity."

After Ignacio had left, Angie came back in the room, accompanied by May, who saw me, squeaked, and in contrast to her previous behavior, threw herself at the bed and onto my chest while wailing in a mix of Cantonese and English as both her eyes and nose ran.

"**Ow, ow, ow.** May, if you want to finish me off, please go find Boris' gun and shoot me now. It will be more humane. Angie, what's she saying?"

"Sorry," she said, moving May to the side so the liquid pool accumulating on my dressings could evaporate. "It's a little hard to make out, but she's pleading for Boris' life, his freedom, his return to her, does he still have a job..."

"God. The Chinese. Practical to the end. Tell her a) no one is going to take Boris' life, b) we'll spring him eventually, c) it's obviously inadvisable to separate them and, d) Boris can keep his job and his options if he agrees to never ever shoot me again. No pointing guns at you, either.

It's impossible to replace his level of technical talent. By the way, what's she doing here?"

"The immigration issue has been settled. May's sister is actually her legal stepsister. Her mother married her stepfather years before she was 18, but no one bothered to change the surnames."

"Not surprising in a country where everyone's last name is Wang, Wong, and Wu." Angie gave me a look. "With the occasional 'Song' thrown in for variety. Just tell her everything is going to be fine. Who's she staying with?"

"Us."

"Of course. Take her home. She's drenching the bed."

"Sorry." There was a brief burst of Cantonese between the two, May bestowed upon me a look of infinite gratitude, and the two of them left to allow me time to dry out and my chest stop aching.

My next visitor was Mom. She came with Ignacio.

"Hi, Mom. Thanks for coming."

"Nate, what happened to you?"

"I was shot, Mom. It was a misunderstanding. I'm going to be fine."

"Did Annie shoot you?"

"No, Mom. Angie didn't shoot me. Have you seen your grandson? Livingston?"

Her face softened. "I did. He's so tiny. Much smaller than you were."

"He's a pound lighter than I was."

Her expression became stern. "He's Chinese, isn't he."

"No, Mom. He's Blended Caucasian."

"Oh. Well, that's something. Nate, that Annie is wearing your grandmother's ring and I want to know..."

"Ignacio? Could you take Mom to the gift shop and help her pick out a nice present for the baby? I'm sure Angie will appreciate it."

"Sure, Nate." He escorted Mom out of the room.

In the afternoon I had a surprise visitor, Sister Mary Gael.

"Sister!" I said. "This is an unexpected treat. Thank you for visiting me."

"I hope I'm not intruding. When I read about what had happened, I decided to visit you. How are you feeling?"

"Surprisingly well, all things considered. By the way, I just want you to know the Order can anticipate receiving a fat check from Reliqueree. You provided me with inspiration and comfort when I most needed it. I made a promise to Mother Cabrini that if she came through for me, I'd do the same for her."

"The Mother comes through for all of us, Nate, if you ask her. She can't be bought."

"I understand, but as we discussed, you and I live in a material world and matter must be maintained. If our donation is used to fix the sidewalk in front of the Shrine or to keep her mural looking beautiful, I don't think the Mother will mind, do you?"

"I have to say I don't think she will."

"Do you know I went into cardiac arrest twice? I hoped I'd have seen a vision of her, but I can't remember anything."

"She was probably in a different location from the one you were looking at. Or perhaps she was directing her attention to another problem. I talked briefly with your fiancée about an immigration problem you were having with one of your employees. The Mother **is** the patron saint of immigrants."

"Sister, I hadn't thought of that. By the way, May is not an employee."

We talked a bit more before she left. I made a note to swing by the Shrine again the next time I went to see Mom. I'd be carrying that check.

A smart entrepreneur is always willing to pay for real value.

My last visitor was Illarion. "How is Boris doing?" I said when he came into the room.

"He is recovering. I have fired the doctors who treated him. They were incompetent. They were supposed to help him sleep and feel better, not transform him into a madman."

"How is he feeling?"

"Much better. He has no memory of the shooting. He is extremely anxious to see you and apologize. This morning I visited to tell him

May has been released. He will be able to see her in a couple of days. I believe this is the cure he needs."

"What's his legal status?"

"He has been charged with attempted second-degree murder and illegal possession and discharge of a firearm. The Great White Blonde is working to have the criminal charges dismissed on the grounds of insanity and have him released into my custody. She tells me if you do not press charges and refuse to testify against Boris, this will strengthen her position."

"Not a problem. I saw his eyes before he shot me. I don't think he knew me from Steve Jobs."

"Thank you."

"In return, I have a favor to ask you."

"What is it?"

"I want a 50/50 equity split."

"Fifty five/forty five. It is fair."

"**Two** bullets, Illarion. One next to my heart."

There was a long sigh, then he said, "50/50."

It had been worth being shot. To an entrepreneur, equity is life itself.

"By the way. Ignacio told me there was a major opportunity you wanted to discuss with me?"

"Yes," he said. "The Pope is dying. The Vatican wants to talk."

★ ★ ★

Thank you for reading *Selling Steve Jobs' Liver.* If you enjoyed it, please take a moment and post a **review** on the book site of your choice. If you'd like to comment on *Liver* or ask about my background in high tech (and yes, I did meet Steve Jobs personally, once, in Pittsburgh in either 1989 or 1990), please post on my professional website, www.softletter.com.

GLOSSARY OF PEOPLE

Gil Amelio. Apple's CEO immediately preceding Steve Jobs' reascension to executive control of Apple in 1996. While a competent financial steward and capable of managing a commodity-scale technology firm, Amelio was out of his depth as Apple CEO. After his overthrow by Jobs in a boardroom coup, he wrote a book called *On the Firing Line* in which he described creating a Distinctly Superior User Value Task Force which was responsible for monitoring the Macintosh UI, performance, and networkability. The group was run by a…lawyer. (Yes, I know.)

John Atanasoff (October 4, 1903 – June 15, 1995). John Atanasoff is recognized as the inventor of the first machine that can be regarded as an electronic digital computer. The machine, the ABC, was a specialized binary device and did not incorporate a CPU.

Charles Babbage (December 26, 1791 – October 18, 1871). The father of all computers. Babbage developed two partial prototypical mechanical computers in the 1820's and 1830's named "Difference Engines." No complete computer was ever built from his plans and designs while he was alive, but working models have been constructed from his original notes using 19th century technology. Had any of his units gone into widespread use, they would probably have accelerated the adoption of computing technology by 50 to 100 years.

Chrisann Brennan. Brennan is currently a well-respected painter, but is best known as Steve Jobs' high school girlfriend and subsequently the mother of his first child, Lisa. In 2013 she released a book, *The Bite in the Apple: A Memoir of My Life with Steve Jobs*, some of which makes for painful reading for Jobs' admirers.

Edgar Frank "Ted" Codd (August 19, 1923 – 18 April 18, 2003). Ted Codd is the father of relational database management systems (RDBMS). Developed by him in the 1960's and 1970's, relational technology swept through the computing world in the 1980's and today is the primary model for data and transaction management. Codd's 12 rules for defining what constitutes a relational database serve as the canon for the technology.

Philip Don Estridge (June 23, 1937 – August 2, 1985). Known in the industry as Don, Estridge is regarded as the father of the IBM PC. When the first model, the 5150, was introduced in 1981 by Estridge's Entry Systems Division, it quickly overtook the Radio Shack Model One, various CPM systems, and the Apple II as the microcomputer hardware standard. Don Estridge and his wife died tragically in 1985 in an airplane crash on a flight to Dallas. To this day, 90 percent plus of desktop and laptop computers are built around the descendant of the original IBM PC standard.

Lee Felsentein. Lee Felsenstein is one of the seminal figures in the history of modern computing. He was one of the lead developers and funders of Community Memory, an experiment in providing distributed and networked computing to the public. He designed the Osborne 1, the first fully functional portable computer and the ancestor of every laptop and notebook in use. Other notable designs included the PennyWhistle modem and the Sol-20 Personal Computer, an 8-bit CP/M desktop system. Felsenstein's design philosophy centered around the concepts of simplicity, serviceability, and creating an effective balance between performance and cost.

Jean-Louis Gassée. In many respects, Gassée was responsible for the ultimate success of the Macintosh platform as he drove (and hid its existence from Steve Jobs until after he left the company) the development of the Macintosh II, an "open" system that rejected many of Jobs' original design mandates but sold extremely well. After yet another Apple power struggle, Gassée left the company in 1990 and founded Be, Inc. Be's principal product was the BeOS, which was powerful and ahead of its time. Gassée was in the happy position of being first in line to sell his company and the OS to Apple in the 1996 timeframe as the company was in desperate need of an upgrade to the Mac OS and had proven incapable of developing one internally. Unfortunately, Gassée could not stop himself from being French and annoying and the deal broke down, to the happiness of Steve Jobs and NeXT, who swooped in and took advantage of the opportunity.

Grace Hopper (December 9, 1906 – January 1, 1992). Rear Admiral Grace Hopper developed the first computer language compiler, was a seminal figure behind the development of COBOL, is widely credited with inventing the concept of "debugging," and was an early advocate of distributed computer networking.

Gary Kildall (May 19, 1942 – July 11, 1994). Kildall was the CEO of Digital Research and the developer of CP/M, perhaps the most important of the 8-bit operating systems of the 70's and 80's. He was also a major contributor to the development of optical content standards and the moving force behind GEM (Graphical Environment Manager), a PC-based Macintosh alternative Apple sued out of existence. Kildall is best known for failing to strike a deal with IBM to bundle a 16-bit version of CP/M with the original IBM PC.

Daniel Kottke. Daniel Kottke was Apple employee number 12 and at one point a close friend of Steve Jobs, meeting him at Reed college and accompanying him on a trip to India before Apple's founding in 1976. Kottke was heavily involved in the testing and production of the

Apple II computer, the company's first major hit and one of the three dominant eight-bit computer platforms of the era. Kottke was close with Chrisann Brennan and assisted her in early efforts to care for her daughter, Lisa. In a (in)famous incident, Jobs refused to award stock options to Kottke while Apple was preparing to go public. Steve Wozniak decided to award Kottke and other early employees $10 million in options from his own shares.

J.C.R. Licklider (March 11, 1915 – June 26, 1990). J.C.R. Licklider was a technology visionary and computer scientist who did pioneering research and analysis in the areas of graphic user interfaces, networking technology and protocols, and interactive computing. Many people in the industry regard him as the Father of the Xerox Alto, the computer both Steve Jobs and Bill Gates "emulated" on their path to business success.

Ada Lovelace, The Countess of Lovelace (December 10, 1815 – November 27, 1852). Ada Lovelace was the daughter of Lord Byron. She had an ongoing professional collaborative relationship with Charles Babbage and during her correspondence with him on the abilities of his Difference Engine, conceived the concept of programing the machine via algorithmic instructions. In her famous note 'G,' she wrote (diagrammed) the first computer program, a process for computing Bernoulli numbers.

Presper Eckert (April 9, 1919 – June 3, 1995) and John Mauchly (August 30, 1907 – January 8, 1980) jointly developed ENIAC, the first general-purpose programmable computer, in 1944. They also founded the first computer company in 1947. Eckert was the hardware specialist of the team while Mauchly focused on system software.

Mike Markkula. Mike Markkula was Apple's first major investor and its second president till 1983, when he was replaced by John Sculley and became the chairman of Apple's board. In this position, he played a key role in the company's strategic management decisions. In

1985, he decisively backed John Sculley over Steve Jobs in the fight for control of Apple, with Jobs leaving soon after the company's board of directors reaffirmed its confidence in Sculley. Markkula was also a key figure in Sculley's removal from Apple and the subsequent hiring of Michael Spindler and Gil Amelio, both of whom proved inadequate to the job of running the company. In 1996, after regaining control of Apple, Steve Jobs quickly escorted Markkula and most of the board of directors out the door. Markkula has a degree in electrical engineering and also wrote several early Apple II and III software products.

Adam Osborne (March 6, 1939 – March 18, 2003). Adam Osborne was a well-known and respected writer and popularizer of computing technology in the 1970's and 1980's. In 1981 he founded Osborne Computer Corporation, manufacturer of the Osborne 1, the first commercially available portable computer. (Portable by the standard of the time. The O-1 weighed 24 lbs.) Designed by Lee Felsenstein, the Osborne was regarded as a remarkable value because of the amount of software bundled with it, which included WordStar, SuperCalc, Personal Pearl, dBase II, BASIC and the CP/M operating system. The actual bundle contents varied based on the deals struck with software vendors. The Osborne Computer Corporation grew quickly and collapsed even more rapidly because of cash flow mismanagement and the growing power of the IBM PC standard in the marketplace.

Jef Raskin (March 9, 1943 – February 26, 2005). Apple employee number 31, Jef Raskin worked at Apple as a tester and documentation specialist. He conceived of the original Macintosh in 1979 as a simple, "appliance" type computer for the masses. The project was taken over by Steve Jobs in 1981, who retained the original appliance philosophy but redirected the development effort to incorporate a graphic UI. Raskin's relationship with Steve Jobs remained problematic over the years. In an example of cosmic irony, he died of pancreatic cancer in 2005.

Rob Schoeben. Rob Schoeben was reportedly relieved in public of his responsibilities by Steve Jobs as punishment for the serious problems afflicting Apple's MobileMe service upon its first release. (Schoeben has denied this and no one else has stepped up to be identified.) The MobileMe system was a paid sync-and-storage offering Apple eventually discontinued. During a review of its problems with the MobileMe group, Jobs is reported to have told them "You should hate each other for having let each other down." As CEO of Apple and the person in charge of Apple products, there is no report he sent himself a nasty email after this observation.

John Sculley. John Sculley was hired by Apple and Steve Jobs from Pepsi-Cola to be CEO in 1983. The original plan was for Sculley to "mentor" Jobs along the path to becoming a well-rounded chief executive and at some point hand the reigns of the company back to the Apple co-founder. This plan was disrupted by the release of the original Macintosh, which was a sales flop because it lacked enough memory, storage, and applications to be useful. After an initial burst of early enthusiasm, sales of the system slumped severely. Jobs' answer to the problem was for Apple to cease advertising the company's cash cow, the Apple II, and focus all marketing programs on the Macintosh. Sculley quite rightly rejected this disastrous approach because everyone knew the problem with the Mac wasn't that people didn't **know** about the system, but rather you couldn't do much **with** it. In the ensuing corporate shootout, Jobs lost and was stripped of all operational responsibility at Apple and in turn resigned from the company in 1985. He returned in 1996 to engineer what is probably the most remarkable turnaround in American business history. Sculley by all normal metrics was a very successful CEO, driving sales from $800M to $8B during his tenure. He was kicked out of Apple by the board of directors in 1993 over disagreements in the direction of the company and slowing sales.

Michael Spindler. John Sculley's successor as CEO of Apple. His background at Apple was primarily in sales, at which he was very successful.

Nicknamed "The Diesel," he proved to be totally unequal to the task of managing Apple and was removed by the board as CEO in 1996.

Jack Tramiel, (December 13, 1928 – April 8, 2012). Liberated from Nazi death camp Auschwitz while in his teens, Jack Tramiel was the founder of Commodore Business Computers and responsible for the brief resurgence of Atari as a force in computing in the mid-1980's through the mid-1990's. Famous for his statement "business is war," under his leadership Commodore developed a scorched earth pricing policy that periodically wreaked havoc in the marketplace, particularly in what was once the "home computer" segment, whose prominent players were Texas Instruments, Atari, Sinclair, Coleco, IBM with the PC Junior, and others lost to history. The company's most famous product was the Commodore 64, which at approximately 23 million units shipped, is believed to be the best selling desktop computer of all time. An active and engaged community of enthusiasts keeps the C 64 flame alive via software emulators and the Commodore 64x, a Linux PC that mimics the look of the original unit and ships with various emulations integrated with the system's hardware.

Thomas Watson, Jr. (January 14, 1914 – December 31, 1993). Thomas Watson, Jr. succeeded his father as the second president of IBM. Watson, Jr. recognized early the impact that computing would have on business and society. Under his management, IBM became so dominant in the computing industry that its rivals were referred to as the "Seven Dwarves." No company in history (including Apple) has ever possessed the almost imperial power and hold on the imagination of the public that IBM enjoyed up through the mid-1990's, at which time "Big Blue" lost its grip on the market to Microsoft.

ABOUT MERRILL R. CHAPMAN

Rick Chapman is the managing editor and publisher of Softletter. He is also the author of *In Search of Stupidity: Over 40 Years of High-Tech Marketing Disasters*, *SaaS Entrepreneur: The Definitive Guide to Succeeding in Your Cloud Application Business*, *The Product Marketing Handbook for Software*, and *Rule-Set: A Novel of a Quantum Future*. *Selling Steve Jobs' Liver* is his second novel. The technology, attitudes, terminology, and industry history referenced in *Liver* are accurate. Rick denies having ever used the word "ideate" in an actual sentence.

Rick has worked and consulted in the industry for such industry pioneers as MicroPro (WordStar) and Ashton-Tate (dBase) and consulted for a wide variety of software and high technology firms including IBM, Novell, Microsoft, Sun and many others. In his career, Rick has held the title of programmer, sales engineer, product manager, and VP of marketing and product management. He remains firm in his conviction that WordStar was the greatest word processor ever created.

OTHER BOOKS BY MERRILL R. CHAPMAN

Rule-Set: A Novel of a Quantum Future

Read more at: www.softletter.com

In 2087, Clarence Hamilcar, ex-Marine lieutenant, decorated veteran of The Koumintang War, associate professor of Asian literature studies, and failed tenure candidate at Black Hills University, South Dakota, is flown under contract by the U.S. Army to Waxahachie, Texas. His destination is the Hyperconducting Hyper Collider, the world's most powerful particle accelerator, built on the remains of the Superconducting Super Collider, abandoned in 1993 after the US government spent $2 billion to excavate 14 miles of tunnels and 17 access shafts 200 feet below the north Texas plains.

Clarence's contract requires him to immerse and "liaise" with Hanabusa Narihisa, an AI extracted from one of the 42 simulations executing on

Colossus. Narihisa's character is based on a Japanese manga and combines combines beauty with a bad temper and a very sharp katana. In the tunnels of the HHC 200 feet below Waxahachie, Clarence and Narihisa will engage in a battle of skill and wits whose prizes are the secrets of Colossus and Rule-Set.

"Make no mistake; the novel's pervasive theme of Japanese mysticism is underpinned by (well-researched) hard science. This work is literally a "quantum leap" in the exposition of future virtual reality.

In addition, it contains something both rare and welcome in hard SF: a sprinkling of ROFL humor. You'll be begging for the sequel."

Joe Dacy, II, The Kindle Book Review

In Search of Stupidity: Over 40 Years of High-tech Marketing disasters

Read more at: www.softletter.com

"'In Search of Stupidity: Over 20 Years of High Tech Marketing Disasters' is a most valuable book and is a wonderful read for anyone in the software industry. For those in sales and marketing, it is clearly required reading, and in fact, should be reread periodically. While 'In Search of Excellence' turned out to be a fraud, 'In Search of Stupidity' is genuine, and no names have been changed to protect the guilty."

Ben Rothke, Slashdot.org.

"'In Search of Stupidity' is a delightful and deceptively useful chronicle of what went wrong in the high-tech industry. Having followed many of these companies and products over the years, I'd often wondered why such smart people made such weird choices. Rick Chapman has many of the answers. Anyone who has ever yelled at the computer screen will enjoy this book".

James Fallows, National Correspondent for The Atlantic Monthly, author of Free Flight: Inventing the Future of Travel (2001) and former editor of US News & World Report

SaaS Entrepreneur: The Definitive Guide to Succeeding in Your Cloud Application Business

Read more at: **www.softletter.com**

SaaS Entrepreneur: The Definitive Guide to Succeeding in Your Cloud Application Business is the most comprehensive guide you will find to understanding and succeeding in building SaaS (Software as a Service) businesses and services. Its case studies, operations analyses and timely data provide critical insights and information that will help you build and grow a successful new SaaS business. Its focus is on those areas of community and product management, sales, marketing, compensation, customer service, and operations and infrastructure where SaaS B2B companies sharply diverge from their on-premise counterparts.

Rick's book is a must. There has been a need for a resource like this for quite a while, so I am very pleased to see SaaS Entrepreneur brought to the market. What makes this book different from so many others is that it combines extensive and fresh statistical data on the current SaaS market combined with well written, practical text. I would highly recommend this book to anybody that is considering entering the SaaS market and for the firms who need to improve their business operations and processes. The included Virtual DVD includes a huge amount of valuable material for anybody working in the SaaS domain.

Dr. Petri I. Salonen, CEO, TELLUS International, Inc

CONNECT WITH MERRILL R. CHAPMAN

Merrill R. (Rick) Chapman can be emailed rickchapman@softletter.com

He can also be reached on the following social platforms:

Instagram

LinkedIn

Facebook

Goodreads

Rumble

Twitter (X)

Made in the USA
Columbia, SC
14 October 2024

43558255R10172